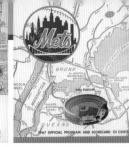

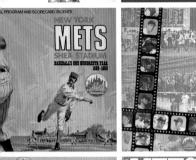

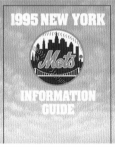

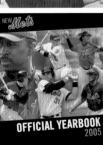
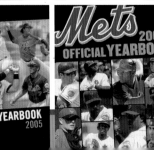

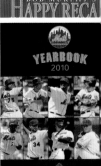

NEW YORK METS

The Complete Illustrated History

Matthew Silverman

MVP
BOOKS

First published in 2011 by MVP Books, an imprint of MBI Publishing Company and the Quayside Publishing Group, 400 First Avenue North, Suite 300, Minneapolis, MN 55401 USA

MVP Books titles are also available at discounts in bulk quantity for industrial or sales-promotional use. For details write to Special Sales Manager at MBI Publishing Company, 400 First Avenue North, Suite 300, Minneapolis, MN 55401 USA.

To find out more about our books, visit us online at www.mvpbooks.com.

ISBN-13: 978-0-7603-3960-2

Library of Congress Cataloging-in-Publication Data
Silverman, Matthew, 1965-
  New York Mets : the complete illustrated history /
Matthew Silverman.
    p. cm.
  Includes index.
  ISBN 978-0-7603-3960-2 (plc)
 1. New York Mets (Baseball team)--History. 2. New York Mets (Baseball team)--History--Pictorial works. I. Title.
  GV875.N45S56 2011
  796.357'64097471--dc22
                              2010035348

Editor: Josh Leventhal
Design manager: Katie Sonmor
Book designer: Erin Fahringer
Cover designer: Matthew Simmons

Printed in China

Acknowledgments

Thanks to William A. Shea for doing the dirty work to bring the National League back to New York. Plenty of others were helpful in telling the story that Bill Shea began.

I retraced much of the early history of the Mets through the *New York Times* and through the work of Jack Lang, who covered the club from day one for the *Long Island Press* and later the *New York Daily News*. The *2010 New York Mets Media Guide*, along with a crate full of previous editions, helped tremendously in my research, as did the websites baseball-reference.com, mets.com, ultimatemets.com, and ESPN New York. Numerous independent sites, which are the lifeblood of the Mets fanatic in the twenty-first century, were equally informative, notably Centerfield Maz, Faith and Fear in Flushing, Mets Blog, Mets by the Numbers, Mets Police, Mets Report, On the Black, and Ted Quarters. There are dozens more sites, including my own site, metsilverman.

com, where you'll find updates and other follow ups on the Mets that could not fit into this book.

Thanks to Pete Flynn, Keith Hernandez, and Rusty Staub, among others, for their thoughts of what it was like on the field at Shea Stadium, and to Lorraine Hamilton at the Mets for her help. Eddie Boison, AKA Cowbell Man, is the new century's Sign Man and generously shared his experiences. Special thanks for additional input from Greg W. Prince, Greg Spira, Alec Dawson, Paul Lovetere, and Mark Simon, and photography assistance from Dan Carubia, Lynn Cohen, Andy Esposito, Andy Fogel, Dwayne Labakas, Gene Caputo, Jacob Kanarek, and the Hall of Fame's John Horne. In terms of patience, thanks as always to Deb, Jan, and Tyler, and especially my editor and publisher, Josh Leventhal, who contacted me for this task and helped me to corral the half century of nonstop drama, unforeseen miracles, and frequent heartache that is New York Mets baseball.

Contents

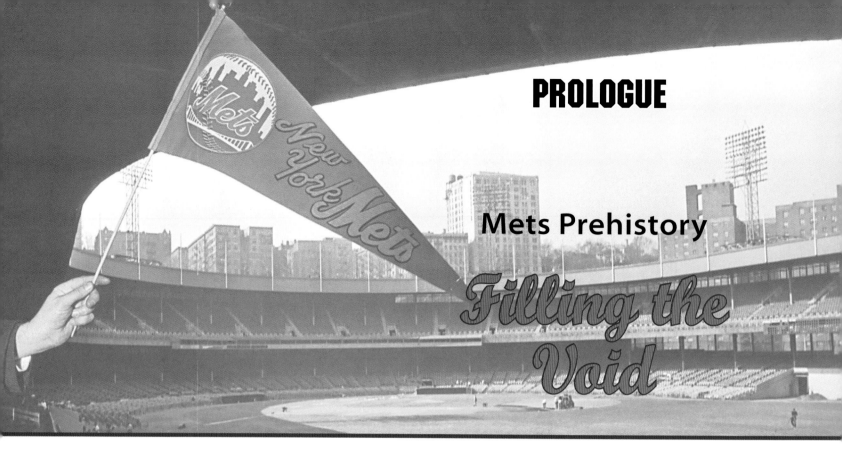

Mets Prehistory

Filling the Void

Diamond Images/Getty Images

A display of baseball equipment stands as a monument to the departed Dodgers at Ebbets Field in April 1958. *John Rooney/AP Images*

In the beginning there were Giants and Dodgers. Before there was Shea Stadium, before Ebbets Field, before even Casey Stengel was born, there was an intense National League rivalry that predated not only the Yankees, but the American League, the automobile, the airplane, and the motion picture.

Manhattan and Brooklyn were separate cities rather than interlocked boroughs, and the clubs were known as the Gothams and the Bridegrooms, when the baseball rivalry began in the 1880s. Seven decades later, when the teams left for California arm in arm, the Giants and Dodgers stranded two intensely loyal fan bases. The only team left in town was the dominant club of the American League, the Yankees. After years of street-corner arguments and October rivalries, many New Yorkers would rather quit the game than switch allegiances to the Bronx Bombers. A brave few challenged the powers that be to grow something new out of the baseball Armageddon that had taken away two of the sport's most storied franchises.

It took cajoling, cunning, and conniving, but the idea of a third major league finally set the wheels in motion to bring National League baseball back where it belonged.

Shea Hello

Two months after the Brooklyn Dodgers and New York Giants played their last games in the Big Apple, Mayor Robert F. Wagner appointed a four-man committee to try to bring a team to New York. The lineup: real estate executive Clint Blume, former postmaster general and Coca-Cola board chairman James Farley, department store maven Bernard Gimbel, and William A. Shea, senior partner in the law firm of Manning, Hollinger & Shea. The mayor tabbed Shea to chair the group. He had his work cut out for him.

The Cincinnati Reds did some saber rattling about relocating due to problems at their Crosley Field. Nothing came of it. The Pirates and Phillies were queried about relocating but weren't tempted. After Wagner and Shea met with major league owners in Baltimore in July 1958, Bing Devine, then general manager of the St. Louis Cardinals, summed up the situation succinctly in the *New York Times*: "There is no indication that anybody wants to go to New York at this moment."

The Mahatma. Branch Rickey enjoys a trademark cigar while wheeling and dealing on the phone, circa 1962. *Robert Riger/Getty Images*

On November 13, 1958, almost a year after its formation, the committee threw down the gauntlet: If they couldn't get a team from the National League, they would create a new league. But ever the diplomat and backroom negotiator, Shea never burned his bridges with the major leagues even as he set fires to get a reaction. Shea declined a July 1959 invitation from Senator Estes Kefauver, chairman of the Senate antitrust committee, who had proposed a bill that would aid in the formation of a third major league by limiting the number of players major league teams could control. Commissioner Ford Frick spoke positively of Shea's demurring Kefauver's offer and the new league's intention of operating within organized baseball, not as an outlaw league like the American League during 1901–1902 or the Federal League during its two-year run (1914–1915).

Five cities deposited $50,000 apiece to join the Continental League as charter members: Houston, Toronto, Denver, Minneapolis–St. Paul, and New York. Owners were lined up, and the linchpin was New York's group, which was made up of a trio of well-heeled fans: Dwight Davis, rabid Dodgers fan Dorothy Killam, and Joan Payson, a Giants stockholder. The league planned a 154-game schedule starting in 1961 with eight teams; almost a dozen cities were vying for the remaining three spots. By the time major league representatives met with the Continental League on August 18, 1959, the two sides were almost cordial—and if they weren't, there was a

Man on a Mission
WILLIAM A. SHEA

William A. Shea was more than just the man for whom Shea Stadium was named. He was the primary force behind getting a National League team back in New York after the Dodgers and Giants departed in 1958.

Born in Manhattan in 1907, Shea attended George Washington High School and went on to attend New York University on a basketball scholarship. He then went to Georgetown University on another athletic scholarship and was a starting forward for three years. The six-footer was Georgetown's second-leading scorer as a senior in 1931. Shea was admitted to the District of Columbia bar that year and followed suit in New York in 1932.

A lifelong lover of sports, Shea owned a Long Island minor league football franchise for the Washington Redskins, was a part owner in the short-lived Boston Yanks of the NFL in the 1940s, and was an avid Brooklyn Dodgers fan—and he was not afraid to play hardball as a lawyer. His ability to get people's ears and broker deals served him well in his law practice and in life, but it served the city of New York and its forlorn baseball fans of the late 1950s best of all. Appointed as head of Mayor Robert Wagner's committee to bring an NL team to New York, he initially struck out in his attempt to get three existing teams to relocate. While in the office of Phillies owner Bob Carpenter, Shea had a realization. "I begin to see that I am placing myself in the position of asking him to do the very thing I would never do: Pull out of your own town," Shea later recalled. "That cured me. From then on, I stopped bothering other teams. I was not going to be a party to moving any club, so long as that city had people willing to support it."

With expansion as his new aim, Shea came to his next realization: The National League wasn't interested in adding more teams. So Shea took a third route and decided to start a new league, with New York as the flagship franchise. While NL owners chuckled at the concept of the Continental League, they weren't laughing so hard when Shea hired Branch Rickey to be commissioner. Shea worked hard behind the scenes while Rickey kept reporters writing and put pressure on the NL. Finally, in August 1960, Shea and Rickey were summoned before the owners and brokered a deal that resulted in New York and Houston receiving expansion franchises in the National League.

Flushing Meadows had long been the spot favored for a stadium by New York's "master builder" Robert Moses. The higher-ups in the city administration decided on the name as well: Shea Stadium. The New York power broker was truly humbled by the honor. A boisterous booster at Mets games, Shea presented a floral horseshoe to the team in each year of the stadium's life—a tradition carried on by his family after his 1991 death following a stroke.

The Mets, who inducted Bill Shea into their hall of fame in 1983, even brought the name along when they left the stadium behind. The franchise founder's name went up on the wall with the club's retired numbers for the last year at Shea Stadium in 2008 and was in play in left field for the first pitch at Citi Field.

William A. Shea, 1959. *New York World-Telegram and the Sun Newspaper Photograph Collection, Library of Congress*

FLAGSHIP FRANCHISES, PAPER LEAGUE

The original five cities proposed for the Continental League all eventually got major league franchises, though some had to wait longer than others.

Minneapolis–St. Paul	Twins, relocated from Washington in 1961
New York	Mets, formed in 1962
Houston	Astros, formed in 1962
Toronto	Blue Jays, formed in 1977
Denver	Rockies, formed in 1993

Mahatma present to get their attention. Branch Rickey was announced as president of the new league.

The man who helped to break major league baseball's color barrier by signing Jackie Robinson—not to mention the founder of the farm system and creator of the modern spring training complex—was still a cleanup hitter. National League owners, many of whom had been outmatched in dealings with Rickey, knew that he was not someone to take lightly. And there was no shortage of newspapermen to charm. When asked where his office would be located, Rickey let out a puff of smoke from his ever-present cigar and replied, "In my coat pocket. Where else?"

Three's a Crowd

The two established leagues and the proposed new entry went from ally to adversary and back as new issues cropped up and threatened their tenuous peace. Perhaps the biggest foreseeable roadblock was minor league baseball's insistence on steep indemnification for lost territories, since all of the Continental League's proposed cities had existing minor league teams. But as the 1959 season concluded, New York fans were jarred by a sudden change in tactics.

The American League jumped ship and now wanted expansion. The Associated Press reported that the AL would initiate interleague play, expand, move the Senators from Washington to Minnesota, put a new team in Washington, and add a second team in New York, only to swap that Big Apple franchise with the National League for one of its Pennsylvania teams. NL president Bill Giles continued to insist that his league was not interested in expansion, but Frick was more to the point: "I'm not going to get into any controversy. I'm for expansion and I don't care how it's done."

Shea's calculated dealings and peace offerings were in danger of leaving his group out in the cold. The concept of an outlaw Continental League returned. The player raids

of the distant past conjured unpleasant visions of increased salaries and severe damage to each league. The American and National Leagues hashed out their differences, and the AL announced that it could not expand if the NL was not willing to follow suit. A new $15 million stadium in Flushing Meadows, contingent to any New York baseball bid, was now approved by the city's board of estimate. The Continental League was back on as part of organized baseball.

Shea and his proposed league got a major boost from Congress, where a hearing investigating Major League Baseball's antitrust exemption got some owners nervous. The long dance between three leagues to bring a new team to New York was awkward at times, but it eventually achieved the desired result. On August 2, 1960, New York and Houston were named National League expansion teams, pending a final vote. The man who started this crusade got what he'd originally sought. "My principal mission from the start has been to assure New York of having everyday baseball again," Bill Shea said.

Once official approval was given in October, the next pressing issue was when the expansion clubs would debut in the Senior Circuit. The new Queens stadium started behind schedule and remained that way, opening two years after the team debuted. Given the stadium's eventual name, Wagner's statement to the NL was prophetic: "Any questions regarding the stadium can be answered by the chairman of my baseball committee, William A. Shea."

Now We Just Need Everything Else

New York was overjoyed. Houston, too. Washington and Los Angeles were getting more baseball, and Minnesota was getting its first major league club. (The original Senators moved to Minnesota to become the Twins, the expansion Senators took their place in the nation's capitol, and the Los Angeles Angels filled out the American League with 10

Club president George Weiss, National League president Warren Giles, baseball commissioner Ford Frick, majority owner Joan Payson, and board chairman M. Donald Grant christen the new Mets franchise with a bottle of champagne in May 1961.
AP Images

WHAT'S IN A NAME?

Joan Payson, owner of New York's National League expansion franchise, could have named the team anything she wanted—Meadowlarks was her preference—but she decided to leave the final decision to the public.

Out of 9,613 suggestions, a list of 644 names was sent to the new team's Fifth Avenue offices, and the list was further whittled down to a top 10 in February 1961. The finalists were:

Avengers	Metropolitans
Bees	NYBs
Burros	Rebels
Continentals	Skyliners
Jets	Skyscrapers

Somehow, Payson's favored Meadowlarks didn't make the list.

Obviously, the final winner was Metropolitans, eventually shortened to Mets, which, um, met most of the criteria the club set forth when board chairman M. Donald Grant made the official announcement at the Savoy Hilton Hotel on May 8, 1961. Besides fitting neatly into newspaper headlines and having some local history as the name of an American Association team from the 1880s, Mets was chosen by the most people writing in. The people's team indeed.

teams.) The AL moved forward with expansion in 1961 and instituted a 162-game schedule. The NL played one more year with 154 games and 8 teams before entering the world of 10 teams and 162 games. What would New York's new team do with that extra year?

Well, there was plenty to do, not the least of which was find a name. Out of thousands of suggestions, the one that came up most often was Mets, like the long-dead American Association team of 1883–1887. Influential *New York Times* sports columnist Arthur Daley dismissed it. "This nickname rings no bells, throws off no sparks." That's where Casey Stengel came in.

Stengel had been first choice of the Angels, but the club's rushing from birth to debut in four months was a little quick for the 70-year-old Stengel, who'd been "retired" against his wishes by the Yankees despite 10 pennants in 12 years. Though the Angels job would have kept Casey at home in Glendale, California, he would have had all of one day to sign a contract and then head to the AL's first expansion draft and pick from a crop of Junior Circuit flotsam. He also turned down the Tigers, among other inquiries, but throughout 1961, Stengel seemed set to return to New York and show his old employer that he could still manage. He officially said yes to the Mets on the final weekend of the '61 season.

After four years of politicking, meeting, bluffing, and badgering to bring a new baseball team to New York, everything moved aside for something that fans of all ages could relate to: ballplayers. The Mets had signed minor leaguers through their affiliates in Mobile, Raleigh, and Lexington, North Carolina. Each of the eight National League teams submitted a list of players that the Mets and Houston Colt .45s could draft. The bounty was far from inspiring.

Before the draft was even held, Houston GM Paul Richards was given a gag order by the league to stop complaining about the paucity of talent available. Observers

Ma Met
JOAN PAYSON

What do you get the woman who has everything? Her own baseball team.

Joan Payson wasn't just the money behind the New York Mets; she was the matron and pillar of patience and pride as the Mets of the 1960s ran the gamut from stupendously bad to, as patron Casey Stengel put it, "Amazin', amazin', amazin'."

Born into the gilded Whitney family, Payson had one set of ancestors who came over on the *Mayflower* and another that arrived on the *Arbella*, which sailed into Plymouth Colony in 1630. Her nineteenth-century forebears included a senator, a secretary of the navy, and an ambassador to Great Britain; the latter post was later served by Joan's brother, John Hay "Jock" Whitney, publisher of the *New York Herald Tribune*. The 21-year-old Joan wed Charles Shipman Payson on July 5, 1924, and they eventually had three daughters and two sons; the eldest boy, Daniel Carroll Payson, was killed at the Battle of the Bulge.

Joan Payson had an eye for paintings and horses, opened a children's bookshop, invested in the film *Gone with the Wind*, and gave vast sums to charity, the arts, and civic causes. But most of all, her passion was baseball. An avid follower of the New York Giants since her youth, Payson shared with her stockbroker and representative in baseball matters, M. Donald Grant, the dream of running a ballclub. Payson bought Grant's one share in the Giants and owned 10 percent of the team by 1957, when she was the lone dissenting vote on the team's decision to move to San Francisco. That ship sailed without her.

Payson was the perfect ownership candidate for William A. Shea's Continental League franchise in New York. By the time the National League allowed New York and Houston entry into the league, Payson was the majority owner of the new franchise, the first woman to purchase a major league team. (Helene Britton had inherited ownership of the St. Louis Cardinals from her uncle in the 1910s.) Payson eventually owned 80 percent of the club.

She stayed positive during the team's ghastly 40–120 maiden voyage, even joking, "If we can't get anything, we are going to cut those losses down—at least to 119." The 1963 Mets cut their losses down to 109. The team on the field wasn't much improved, but the shift from the decrepit Polo Grounds to Shea Stadium in 1964 helped make the moribund Mets a hot ticket.

Shea Stadium outdrew Yankee Stadium in attendance for the rest of Payson's life. And though her club couldn't attract more fans than the Los Angeles Dodgers, the Mets did far better than the relocated Giants in San Francisco. Of course, the greatest success that Payson enjoyed during her time as Mets owner was the miracle run to a World Series championship in 1969. She presided over another improbable pennant in 1973, although that dream came to an end with a loss to Oakland in the Fall Classic.

By then, Payson's health was failing, and her appearances next to the Mets dugout became increasingly rare. A stroke in mid-1975 left her incapacitated, and she died on October 4 at age 72, just one week after Casey Stengel's death from cancer. The two were enshrined in the inaugural Mets Hall of Fame class in 1981.

Joan Payson enjoys one of the brighter moments of her tenure as Mets owner: the 1969 World Series. *Focus on Sport/Getty Images*

Play It Again, Guys
CASEY STENGEL AND GEORGE WEISS

Casey Stengel and George Weiss spent 17 seasons together in New York. In this duet, it was pretty obvious who was the comedian and who was the straight man.

George Martin Weiss put his Yale education to use on the diamond. His native New Haven sandlot team did so well he was offered the local franchise in the Eastern League. He had moved to the International League as general manager in Baltimore when Yankees owner Colonel Jacob Ruppert hired him to organize his franchise's farm system. Weiss did much of the work for stockpiling the players that dominated baseball for the Yankees. In 1947 he was named general manager of the big league club, replacing the combative Larry MacPhail, who had fired Weiss 12 hours earlier. Weiss' teams went on to win 11 pennants, 10 of those thanks to his controversial managerial choice: Casey Stengel.

Charles Dillon Stengel was as loud as Weiss was quiet, but like his boss, Casey was a baseball man to the core. His Kansas City hometown provided his nickname, and Casey did the rest. While his mother wanted him to be a dentist, he wound up a Dodger instead. Stengel learned at the knee of colorful sage Wilbert Robinson and led Uncle Robbie's troops with a .364 average in the 1916 World Series loss to Babe Ruth's Red Sox. Stengel later studied under John McGraw with the New York Giants and even contributed the first World Series home run at Yankee Stadium, a game-winning inside-the-park job to give the Giants the 1923 series opener. Two days later he delivered the second Yankee Stadium World Series clout—clearing the right-field wall in the 10th inning for the only run of Game 3. The Giants lost the series despite Stengel's .417 average, again with the Babe pacing the opposition.

A born manager, Casey spent six years apprenticing in the minors before returning to the major leagues in the same place he began as a player: Brooklyn. He managed nine years with the second-division Dodgers and Braves, only once leading his team to a winning record. Stengel returned to the minors, and his success with the Oakland Oaks of the Pacific Coast

Team president George Weiss and manager Casey Stengel compare notes in the dugout at spring training, March 1962. *Donald Uhrbrock/Time Life Pictures/Getty Images*

League convinced Weiss to make Casey the choice to take over the Yankees in 1949. He won 90 or more games in each of his first 10 seasons in the Bronx, including an unprecedented five consecutive world championships (1949–1953). After winning 103 games but finishing behind the 111-win Indians in 1954, the Yankees won four more pennants in a row.

The Yankees won 97 times in 1960 and then dominated the Pirates in the World Series. New York outscored Pittsburgh 55–27 in the seven games, but when Bill Mazeroski's ninth-inning home run won the finale, the Yanks had lost. So had Stengel and Weiss.

A newly enforced Yankees "policy" requiring all employees age 65 or older to retire forced out Stengel and then Weiss. Weiss' Yankees contract stipulated that he could not serve as general manager anywhere for one year, so the Mets named him president in March 1961. He took over the role from owner Joan Payson's stockbroker, M. Donald Grant. Weiss' appointment also ended speculation that the 80-year-old Branch Rickey would serve as president, with Leo Durocher as manager.

Stengel had an even stranger contract—with the *Saturday Evening Post*. A series of articles required author Stengel to be unaffiliated with a club, so all of New York waited for the articles to come out and for Casey to come out with it. Stengel had first hinted in March that he had talked with the still-unnamed New York team; it was the last week in September when Casey stopped being coy, though his challenged syntax was just a sampling of what the press and public could expect. "You can say I'm happy going back to the Polar Grounds," Stengel said, in between references of his new team, "The Knickerbockers."

Weiss and Stengel would build a New York franchise that had nothing in common with the one from which they had come. But it would be fun, and Casey made sure of that. In the last go-round in their Hall of Fame careers, these two "retired" men put together a team that New York desperately wanted. The fans rewarded them with unquestionable love and loyalty, despite a baseball product that was the worst of the century. You can't have everything.

NATIONAL LEAGUE EXPANSION DRAFT, OCTOBER 10, 1961

PRICE	PICK/NAME (PREVIOUS TEAM)	POSITION	YEARS WITH METS
$75,000	1. Hobie Landrith (Giants)	catcher	1962
	2. Elio Chacon (Reds)	infielder	1962
	3. Roger Craig (Dodgers)	pitcher	1962–63
	4. Gus Bell (Reds)	outfielder	1962
	5. Joe Christopher (Pirates)	outfielder	1962–65
	6. Felix Mantilla (Braves)	infielder	1962
	7. Gil Hodges (Dodgers)	infielder	1962–63
	8. Craig Anderson (Cardinals)	pitcher	1962–64
	9. Ray Daviault (Giants)	pitcher	1962
	10. John DeMerit (Braves)	outfielder	1962
	11. Al Jackson (Pirates)	pitcher	1962–65, 1968–69
	12. Sammy Drake (Cubs)	infielder	1962
	13. Chris Cannizzaro (Cardinals)	catcher	1962–65
	14. Choo Choo Coleman (Phillies)	catcher	1962–63, 1966
	15. Ed Bouchee (Cubs)	infielder	1962
	16. Bobby Gene Smith (Phillies)	outfielder	1962
$50,000	17. Sherman Jones (Reds)	pitcher	1962
	18. Jim Hickman (Cardinals)	outfielder	1962–66
$125,000	19. Bob L. Miller (Cardinals)	pitcher	1962, 1973–74
	20. Jay Hook (Reds)	pitcher	1962–64
	21. Don Zimmer (Cubs)	infielder	1962
	22. Lee Walls (Phillies)	outfielder	none

noted that because the National League had a year's notice of the expansion draft, existing teams could maneuver players and prospects so they would not be exposed to the draft, whereas the previous year's American League draft, held with less than a month's notice, offered far more talent for the expansion Senators and Angels to choose from. (Indeed, after two miserable seasons by the new NL clubs, the league permitted a make-good draft with a handful of players in 1963.)

Though he'd been on the job less than two weeks by the day of the expansion draft, Casey Stengel's wit was in midseason form. "I want to thank all these owners for giving us all those great players they did not want. Those lovely, generous owners."

Those owners also made a few bucks off their new colleagues. The draft, held the day after the Yankees beat the Reds in the 1961 World Series, took place in Cincinnati (the league headquarters at the time). Each of the eight existing teams had to leave 15 men unprotected on their 40-man rosters. Seven of the players had to have been on a team's 25-man roster as of August 31, while the remaining eight came from the farm system. New York and Houston could each choose 16 players from the first pool at a price tag of $75,000 apiece. Next, the teams could select two players from a second pool at $50,000 each. Finally, four premium picks could be made for $125,000 per man. The spending spree totaled $1.8 million.

The Mets went shopping with their eyes on familiar names and faces. Gil Hodges, Don Zimmer, and Roger Craig were all former Brooklyn Dodgers left unprotected. Lee Walls and Gus Bell were both former all-stars, and Ed Bouchee and Felix Mantilla were still in their primes, but their previous employers all saw them as expendable, and time would show that to be wise. Without having to worry about fans with memories of past heroes, Houston went for most of the younger talent.

The Mets squandered their first pick on Giants catcher Hobie Landrith. "You gotta have a catcher or you're going to have a lot of passed balls," Stengel quipped as he gabbed with scribes between picks—but that line was all that was memorable of Landrith's brief stay in New York. The only youthful everyday players the Mets got out of the draft were Jim Hickman and Joe Christopher. They got lucky with Al Jackson, but the southpaw didn't have much luck in return, since the team behind him displayed some of the worst fielding since the development of the baseball glove.

Granted, the available players were generally poor, but the team's drafting strategy was even more questionable. "Our main aim had been to get men of experience," Mets general manager George Weiss said. "And while there now remains a tremendous amount of work to be done, I honestly believe we have the nucleus around which we can build an interesting ballclub." The 1962 Mets were certainly not dull.

1 Former Brooklyn and Los Angeles Dodger Gil Hodges was one of the old heroes brought back to join New York's newest National League franchise. Here he shows off his freshly signed contract in front of an artist's rendering of a planned new ballpark for the Mets. *John Lindsay/AP Images*

2 One of the few everyday players to emerge from the expansion draft, Joe Christopher spent four seasons with the Mets and had his best season in 1964, when he batted .300 and led the team with 76 RBI. *Rogers Photo Archive/Getty images*

3 Hobie Landrith was the Mets' first pick in the 1962 expansion draft. The catcher played a grand total of 23 games for the club. *Rogers Photo Archive/Getty images*

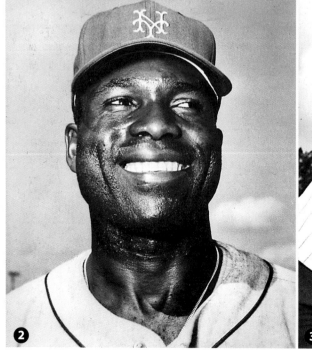

4 The Ol' Perfessor, Casey Stengel. *Donald Uhrbrock/Time Life Pictures/ Getty Images*

5 Happy to be back in New York, Frank Thomas, Gil Hodges, Don Zimmer, and Roger Craig whoop it up at the Polo Grounds prior to the start of the 1962 season. The positive outlook would be short-lived. *Pat Candido/NY Daily News Archive/Getty Images*

6 Team president George Weiss (in trench coat), Mayor Robert Wagner, and manager Casey Stengel gather with the inaugural-season New York Mets at a City Hall reception in April 1962. *Phil Greitzer/NY Daily News Archive/Getty Images*

CHAPTER 1

1962–1969

Meet the Mets

AP Images

MVP Books collection

METS

10TH PLACE · NATIONAL LEAGUE

WORLD CHAMPIONS

O n October 26, 1961, infielder Ted Lepcio became the first major league player signed to a contract by the New York Mets. On April 6, 1962, he became the last Met cut before the team headed north for the first time. Lepcio, a 32-year-old veteran of 10 major league seasons coming off a .167 season, never played professional baseball again. The Mets saved him from the ultimate humiliation.

Good players were hard to come by, especially if you were a nobody. As general manager of the Yankees from 1947 to 1960, George Weiss was used to fleecing the overeager suitors who begged for his prized talent in both the major and minor leagues. Now heading the Mets, Weiss was the supplicant, and opposing GMs licked their chops.

With nothing of value to trade, Weiss had to spend freely to acquire names that would ring true to reporters and fans who hadn't followed the National League in four years. Frank Thomas, Charlie Neal, and Richie Ashburn were all acquired in six-figure deals, joining a host of old Dodgers and Giants on the roster (and that's after Bill Loes and Johnny Antonelli retired rather than join the expansion club). The prospects, suspects, and rejects all met in St. Petersburg for spring training.

With reporters jotting down every first for the new club on day one of camp on February 18, 1962, pitcher Ken MacKenzie went in the books as the first Met with a muscle cramp. Owner Joan Payson, who'd flown from West Palm Beach for the day, held a parasol and cooed, "We're finally here." Here turned out to be the Catskill-style Colonial Inn, which traveling secretary Lon Niss switched to upon learning that the Soreno Hotel, their first choice, did not allow blacks.

When the Mets moved into their first ballpark, they had a roommate. The expansion club shared Miller Huggins Field with the Cardinals, who had called St. Petersburg their spring home since 1938 (save for three springs during World War II). The Mets were hospitable guests, and Stengel initially had his players take off their spikes in the clubhouse so as not to ruin the carpeting.

It was a busy camp, what with the dozens of players who would have been out of baseball entirely if not for expansion. A Police Athletic League veteran from Astoria, Queens, John Pappas had practiced his pitching that winter under the Triborough Bridge and demanded a tryout in person. Former big league relief ace Johnny Murphy, now an administrative assistant with the Mets, told him if he found his own field and rounded up his own catcher, they'd look at the kid pitcher. Murphy probably should have known better, but he'd also gotten a look at the arms the Mets had invited to camp. The inaugural intrasquad game ended in a tie—the only team that couldn't beat the '62 Mets was the '62 Mets.

Still, the Mets were an almost-mediocre 12–15 in Florida. The highlight was the first Mets–Yankees contest on March 22. Stengel pulled out all the stops in his first game against the club that had fired him a year and a half earlier, using his top two pitchers to face the world champion Yanks, who had won 10 of their first 11 spring games. The Yankees tied the game in the top of the ninth, but Joe Christopher tripled to lead off the bottom of the inning and Richie Ashburn singled him home to clinch the win. Stengel soaked in the applause of the 6,277 fans at Al Lang Field.

"As far as this game is concerned, it really doesn't matter," Stengel said. "When we meet each other in the World Series next fall, it will matter."

Stengel knew full well that this Mets team was the worst team he'd ever been handed—and he'd managed some pretty bad teams in his pre-Yankees days. So from the moment he arrived at spring training, the Ol' Perfessor made himself the show. "He regularly rambled on for hours and hours, telling anecdotes from the past, relating humorous yarns, and generally 'selling' the Mets as a new and promising franchise that would bring joy to long-starved National League fans in New York," wrote *Long Island Press* reporter Jack Lang.

The press played along, doting on the minor successes and characters, dropping hints and asides about the team's overall lack of talent. The reporters, Lang wrote, "were aware that fans back home were nourishing hope for their new team and wanted only good news. Why spoil it with bad news? The Mets had not lost their first game."

That would quickly change.

Messy, Messy, Metsy

The 1962 Mets wrote the book on abysmal baseball. In fact, Jimmy Breslin's seminal account of the team, *Can't Anybody Here Play This Game?*, made them into folk heroes. Anybody can lose; the original Mets were spectacular at it.

So how on earth did New York fall so hard for this historically horrific team? Breslin said it best:

> This is a team for the cab driver who gets held up and the guy who loses out on a promotion because he didn't maneuver himself to lunch with the boss enough. It is the team for every guy who has to get up out of bed every morning and go to work for short money on a job he does not like. And it is the team for every woman who looks up ten years later and sees her husband eating dinner in a T-shirt and wonders how the hell she ever let this guy talk her into getting married. The Yankees? Who does well enough to root for them, Laurance Rockefeller?

After the Mets dropped the first nine games of their existence, the *New York Times* asked a psychologist about the state of the club's followers. The doctor's diagnosis was that "becoming emotionally involved with them is a kind of masochism. A kind of painless flagellation." Nine-year-old Billy Grady was more succinct, if mathematically inaccurate: "I got two words for the Mets: They are lousy."

Lousy indeed. The Mets' 120 losses in 1962 were the most by any team in the twentieth century, and their .250 winning percentage was the worst since the 1935 Boston Braves (38–115, .248). They collected fewer base hits than any other major league club in 1962, finishing with a league-low team batting average of .240. The pitching staff was no better, posting a 5.04 ERA (worst in the majors), allowing 192 homers (most in the NL), and throwing 71 wild pitches (second most in the majors). The Mets committed 210 errors

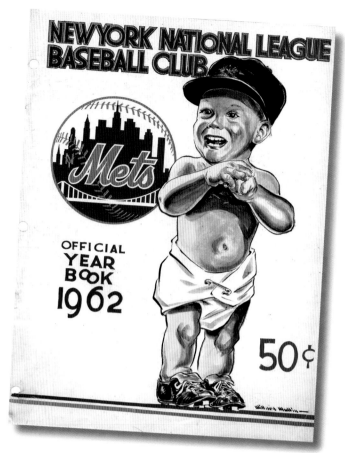

MVP Books collection

in the field to become only the fourth team since 1946 to boot more than 200 balls in a season.

The 1962 Mets had only one player bat over .300 (Richie Ashburn, .306), and they just missed becoming the first team since the 1916 Philadelphia Athletics to boast three 20-game losers on the same staff. Roger Craig (10–24) and Al Jackson (8–20) took the honors, but Jay Hook, ironically the first Met to win a game, came perilously close at 8–19. He took losses in nine of his last 10 decisions, and by all rights, he should have made it a 20-loss trio. Jay was taken off the hook, if you will, on August 15. The Mets, trailing the Phillies 6–1 when Hook was removed, rallied to tie it in the eighth in a game that wound up going 13 innings. The Mets lost, of course, but Hook earned a no-decision.

Fans reveled in the absurdity and the newness of it all. The worst players were the best characters. Marv Throneberry, acquired from Baltimore in May, was atrocious in all phases of the game—and was one of the most popular Mets. Fans chanted, "Cranberry, strawberry, we love Throneberry!" They made "Marvelous Marv" one of the most-scribbled sentiments on sheets brought to the Polo Grounds by "The

New Breed," a term that described both those who covered the Mets and those who watched them. With the initials M.E.T., Marvin Eugene Throneberry really was born to be a Met. He'd committed 15 errors over parts of five previous seasons in the majors (three of them with Stengel's Yankees), but he made 17 errors in just 87 games at first base for the '62 Mets. His base running was both atrocious and notorious. Standing on third base after a two-run triple on June 17, he was called out for missing first base. When Stengel went out to argue, first-base coach Cookie Lavagetto told his boss, "Forget it, Casey. He missed second base, too."

Catcher Clarence "Choo Choo" Coleman often forgot which signs he put down for his pitchers. He was uncommunicative for a catcher and, like most of his teammates, couldn't hit a lick, either. Utilityman "Hot Rod" Kanehl was a hustling favorite who defied odds by making the team in spring training and defied logic by playing in 133 games that year despite having more errors (31) than RBI (27).

As a nod to the randomness of baseball, the 1962 Mets did have a hot streak. The newbies went on a 9–3 tear in late May that placed them at the dizzying heights of eighth place. They then proceeded to lose 17 consecutive games. The Mets continued plummeting at a rate of about 10 games in the standings per month. They hit 100 losses the last week of August, then dropped 12 of 13 (plus a tie) to rocket past 110 defeats. The distance from first place crested at 61½ games four times during the final 10 days, but two postponed games not made up, plus the collapse of the front-running Dodgers—not anything the Mets did on the field—kept the '62 deficit from reaching 62 games. The Giants and Dodgers wound up playing a three-game playoff to decide the pennant (won by San Francisco), but Mets fans didn't pay much mind to what was going on in California. New York had the National League back. What else was there?

THE FIRST NEW YORK METS GAME

St. Louis Cardinals 11, New York Mets 4
Wednesday, April 11, 1962
at Sportsman's Park, St. Louis, MO

	1	2	3	4	5	6	7	8	9	R	H	E
NYM	0	0	2	1	1	0	0	0	0	4	8	3
STL	2	0	3	0	1	4	0	1	X	11	16	1

New York Mets	AB	R	H	RBI
Ashburn, CF	5	1	1	0
Mantilla, SS	4	1	1	0
Neal, 2B	4	1	3	2
Thomas, LF	3	0	0	1
Bell, RF	3	0	1	0
Hodges, 1B	4	1	1	1
Zimmer, 3B	4	0	1	0
Landrith, C	4	0	0	0
Craig, P	1	0	0	0
Bouchee, PH	0	0	0	0
Moorhead, P	1	0	0	0
Moford, P	0	0	0	0
Labine, P	0	0	0	0
Marshall, PH	0	0	0	0
Totals	33	4	8	4

2B: Mantilla. **HR:** Neal; Hodges. **SF:** Thomas.
Team LOB: 7
E: Neal; Landrith; Mantilla.

St. Louis Cardinals	AB	R	H	RBI
Flood, CF	4	3	2	1
Javier, 2B	5	3	4	1
White, 1B	4	1	2	3
Musial, RF	3	1	3	2
Landrum, RF	1	0	0	0
Boyer, 3B	4	0	1	2
Minoso, LF	4	0	1	1
Oliver, C	4	1	2	0
Gotay, SS	4	1	0	0
Jackson, P	4	1	1	1
Totals	37	11	16	11

2B: Boyer; Oliver 2; Musial. **SF:** White; Flood. **SB:** Flood 2, Javier.
Team LOB: 5
E: Boyer

Pitching Summary

New York Mets	IP	H	R	ER	BB	SO
Craig, L (0-1)	3	8	5	5	0	1
Moorhead	3	6	5	2	1	1
Moford	1	1	0	0	0	0
Labine	1	1	1	0	0	0
Totals	8	16	11	7	1	2

St. Louis Cardinals	IP	H	R	ER	BB	SO
Jackson, W (1-0)	9	8	4	4	4	2
Totals	9	8	4	4	4	2

Balks: Craig.

Umpires: HP Tom Gorman, 1B Bill Jackowski, 2B Ed Sudol, 3B Al Forman.
Time of Game: 2:53
Attendance: 16,147

IN SEARCH OF WIN NUMBER ONE

"We're aiming for .500 and hope to be pleasantly surprised to go over .500," Mets president George Weiss announced on the eve of the first-ever Mets game in 1962. The baseball gods must have laughed until they cried because the first game in franchise history was rained out. If only the black cloud that followed around the 40–120 Mets could have created a Noah-like flood to wash away the results.

Cardinals 11, Mets 4 (0–1)

The Mets began their existence by going down in order. Richie Ashburn cracked open Mets history by flying out and then caught the first out in the bottom of the first. Later that inning Roger Craig allowed the first run on a balk. Gus Bell had the first hit in Mets history, and Ashburn forced his way into the books again by scoring the first run on a hit by Charlie Neal. Gil Hodges hit the first Met homer; Neal added the second. Craig, given a reprieve when New York tied the game in the top of the third, let the Cardinals retake the lead in the bottom of the inning, and he was batted for in the fourth—Ed Bouchee becoming the first pinch-Met. But for all the firsts under the lights in soggy St. Louis, the only first that really mattered was their introduction to the loss column.

Pirates 4, Mets 3 (0–2)

A day after 40,000 met the Mets in a parade down Broadway, just 12,447 came to see them take the field for the drizzly home opener at the Polo Grounds. Manager Casey Stengel made the players wear their road uniforms for practice that day so as not to dirty the home duds. The Friday the 13th contest was unlucky for the Mets. Sherman "Roadblock" Jones, who had thrown the club's first complete game in spring training, had subsequently burned his eye lighting a cigarette. The Bucs lit him for a single, double, and triple in succession in the second inning to take an early 2–0 lead. The Mets had three wild pitches in a muddy, messy debut in New York.

Pirates 6, Mets 2 (0–3)

Vinegar Bend Mizell handed Al Jackson the first of his 99 career losses in a Saturday matinee. Three weeks later, the Mets acquired Mizell for Jim Marshall—who belted a solo homer off Roy Face in this game. Vinegar Bend didn't win another game for the Pirates, Mets, or anyone else.

Former all-star outfielders Richie Ashburn and Gus Bell nearly collide as a flyball lands safely in front of them during the Mets' third straight loss to open the 1962 season. *Herb Scharfman/Sports Imagery/ Getty Images*

Pirates 7, Mets 2 (0–4)

The first Mets leadoff home run—by Felix Mantilla—gave them their first lead of the season, but the thrill was short-lived. Craig again lasted just three innings, and the 1962 Mets were swept for the first of 25 times.

Colt .45s 5, Mets 2 (0–5)

After the winless expansion club had its second rainout, the Mets' best chance at victory came against a team as old as they were. Expansion Houston, which began its existence with a three-game sweep of the Cubs, was one out from a regulation victory over the Mets when Gus Bell's homer tied the game. New York had a runner thrown out at third base in the 10th inning, and Don Buddin won Houston's first-ever road game an inning later with a three-run home run off Herb Moford.

Cardinals 15, Mets 5 (0–6)

The Mets' spring training host paid a visit and handed New York its second double-digit thumping—the Cards had administered the first as well.

Cardinals 9, Mets 4 (0–7)

The Cardinals improved to 6–0 with yet another drubbing of the hapless, helpless, winless Mets. Ken Boyer homered for the third time in two days, though the Mets kept the Cards under 10 runs for the first time in three meetings. The inaugural Mets homestand ended at 0–6.

Pirates 8, Mets 4 (0–8)

Pittsburgh improved to a 9–0 record while the Mets dropped to 0–8. New York briefly went ahead in the game on Mantilla's two-run double in the fourth inning, but the lead lasted until the bottom of the inning.

Pirates 4, Mets 3 (0–9)

The Mets took their first multiple-run lead, only to see the Bucs rally against Craig in the sixth. A Roberto Clemente error set up the tying run for the Mets in the seventh, but then Clemente scored the go-ahead run on Bill Mazeroski's triple in the eighth. Roadblock Jones fell to 0–3, and the 0–9 Mets stood nine and a half games behind the Pirates.

Mets 9, Pirates 1 (1–9)

Ah, sweet victory. Jay Hook, who had allowed 16 runs in an exhibition game in Florida, allowed just one at Forbes Field to give the New York Mets their first win (ever) and hand the Pirates their first loss of the season. Indeed, Hook outdid the Bucs with his bat as well, driving in two runs and scoring twice. Felix Mantilla and Elio Chacon got things started with back-to-back singles to open the game, and both eventually scored to give New York an early 2–0 lead on this historic Monday evening, April 23. The team's 14 hits and 9 runs in the game were the most in Mets history to that point. All returned to normal the next night, when Mets starter Craig Anderson didn't last past the first inning in Cincinnati, starting a three-game skid.

MVP Books collection

Less of the Same

Joan Payson's cash was the sole enticement for most teams to make deals with the Mets. Though that system was costly, it did net Ron Hunt and Carl Willey from the Milwaukee Braves. Hunt would become the first young Met to show promise, leading the team in most offensive categories in 1963. Willey's 9–14 mark and 3.10 ERA were like a very poor man's version of Sandy Koufax.

Koufax was hardly for sale—and his no-hitter against the Mets in 1962 was like an All-American team beating the junior varsity squad—but New York continued loading up on former Dodgers, purchasing outfielder Dick Smith and catcher Norm Sherry. As the Mets prepared to break camp in 1963 after their first dalliance with winning (a 15–12 spring mark in St. Pete), the roster featured seven former Dodgers, plus an eighth in Triple-A Buffalo, Joe Pignatano—whose last at bat in the majors resulted in a triple play that also ended the big league careers of base runners Richie Ashburn and Solly Drake in 1962. People called the Mets "the Dodgers' B team," but C team would have been more fitting, even after the Mets purchased an April Fool's gift too good to be true: Duke Snider.

New York reunited the Duke of Flatbush with Gil Hodges, giving New York the two most popular still-active stars of the 1955 Dodgers championship club. But these former Bums were on the downsides of their careers. In his last five years in Brooklyn, Snider had surpassed 40 homers each season; in five seasons in L.A., he'd reached 20 once. As a Met in 1963, Snider played more games than he had since his last season at Ebbets Field in 1957. He clubbed New York's first home run of the year, while becoming the first Met to touch home plate in 1963—in the season's third game. Snider, in fact, hit four homers in his first week as a Met, but the team had yet to win. The Mets finally earned a victory in their ninth game, barely avoiding matching their inauspicious 1962 beginning. Snider couldn't stay that hot, and the Mets couldn't be as bad as the previous year's club. His .401 slugging in '63 was his lowest in 16 years, yet it was the highest of any Mets regular.

The reunion of Duke and Gil was short-lived, however. Gimpy and 39, Hodges began his new career as a manager when the expansion Washington Senators hired him and sent back Jim Piersall (though Weiss caused a rift with the press by insisting it was not a straight-up trade). Piersall wanted, but was refused, Casey's uniform number (37). The veteran outfielder, who had spoken unkindly of Stengel when both were in the American League, was released after batting .194 in 40 games.

Attendance increased to 1.08 million, third-best in the league and marking the first time a last-place team exceeded the million mark. The '63 Mets were also the first team to lose 109 games yet have it be an improvement from the previous season (by 22 percent). Fans had a ball in the waning days of the Polo Grounds, reveling in the team's minute successes while marveling at the club's continued failures. Inundated with bed sheets hung by fans at the Polo Grounds, the Mets, who had originally discouraged this practice under Weiss' frowning glare, embraced the fans who saw fit to scrawl their sentiments on their linens. The Mets inaugurated Banner Day in 1963, allowing fans to march on the field between games of a doubleheader, an annual rite that continued for more than three decades.

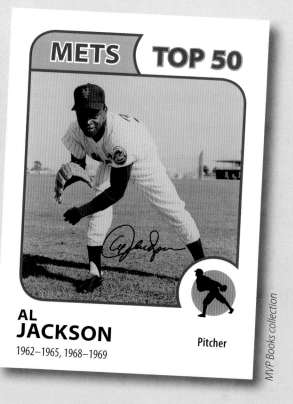

METS TOP 50

AL JACKSON
1962–1965, 1968–1969

Pitcher

In 1962, Ray Charles recorded a version of a song of the luckless lover: "Born to Lose." The song perfectly fit that year's 120-loss Mets. Al Jackson, taken from the Pirates with New York's 11th pick in the expansion draft, got to pitch every fourth day as a Met, but, oh, the losses would come: "Born to lose, and now I'm losing you."

The youngest of 13 children, Alvin Neill Jackson didn't dwell on defeat. He threw the first (and only) four Mets shutouts in '62, and he earned the team's first win and shutout at Shea Stadium in 1964. The tough Texan had 10 shutouts and 41 complete games in four seasons, the most until Tom Seaver and Jerry Koosman arrived. A pair of 20-loss seasons assured that Jackson's club record for losses would last well into the 1970s.

He was traded to St. Louis for Ken Boyer after the 1965 season and then was reacquired by New York the day after the Cardinals won the 1967 World Series (Jackson saw no Series action), but the Mets were neither as bad nor Jackson as good as when they first parted ways. By mid-1969, the suddenly contending Mets sold their former star to the Reds. Jackson once again missed pitching in a World Series, but he would come back to the Mets. He spent most of the next four decades working with the club's minor leaguers, and he was bullpen coach for the only back-to-back postseason appearances in Mets history in 1999–2000.

Jimmy Piersall was a legendary character, and former all-star, with the Red Sox and Indians in the 1950s and early 1960s, but his time with the Mets was brief. After hitting his one hundredth career home run, Piersall (wearing number 34) circled the bases backward. It was his only homer as a Met. *AP Images*

The 1963 Mets enjoyed what was arguably the most fan-friendly season to that point in baseball's long and staid history. The Mets had an official mascot named Homer, a beagle sponsored by Rheingold, with his own platform behind home plate. The image of Mr. Met debuted on the yearbook and was also featured on the record sleeve of the team's musical anthem, "Meet the Mets." The catchy tune, written by Ruth Roberts and Bill Katz, was sold as a 45-rpm record at the ballpark for a buck. It summed up the city's enthusiasm about this terrible team. The sentiment has held steady for a half century.

> *Meet the Mets, Meet the Mets,*
> *Step right up and greet the Mets.*
> *Bring your kiddies, bring your wife,*
> *Guaranteed to have the time of your life.*
> *Because the Mets are really socking that ball*
> *(CRACK!)*
> *Knockin' those home runs over the wall.*
> *East Side, West Side, everybody's coming down,*
> *To meet the M-E-T-S Mets, of New York town.*
>
> *Oh, the butcher and the baker and the people on*
> *the street.*
> *Where did they go? To MEET THE METS!*
> *Oh, they're hollerin' and cheerin' and they're jumpin' in*
> *their seats.*
> *Where did they go? To MEET THE METS!*
> *Oh, the fans are true to the orange and blue,*
> *So hurry up and come on down,*
> *'cause we've got ourselves a ballclub,*
> *The Mets of New York town!*
> *Give 'em a yell! Give 'em a hand!*
> *And let' em know you're rooting in the stands!*
> *Come on and ...*
> *(Repeat first verse)*

The obscure second verse may be known only to the round-the-bend diehards, but the song has served to indoctrinate children into the world of the Mets for generations. Once heard or sung, "Meet the Mets" is practically impossible to dislodge from memory. Its breeziness defies even inbred levels of pessimism, at least for a few moments after singing.

Mr. Met was introduced as the team mascot in 1963, although riding a bicycle during a parade was not part of the job description for the top-heavy mascot. *Ossie LeViness/NY Daily News Archive/Getty Images*

After two years and 231 losses, a far-off concept of greatness, or at least mediocrity, was somewhere out there, but far, far into a future that was hard to imagine. As the Yankees continued racking up pennants, the question for the Mets as they departed the Polo Grounds for the last time was this: Could they sustain this high level of fan interest in a new home when it was blatantly obvious that the team would not be good for years to come? Announcer Lindsey Nelson provided an answer while narrating the club's 1963 highlight film, which was shown to organizations large and small throughout the tri-state area as a way of keeping the Mets drums beating. "Winning is important, of course," Nelson said, "but not out of proportion to the fun of the game." These would prove words to live by.

Mets Meet World

The 1964 season was about timing. Though the Mets' new home, Shea Stadium, opened a year behind schedule, it turned out to be right on time. That the Mets went on to post the worst record in baseball for the third year running hardly mattered. They would be seen by more people than any team in baseball other than the Dodgers. The Mets' attendance of 1,732,597 was better than 400,000 more than the Yankees, who won their fifth straight pennant in 1964. Given Shea

Shea Stadium was only about one-third full when the Braves came to town for a series in May 1964, but the Mets finished the season number two in the National League in attendance in the first year of their new ballpark. *AP Images*

Stadium's location next to the World's Fair, it's safe to say the Mets had more people who knew nothing of baseball watch their games than any major league club. Those spectators were the lucky ones.

The 1964 Mets were as dreadful as their predecessors. Though they won two more games than the previous year's club, for every tiny step forward, it seemed another humiliation was added. Still, the move from the drab Polo Grounds to bright, new Shea Stadium was like trading in a black-and-white television for a color set. While demolition of the old stadium went on in Harlem, the Mets opened Shea Stadium against Pittsburgh on April 17. Pirate Willie Stargell christened the place with a home run, and Bucco Bob Friend (who had gotten the win the day the Giants closed the Polo Grounds in 1957) beat the Mets at their new home, 4–3. The Mets secured their first win of the season in record time—only five games!—when Al Jackson tossed the first shutout on the first Sunday at the colorful new ballpark.

Blue and orange steel panels hung in mid-air on Shea Stadium's exterior. Inside, every level had a different seat color: Field Level—yellow; Loge—red, Mezzanine—blue, Upper Deck—green. Green was also the color of what the new place was raking in. In the first nine games at Shea, 238,532 paid their way in—a quarter of the previous year's

Getty Images

SHEA STADIUM
A Home of Their Own

In 1964, baseball was filled with ballparks that were older than the parents of many of the "New Breed" (as Mets fans were known in the early days), but Shea Stadium was the epitome of ballpark innovation and New Frontier planning. Publicly funded, over budget, and behind schedule, the stadium nevertheless opened to great fanfare. No poles obstructing views, escalators took fans where they needed to go, ramps made for easy access in and out, and plenty of parking for everyone, plus subway and commuter railroad stops. And if the losing got to be too much, fans could slide over to the World's Fair at Flushing Meadows for a Belgian waffle and a ride on "It's a Small World."

Shea Stadium, home of 3,609 Metsian dramas (1,882 ending happily) over the years watched in person by nearly 100 million people, also housed the Jets, Giants, Yankees, the Pope, the Beatles, and a "who's who" of rock 'n' roll acts during its 45 years. Mets fans came to defensively call the place "our dump," but it actually began as the city's dump.

The salt meadow along Flushing Creek had been a dumping ground for ashes and soot in the early twentieth century. The site was ghastly enough to be immortalized as the Valley of Ashes in F. Scott Fitzgerald's *The Great Gatsby*, set on Long Island in 1922. At the end of the 1930s, the eyesore ash heap had been cleaned up by master planner Robert Moses for the 1939 World's Fair. While Moses constructed his vision of New York through the building of roads, bridges, tunnels, and the relocation of thousands of its citizens, he never took his eye off Flushing Meadows. When Walter O'Malley wanted to move the Dodgers to a new site in Brooklyn, Moses insisted that the team go to Queens. They went to Los Angeles instead and convinced the New York Giants to head to San Francisco.

Though it was Houston that eventually built a revolutionary domed stadium, New York thought of it first. An 80,000-seat stadium with an enclosed roof had been proposed since O'Malley was still in town. A dome would have run almost $2 million on top of New York's $16 million stadium budget, so the idea was scrapped.

Mayor Robert Wagner had to plead with the state assembly after a stadium measure was rejected in March 1961, and an agreement providing the Mets with a 30-year lease on the Queens site was finally approved that autumn. The official groundbreaking took place on October 28, 1961.

Progress on the stadium was slow and got slower. While the city council agreed in January 1963 to name the stadium after William A. Shea, the ballpark would not be ready for Opening Day as initially hoped. Promises by engineers, politicians, and club officials that the stadium would open for baseball that August were greeted with the *New York Times* headline, "Met Park to Be Ready This Year for Sure, Maybe." Cost overruns, contractor problems, and weather delays finally led officials to concede in July that the stadium would not be ready for the Mets or the American Football League's Jets in 1963. After nearly $29 million and 29 months, it was barely ready for the 1964 opener.

Bill Shea dedicated his stadium by pouring out bottles of water from the Gowanus Canal, the banks of which were near old Ebbets Field, and the Harlem River, which was adjacent to the Polo Grounds. And then the Mets proceeded to stink up the new joint. But it was like driving nowhere in a new sports car: Who cared where you going so long as you were in the newest and fastest thing around?

Baseball's worst team was nearly its most popular. Shea Stadium ranked second in National League attendance in five of its first seven seasons until 1969, when the Mets had the league's highest gate totals four years running and topped two million per season.

Shea was jammed even after baseball was done for the year. Joe Namath, who boldly guaranteed and then delivered a victory in Super Bowl III, made the Jets one of football's best draws. When Yankee Stadium was being rebuilt, the Yankees

Shea Stadium exterior, 1964. *R. Gates/Getty Images*

(1974–75) and the NFL Giants (1975) moved to Queens. Shea was the only venue to play host to an outdoor game in New York in 1975, hosting a staggering 173 regular season sporting events. Between all that sports traffic on the field and the concerts held there, the place aged quickly, and a financially strapped city wasn't able to provide much beyond paint and band-aids.

After Shea attracted fewer than one million fans for the first time in 1979, the Mets were sold and stadium improvements began. The signature orange and blue exterior panels were removed, as were the outdated wooden chairs. Later, touches like a giant apple popping out of a top hat to celebrate home runs, a video scoreboard, and picnic-area bleachers in left field brightened up the place. The workload also lightened when Shea became a one-team stadium after the Jets moved to New Jersey following the 1983 season. Yet nothing did more for Shea's profile than housing a championship team. The Mets became the first New York team to draw three million fans in 1987, the year after they rallied to win the World Series. The Mets led the majors in attendance in 1988 while winning another division title.

But what goes up must come down. The team's misfortunes in the early 1990s stole the luster from Shea. A Nickelodeon amusement park behind the outfield walls in 1994 resulted in the rebirth of Mr. Met and the fun practice of letting kids run the bases after certain games. While the team's first back-to-back postseason appearances in 1999 and 2000 made Shea a happy place, the harsh reality of life after the 2001 terrorist attacks on New York made everyone in the city reconsider their priorities. Shea Stadium served as a staging area for supplies for several days after the attack, and then it hosted the first post-9/11 outdoor sporting event in New York. Mike Piazza's dramatic home run made it a winning and memorable night.

Even as the team subsequently teased its fans with glimpses of greatness and Shea broke its attendance record three years running from 2006 to 2008, those were the last three years of its life. On September 28, 2008, a season of countdowns reached zero. The postgame ceremony coincided with the Mets being knocked out of contention on the last day. As 43 former Mets stood on the ballpark's diamond for the last time, Shea basked in its final curtain call even as its replacement bulged just beyond the fence. "Shea Goodbye" the scoreboard said to an old friend who had taken the multipurpose facility beyond what was ever expected and planted National League baseball so deeply in New York soil that it could not be uprooted again.

ROCK ON, SHEA

In its later years, Shea Stadium's multipurpose past was looked down upon by those who demanded one-sport exclusivity per venue. Shea hosted football for 20 seasons and baseball for 45, but for some people, the place lives on because of something completely different: rock 'n' roll.

Though the stadium hosted Pope John Paul II in 1979, along with many other religious gatherings—not to mention far less sacred proceedings like flea markets and wrestling matches—Shea joined the ranks of legend in just its second year of existence when, on August 15, 1965, 55,600 people helped the Beatles earn $304,000 in one evening. They played for barely half an hour, cranking out a dozen songs at a rate of almost $10,000 per minute. To the people who were there and those born long after who still cherish the music of John Lennon, Paul McCartney, George Harrison, and Ringo Starr, it was a priceless event and the granddaddy of stadium rock.

The Beatles returned a year later on what would be their final concert tour. The Fab Four were a tough act to follow, but the shows went on. In 1971, Grand Funk sold the place out even faster than the Beatles, and a year before that the Festival for Peace featured one of the last appearances by Janis Joplin. Unlike the Beatles concerts, which had confined the band to the infield and the crowd to the stands, promoters discovered that there was even more money to be made by putting the stage in the outfield and letting the fans crowd onto the field. The Who came to Shea in October 1982, which made the trashed field the Jets' problem, but concerts by Simon and Garfunkle and The Police over a two-week span in August 1983 left the field in absolute shambles. The last-place Mets weren't in much better shape.

The Rolling Stones played Shea for six shows in 1989, and Elton John and Eric Clapton played two shows together in 1992. The damage done to the field helped put a moratorium on concerts at the stadium until Bruce Springsteen played three nights there in October 2003. Shea's final year saw one final concert—and then two after the first one sold out in minutes—as Billy Joel played twice in July 2008. He even ceded the stage and final song to Paul McCartney, who had played the first Shea show and would play the first concert at Citi Field a year later.

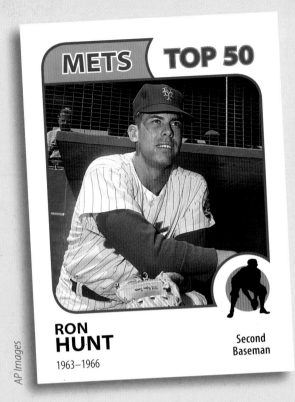

METS TOP 50

RON HUNT
1963–1966

Second Baseman

Ron Hunt was hit by a record 50 pitches in a season while with Montreal in 1971—and 243 times in his career—but as a Met, he was known for his ability to produce hits during the club's formative years. He led the Mets in batting in three of his four years in New York. His .303 mark in 1964 was the highest by a Met until Cleon Jones hit .340 in 1969.

Ronald Kenneth Hunt grew up in St. Louis and was signed by the Milwaukee Braves as an 18-year-old in 1959. The Mets purchased the minor league second baseman after their disastrous 1962 debut season. He finished second to Pete Rose in 1963 in National League Rookie of the Year voting, and his 10 homers and 42 RBI were numbers he matched just once more in his 12-year career. In 1964 he became the first Met to start an All-Star Game. He singled off Dean Chance in the National League's dramatic win at Shea Stadium.

Injuries derailed Hunt's 1965 season, but he hit .288 a year later and was an all-star again. (His bunt set up Tim McCarver's game-winning single in the 10th inning.) Hunt's .282 average as a Met was the club standard when he was traded, with popular Jim Hickman, to the Dodgers for Tommy Davis. Two generations later, he still ranks in the club's top 10 in average, but no Met has surpassed Hunt's 41 hit by pitches. That's a record no one's anxious to break.

take at the Polo Grounds—and the Mets hadn't yet hosted the top draws, the Dodgers and Giants.

The Giants made their first trip to Shea Stadium at the end of May, and the cellar-dwelling Mets won the first two games of the weekend series with San Francisco behind Jack Fisher and Tracy Stallard. The Mets took the field for the Sunday doubleheader with Ed Kranepool, fresh off a doubleheader in Triple-A Buffalo the previous day, arriving just in time to be in the lineup against San Francisco's Juan Marichal. Not surprisingly, the Mets lost the opener. With the Mets trailing

As the Giants and Mets enter the 18th inning of their contest on May 31, 1964, the Shea scoreboard announces it as the longest game of the year. The teams would go on to play six more innings before San Francisco secured an 8–6 win. *John J. Lent/AP Images*

6–1 in the nightcap, Kranepool's triple started a sixth-inning rally, and Joe Christopher's three-run shot in the seventh tied the game. It stayed tied for the next 16 innings. In the course of the marathon contest, the Mets turned a triple play, Willie Mays played shortstop, and a dozen players came to the plate 10 times in the game. Gaylord Perry, a struggling 25-year-old hurler without a start to that point for the '64 Giants, entered the game in the 13th and threw 10 innings of shutout ball. Del Crandall, batting for Perry in the 23rd inning, hit a two-out double to bring home Jim Davenport in the game's seventh hour and make this the longest game yet played to a conclusion (a record the Mets would twice break in the next decade). Perry earned the win and hard-luck Galen Cisco took the loss, just as the two pitchers had in a 15-inning game in San Francisco 15 days earlier.

Shea Stadium hosted its first—and only—All-Star Game on July 7, 1964, a thriller decided on a ninth-inning homer by Philadelphia's Johnny Callison. By then, Callison had already homered three times at Shea Stadium, the second coming during Jim Bunning's perfect game on Father's Day. It was the first 27-up, 27-down outing in the National League in 84 years.

Even though the Mets kept making history for all the wrong reasons, the fans loved the team and its new home. The Mets drew 30,000 or better for 24 of their first 69 home contests at a time when the league's average attendance was less than 15,000 per game. Yet the Mets responded with a 33–48 mark at home—worst in the NL, again. (That was, however, better than two AL clubs.)

The road was even more foreboding. Despite twice beating the eventual world champion Cardinals in St. Louis in the last series of the year—the Cards rallied to win the final game on Sunday to clinch the pennant—the Mets won just 20 of 81 games away from Shea. That .247 road percentage was the highest in the history of the team to that point.

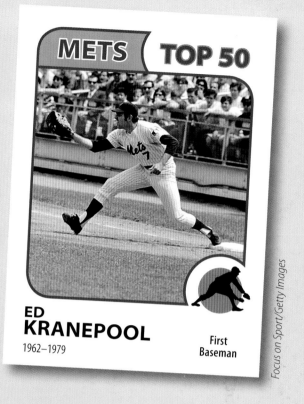

METS TOP 50

ED KRANEPOOL
1962–1979

First Baseman

In the team's first two decades, the Mets went from terrible to Amazin' to terrible again. Ed Kranepool saw it all.

Recruited by colleges out of James Monroe High School in the Bronx for both baseball and basketball, Edward Emil Kranepool Jr. chose the expansion Mets in 1962 and their $80,000 bonus, plus incentives for reaching each level of the minor leagues. He achieved them all by September, debuting at the Polo Grounds at age 17.

By the time he was 18, Kranepool was the number-three hitter and starting right fielder. Sent to the minors for more seasoning, the lefty returned as an all-star at age 20. He homered in the 1969 World Series but a year later was back in the minors. He raised his average 110 points in 1971 and made a successful transition to pinch hitter. "Steady Eddie" batted .486 off the bench in 1974 and clubbed three pinch homers in 1978. His 90 career pinch hits remain the club record.

Kranepool played in each of the first 18 seasons of the Mets franchise. In his last at bat in the 1979 season finale, he rapped career double number 225—securing one of the many team records he held upon his retirement. Although his doubles total has since been surpassed (by David Wright), Kranepool still holds the franchise marks for games, at bats, hits, and total bases. A successful businessman, he was also part of a group that tried, unsuccessfully, to buy the team in 1980.

1 Returning Brooklyn hero Duke Snider joined the Mets in 1963, but the New York reunion lasted only one season, as the future Hall of Famer struggled with a .243 average and 14 homers in 129 games. *Herb Scharfman/ Time Life Pictures/Getty Images*

2 Seen here driving the ball deep against the Phillies in 1965, Ed Kranepool was a Mets mainstay for nearly two decades. *Louis Requena/ MLB Photos/Getty Images*

3 Seen here wearing unlucky number 13, Roger Craig lost a combined 46 games for the Mets in 1962 and 1963. He also completed a team-best 27 games over those two seasons. *Herb Scharfman/Time Life Pictures/Getty Images*

4 Cleon Jones (21), Tommie Agee (20), and Ron Swoboda (4) formed the core of the Mets outfield throughout the second half of the 1960s. *Frank Hurley/NY Daily News Archive/Getty Images*

5 Shown here during a May 1962 Mets–Braves game, the Polo Grounds served as the young franchise's home while a new stadium was being built in Flushing, Queens. The old home of the New York Giants was showing its age, but more than two million fans came out to watch the Mets in the team's two seasons at Coogan's Bluff. *Charles Hoff/NY Daily News Archive/ Getty Images*

6 Aerial view of Shea Stadium, hosting baseball but still under construction, in April 1964. *Ted Russell/ Time Life Pictures/Getty Images*

"A Real Cliff Dweller"

Quietly in the front office, and sometimes louder in the press, questions arose about whether Casey Stengel should be sent home, like a wet nurse after the newborn reaches a certain size. The Mets were still size 109—losses, that is, in 1964. Box-office appeal was no permanent guarantee. All the Mets had to do was look to Milwaukee, which had supported the Braves hysterically, averaging almost two million annually in the first seven seasons after the franchise left Beantown for Beer City in 1953; by the mid-1960s the Braves—a far more successful organization than the Mets—faced dwindling interest and soon made another move, to Atlanta.

A movement was afoot to replace Stengel, led by young WABC radio announcer Howard Cosell. There was no shortage of candidates to take the reins. Giants manager Alvin Dark was an intriguing option until he questioned the intelligence and desire of his minority players, which included future Hall of Famers Willie Mays, Willie McCovey, Orlando Cepeda, and Juan Marichal. Dark denied the assertion, but the Mets crossed him off their list. Dodgers coach Leo "the Lip" Durocher, who had managed both the Giants and Dodgers in New York, was embroiled in legal troubles after breaking the jaw of a fan who had made disparaging comments about his personal life. In addition, rumors had Stengel considering a return to his Glendale, California, home, where he was director of a bank; some newspapers had Casey going to the Angels or Dodgers.

The Mets, for their part, insisted that the decision hinged on Stengel's plans. At the end of the 1964 season, the team announced that Casey was staying. "He's been our boy and he's still our boy," board chairman M. Donald Grant declared at the press conference. "He told us yesterday that he wanted to manage again, and that was that."

Stengel's career abruptly ended on the eve of his 75th birthday celebration in July 1965. He broke his hip after a party in his honor at Toots Shor's Restaurant. An operation inserted a ball prosthesis to perform the movement of his hip joint. The initial prognosis was that he would miss two months. It soon became apparent that he would not be back at all.

To the surprise of many, Stengel decided from his hospital bed that Wes Westrum, a former New York Giants catcher, would be interim manager instead of another longtime New York catcher: Yogi Berra. Going back to his days with the Yankees, Stengel had called Berra his "assistant manager." Like Stengel, Berra had been fired as manager of the Yankees after winning a pennant, although Stengel had been 70 at the time of his dismissal and Berra was a 39-year-old rookie skipper when he was fired after taking the Yanks to the World Series in 1964.

Berra signed with the Mets as a player/coach that offseason, as did another future Hall of Famer: Warren Spahn. Whereas Spahn left the Mets to continue pitching elsewhere—and Westrum assumed Spahn's role as pitching coach—Berra hung up his catching gear after nine at bats (and two hits) to become a full-time coach. Berra was among those considered for the full-time manager post at the end of 1965. Also in the running were director of player development Eddie Stanky, Gil Hodges (currently managing the Washington Senators), and Durocher, who was eventually hired to manage the Cubs that October. George Weiss, after exercising the option in his contract to remain with the Mets for a sixth year, decided to promote Westrum from interim to full-time manager for 1966.

The second manager in Mets history had no previous managing experience, and he was not even an old friend of Stengel's; they'd known each other for barely a year. Reporter Jack Lang and Stengel had been making the rounds of Cleveland watering holes the night before the 1963 All-Star Game when they came across Westrum, then a Giants coach, and asked him to join them at their table. The generally quiet Westrum at first demurred, but he eventually came over. "Soon he and Casey were deep in baseball conversation," Lang later wrote. "I left them around 2 a.m., and Westrum told me the next day they remained until closing." When coach Cookie Lavagetto wanted to be near his home in Oakland after the '63 season, the Mets arranged a swap of coaches with San Francisco: Lavagetto for Westrum.

Westrum may have been baseball smart, but he did not excel at expressing that knowledge to the press. Reporters were used to Stengel, who could fill up a notebook with a response to a query about the time of day. Westrum was a far tougher interview whose malaprops made him look uneducated, whereas Casey's mangled syntax, lovingly labeled "Stengelese," made the Ol' Perfessor appear charming, or better yet, cunning. After his first exhibition game in the spring of 1966 went extra innings, Westrum returned to his office and told the scribes, "Whew! That was a real cliff dweller!"

The Mets may not have made as good press copy under Westrum, but they were an improved team. Westrum was the first manager to take the Mets above the .500 mark—it occurred just three games into the season, when the team

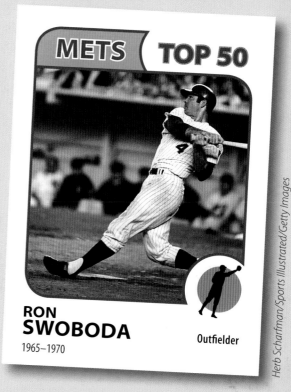

METS   TOP 50

RON
SWOBODA
1965–1970

Outfielder

Herb Scharfman/Sports Illustrated/Getty Images

Big things were expected of Ron Swoboda when he joined the Mets in 1965. Though he never quite lived up to his promise as a superstar, big things were his specialty.

Ronald Alan Swoboda, or "Saboda" as manager Casey Stengel called him, hit 10 homers in his first 90 career at bats. He appeared on the cover of *Sports Illustrated* in May 1968, when the Mets were a perennial bottom dweller. Gil Hodges platooned him with Art Shamsky in right field, and Swoboda did not play at all in the 1969 NLCS sweep because the Braves pitched all righties. Facing the lefty-laden club from his native Baltimore in the World Series, Swoboda batted .400 and delivered the tie-breaking double in the eighth inning of the Game 5 clincher—against a righty, no less.

His two most famous home runs came against "Lefty." Steve Carlton became the first pitcher in history to fan 19 in a game, yet he earned the loss because Swoboda hit a pair of two-strike, two-run homers.

Nicknamed "Rocky" for his so-so defense, he made a legendary backhanded diving catch in the ninth inning of Game 4 of the 1969 World Series. He played his final major league game in center field for the Yankees in the last game at original Yankee Stadium in 1973 before its renovation.

After retiring, the never-shy Swoboda became a broadcaster in several cities, including New York. He made New Orleans his home and broadcast for the Triple-A Zephyrs.

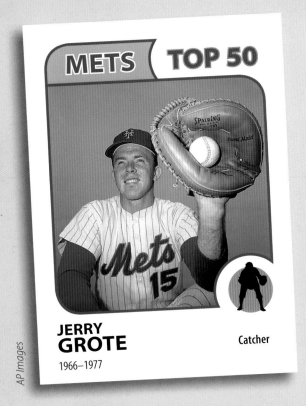

JERRY GROTE
1966–1977

Catcher

AP Images

Cincinnati's Johnny Bench, baseball's pre-eminent catcher of the 1970s, once said that if he and Jerry Grote were on the same team, "*I'd* be playing third base." Lord knows, the Mets could have used Bench or any third baseman with that type of power and talent, but New York did have Gerald Wayne Grote behind the plate.

Born and raised in San Antonio, Grote played in that city in Class AA, but his "red ass" tendencies and inability to hit as a regular with the Houston Colt .45s in 1964 made him expendable. Newly hired Mets scout Red Murff had signed Grote in Houston, and he recommended that New York acquire Grote, who was playing third base after being demoted to Triple A. Among the early Mets' many struggles was the lack of a catcher who could take charge of the young pitching staff. Grote was their man.

Manager Wes Westrum, himself a solid defensive catcher, stuck with Grote despite his continued struggles with the bat. By 1968, Grote was an all-star. Largely because of Bench, Grote made only one more All-Star Game appearance and never won a Gold Glove, yet his old-school catching style, strong arm, and tenacity made him one of the National League's most feared backstops. Grote did not miss an inning in the 1969 or 1973 postseasons, and no Met has ever had more at bats (49) or hits (12) in World Series play than Grote. His 1,235 games overall as a Met are third all-time.

was 2–1—and he was also the first pilot to steer them clear of 100 defeats and last place.

The 1966 Mets boasted a former MVP in third baseman Ken Boyer. Second baseman Ron Hunt returned from an injury-plagued 1965 to hit .288, and youngsters Cleon Jones and Ron Swoboda gained experience in the Shea Stadium outfield. And the pitching staff had not one, not two, but three 11-game winners: Jack Fisher, Dennis Ribant, and Bob Shaw. Of all the young players getting a chance with the Mets, perhaps the most significant was a 23-year-old catcher acquired from the Astros: Jerry Grote. Houston had given up on the fiery Texan because he'd failed with the bat in his first trial. Westrum, a two-time all-star who batted .187 in 1954 yet caught every inning of the Giants' World Series sweep, understood that defense at the position was paramount, whether on a contending team or a developing one. Westrum worked with Grote and took pains to try to rein in his young catcher's temper. Grote raised his average 51 points in 1966 and remained New York's starting backstop for the next decade.

Devine Intervention

Weiss finally stepped aside after the 1966 season and assistant Bing Devine took over as general manager. Devine, St. Louis born and bred, had started with the Cardinals as an office boy and rose through the ranks, serving under general manager Frank "Trader" Lane until he took Lane's place after the 1957 season. Devine built up the St. Louis farm system and pulled off perhaps his greatest deal when he sent Ernie Broglio to the Cubs for Lou Brock in 1964. St. Louis ended an 18-year pennant drought that year, but Devine wasn't there to enjoy it. With the fifth-place Cardinals trailing the Phillies by nine games in mid-August, owner August Busch cleared out the St. Louis front office on the advice of consultant Branch Rickey. This time Rickey was wrong.

While the epic collapse of the Phillies in the final two weeks of 1964 allowed the Cards to steal the pennant, Devine was named assistant to Weiss in New York. To top it off, Devine was later named executive of the year by the St. Louis–based *Sporting News*, his second straight year winning the award; only Weiss (1951–1953) had previously won the award consecutive times.

Bing Devine was the first great hire in Mets history. While serving as Weiss' assistant and heir apparent, he worked tirelessly to bring in players to help this moribund franchise, though some of the players didn't help for four or five years. Devine took Whitey Herzog off the coaching lines and moved him to the front office. Whitey's insights and keen eye for talent continued to help the club long after Devine had departed.

Taking over as GM in November 1966, Devine revisited his Trader Lane roots. He swapped players in and out, trying to find the right mix of cohesion and promise. The Mets employed a then-NL record 54 players during the 1967 season: 27 pitchers and 27 position players. With all that turnover came plenty of failure, such as the Don Bosch center field experiment and the hitless tenures of Sandy Alomar Sr. and Bart Shirley (a combined 0 for 34 with New York). Yet 1967 saw far more triumphs organizationally than on the field. Joining the farm system that year were Amos Otis (plucked from Boston in the minor league draft), Ken Singleton (selected in the first round of the January draft), Jon Matlack (taken in the first round of the June draft), and Gary Gentry (signed out of the third round after he had turned down three teams in past drafts). Devine also acquired future Miracle workers Ron Taylor, Don Cardwell, Cal Koonce, Ed Charles, J. C. Martin, and Art Shamsky. Oh, and add one more name that joined the organization at Devine's behest and debuted in New York during the Summer of Love: Tom Seaver.

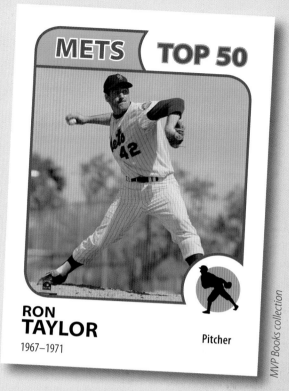

METS — TOP 50

RON TAYLOR
1967–1971

Pitcher

MVP Books collection

Ron Taylor was not a star on the 1969 Mets, but he was vital. He also gave the Miracle Mets their international flavor, having been raised in Toronto.

Ronald Wesley Taylor did things his way, skipping spring training as a rookie with the Indians to pursue his engineering studies. He emerged as a valuable reliever for the world champion Cardinals in 1964, but by 1966 he seemed to be out of gas. Mets GM Bing Devine purchased him from Houston in 1967, and Taylor was reborn. He led the Mets in saves four years running at a time when the potent starting staff completed an average of 45 games per year. Taylor also helped the development of southpaw Tug McGraw, who shared the late-inning bullpen load with the 31-year-old right-hander in 1969.

Taylor went 9–4 with a 2.72 ERA and 13 saves in '69. Since the save became an "official" statistic that year, Taylor was credited with the first certified saves in both League Championship Series and World Series play. The only Met with postseason experience heading into October, Taylor also picked up the Game 2 NLCS victory in Atlanta and finished his career ledger with 10 $\frac{1}{3}$ scoreless postseason innings.

Sold to Montreal after the 1971 season, Taylor was released by the Expos the following April, and so he never pitched for a Canadian team. He worked for one, though. Taylor started medical school at age 35 and served as team physician for the Toronto Blue Jays for more than 30 years, beginning in 1979.

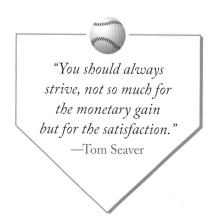

"You should always strive, not so much for the monetary gain but for the satisfaction."
—Tom Seaver

The Franchise Pops Out of a Hat

Tom Seaver came to the Mets by chance and then changed the franchise's fortunes more than any other player in the team's history. The Dodgers drafted the 18-year-old Seaver in the 10th round of the first amateur draft in 1965, but he turned them down to take a scholarship with the legendary baseball program at the University of Southern California. The Braves then picked Seaver third overall in a January 1966 draft for players who had been previously drafted, but the team, in the midst of relocating from Milwaukee to Atlanta, sent Seaver's contract after the Trojans' college season had begun. Major League Baseball commissioner William Eckert stepped in and declared the signing invalid. Now ineligible to play at USC, Seaver threatened legal action, and so Eckert announced that a special draft lottery, open to all teams, would be held for the chance to win the rights to Seaver. The winning team only had to match the offer from the Braves' contract, which was $45,000 plus incentives that brought the total deal to $53,500.

Though the Mets were known to throw around sums that size and larger to purchase washed-up major leaguers, George Weiss was reluctant to put that kind of money up for an unproven college kid. But Bing Devine convinced Weiss to at least get into the lottery. Perhaps other teams had Weiss' misgivings or simply ignored the telegrams informing them of the date, because only the Indians, Phillies, and Mets responded. On April 3, 1966, Eckert assistant Joe Reichler reached into a hat and pulled out a piece of paper

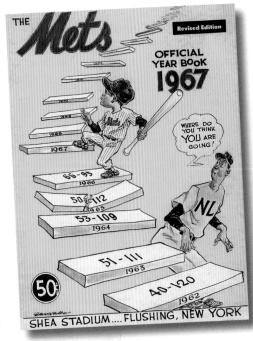

Author's collection

with the Mets' name on it. Scout Nelson Burbank signed Seaver that afternoon. For this sad-sack, laughingstock franchise, "The Franchise" had arrived by sheer luck.

Seaver started at Triple-A Jacksonville in 1966 and threw 210 innings, a figure he surpassed in each of his 11 full seasons in New York. There was little doubt he would be on the major league team in spring training of 1967. Veteran Don Cardwell got the Opening Day assignment (and lost), but Seaver debuted the next day, and the Mets beat Pittsburgh in front of a crowd of 5,005 at Shea. The decision went to reliever Chuck Estrada, his only win as a Met and the last of his career. Seaver had 311 ahead of him.

Seaver's first win came in his second start, when he beat the Cubs at Shea, 6–1. His first road start, at Wrigley Field, showed the 22-year-old ace's mettle. After not getting past the eighth inning in his first two starts, Seaver had a four-hitter with two outs in the ninth and a 1–0 lead over the Cubs. He got all-star Ron Santo to ground to shortstop, but Bud Harrelson's error allowed the tying run to score. The game went to extra innings with Seaver scheduled to lead off the 10th. Not only did he bat for himself, he singled, was sacrificed to second, and raced home with the tiebreaking run on Al Luplow's single. He retired the side in order in the bottom half of the inning to notch the first of his 231 career complete games (171 as a Met, plus two more in the postseason).

Seaver went on to become the first Mets pitcher named to the all-star team—and he threw a scoreless 15th inning to save it for

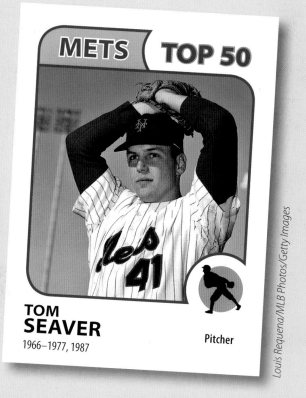

METS **TOP 50**

TOM SEAVER
1966–1977, 1987

Pitcher

the National League in Anaheim—and his numbers for the year surpassed those of any Mets hurler who came before. He established club marks for wins (16), ERA (2.76), and complete games (18)—just the beginning of his ownership of the Mets record book.

All the turnover in 1967, however, made it apparent that the man calling the shots in the dugout was not the man to lead the Mets out of the desert. With the club on its way to 100 losses and no contract extension forthcoming from the front office, Wes Westrum tendered his resignation on September 21. Coach Salty Parker had been in the Mets organization for only one year, but he officially became the third manager in team history when he guided the club to a 4–7 finish.

In the season finale, late-season callup Ken Boswell botched a groundball in the eighth inning that allowed the

tying and go-ahead runs to score for loss 101. As the second baseman later recalled:

> Over in the clubhouse, I was a big hero. It was the last game of the season and a lot of the guys had plane reservations. They were going to Hawaii, Reno, Vegas, and they didn't want to play any more extra innings. They wanted to catch their planes and get out of there. That's how it was over there in '67.

It was New York's fifth 100-loss campaign in six seasons of existence, but the Mets would hit that woeful three-digit number just once more in the next four decades. Under their next manager, the club hit the three-digit win figure quicker than even the most optimistic fan could have imagined.

The arrival of Tom Seaver signaled the New York Mets' rise from the ashes. His hastened departure in 1977 proclaimed the team's descent into the abyss. Without Seaver the Mets were a really bad ball club. With him the Mets were the first expansion team to reach the World Series, and they did it twice.

George Thomas Seaver wasn't considered a big-time prospect coming out of high school. After serving in the Marines, he attended Fresno City College, where scouts began to take notice of him. He was first drafted by the Dodgers in the June 1965 amateur draft, but he opted to attend the University of Southern California on a baseball scholarship. The Braves selected Seaver in the January 1966 draft for previously drafted players, but a snafu with his contract left the young pitcher in limbo. Baseball commissioner William Eckert decreed that any major league team could enter a special lottery for Seaver (only three teams entered). On April 3, 1966, the Mets won the Seaver lottery. The team signed him that same day.

Though the Mets lost 101 times in 1967, Seaver was the overwhelming choice for National League Rookie of the Year.

In 1969, the 24-year-old ace posted a league-best 25 wins to go along with a 2.21 ERA and 208 strikeouts, good enough to win the Cy Young Award. He repeated the honor in 1973 when the Mets claimed another pennant and Seaver won the league ERA (2.08) and strikeout (251) crowns.

TOM SEAVER

Born: November 17, 1944, in Fresno, CA
Signed by New York Mets, 1966
Mets Debut: April 13, 1967
Bats: Right. **Throws:** Right

New York Mets Pitching Record

YEAR	W–L	ERA	G	IP	SO
1967	16–13	2.76	35	251.0	170
1968	16–12	2.20	36	278.0	205
1969	25–7	2.21	36	273.1	208
1970	18–12	2.82	37	290.2	283
1971	20–10	1.76	36	286.1	289
1972	21–12	2.92	35	262.0	249
1973	19–10	2.08	36	290.0	251
1974	11–11	3.20	32	236.0	201
1975	22–9	2.38	36	280.1	243
1976	14–11	2.59	35	271.0	235
1977	7–3	3.00	13	96.0	72
1983	9–14	3.55	34	231.0	135
Mets Totals	198–124	2.57	401	3045.2	2541
MLB Totals	311–205	2.86	656	4783.0	3640

With his league-best 243 K's in 1975, Seaver became the first pitcher to fan 200 batters in eight consecutive seasons; he made it nine straight in 1976. In '75 he also became the first right-handed pitcher to win three Cy Youngs.

Winner of 198 games in a Mets uniform, a nine-time all-star, a *Sports Illustrated* Sportsman of the Year, and one of the most recognizable names in the game—it was heartbreaking to see his time in New York come to an end. An increasingly contentious relationship with chairman M. Donald Grant led Seaver to demand a trade. He was dealt to Cincinnati on June 15, 1977.

Seaver had success with the Reds, but as the "Big Red Machine" was slowing down, Seaver was sent back to the place that wanted him most. The Mets, who had received four players for him in 1977, sent three back on December 16, 1982. He went 9–14 with a team-best 3.55 ERA for the last-place Mets in 1983.

A free agent compensation rule allowed the White Sox to claim Seaver in 1984 after the Mets left him unprotected. It did not have the sting of the '77 trade, but it meant that Seaver would get his 300th win elsewhere—the Bronx, it turned out, while pitching for Chicago in 1985. His career officially ended after a failed comeback attempt with the 1987 Mets. A year later Seaver's number was retired—the only Mets player so honored—and he was inducted into the Mets Hall of Fame. The National Baseball Hall of Fame followed in 1992, with Tom Terrific receiving the highest percentage in history (98.8).

Photo File/Getty Images

Gil

Though generally considered a joke on the field, the Mets were building an organization with some of the brightest young minds—and arms—in the game. What they needed was a leader, someone who would command patience and respect, who could wipe the board clean and begin a new reputation where losing wasn't funny or accepted. What they needed was Gil Hodges.

Hodges, however, was in Washington, where the Mets had traded him during the 1963 season so he could begin his managerial career. The Senators, a 1961 American League expansion club, had improved each year under Hodges, including a 76–85 mark and share of sixth place in 1967. The Senators were not anxious to lose their skipper, but Hodges, who still lived in Brooklyn and owned a bowling alley in town, was eager to be closer to his family.

Assistant general manager Johnny Murphy spent several weeks trying to resolve the problem with Senators GM and former Yankees teammate George Selkirk. They eventually worked out another trade for manager Hodges. Bill Denehy, mentioned as a "kid of high promise" in the same sentence with Tom Seaver in the *New York Times*, went to the Senators, along with $100,000. Denehy was no Seaver. Plagued by personal problems, he never won another game in the majors and finished with a 1–10 career mark.

That wasn't the only change going on that winter at Shea Stadium. Team president Bing Devine resigned so he could return to the Cardinals as general manager, replacing Stan Musial. Devine had never moved to New York and would not accept a contract when he'd taken over for Weiss barely a year earlier. The Mets were shocked, but not unprepared. Murphy—who had been with the club since 1961, had served in nearly every front office capacity, and had been instrumental in getting Hodges back to New York—took over as general manager.

Murphy's first deal in his new role was hand-picked by Hodges, who wanted to buy low from the White Sox on 1966 AL Rookie of the Year Tommie Agee and scrappy infielder Al Weis. The cost? Jack Fisher, Tommy Davis, and two prospects. There was considerable risk involved, however. While the trade offered the Mets a potential answer to the center field conundrum that had plagued them since Richie Ashburn's retirement in 1962, Agee was coming off a poor year in 1967. Weis, an infielder who would be 30 when the season began, had suffered a knee injury and was a paltry hitter at best. Tommy Davis, in his one season as a Met, hit .302 and led the team in nearly every offensive category. Fisher, picked up from the Giants after the '63 season in a make-good draft to ease the NL's conscience for saddling the expansion clubs with so much dead weight, led the Mets three times in innings pitched and, not surprisingly, losses. Yet if the Mets learned one thing under Devine, it was that they were too bad of a team not to take risks.

The first pitch Agee saw as a Met was a fastball off the helmet courtesy of Bob Gibson in the first inning of the first spring training game of 1968. Agee struggled for the first four months of the season. By the end of July, he was batting .168 with three home runs and 10 RBI, and had tied the dubious record set by original Met Don Zimmer by enduring an 0-for-34 slump. (He batted .286 over the last two months to lift his season average to .217.)

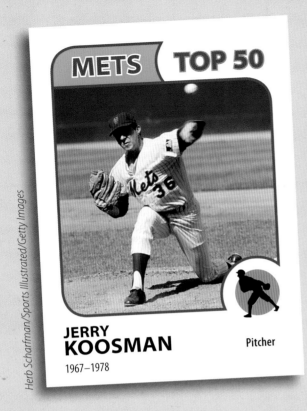

METS TOP 50

JERRY KOOSMAN
Pitcher
1967–1978

Fate intervened, repeatedly, to make Jerry Koosman a Met. Drafted into the army in 1962, Minnesota farm boy Jerome Martin Koosman planned on becoming a helicopter pilot. His dentist, a general in the Minnesota National Guard, helped him transfer to a base where he could pitch. The son of a Mets usher stationed with Koosman passed down a recommendation. New York signed him but considered releasing him except for the matter of a loan he'd taken from the club following a car accident. Granted a reprieve, Koosman mastered the slider.

He went 19–12 with a 2.08 ERA and seven shutouts in 1968, finishing one vote behind Johnny Bench for the NL Rookie of the Year Award. After helping the Mets land in the 1969 World Series, Koosman stole the show. He took a perfect game into the seventh inning of Game 2, allowing just two hits in the victory. Koosman shook off two early home runs in Game 5 to complete the clinching win and jump into Jerry Grote's arms for time immemorial.

Koosman helped the Mets rally back to life in 1973 with a club record 31 ⅔ consecutive scoreless innings. New York again won in both his World Series starts, though they lost the series. Kooz won 21 games in 1976 and followed that with 20 losses in the tumultuous season that followed. Traded to Minnesota at his request, he won 20 in 1979 and remained in the majors through 1985, winning 222 times with a 3.36 career ERA. He was inducted into the Mets Hall of Fame in 1989.

Agee, however, had his high school buddy from Mobile, Alabama, next to him in the outfield. Cleon Jones, seemingly more comfortable after shifting from center field to left, finished sixth in hitting at .297 during a season in which the National League average was .243, the lowest in league history. It was a great year for pitchers, but no pitching staff in baseball needed a turnaround more than the New York Mets.

In five of their first six seasons, the Mets had the league's worst ERA, plus a defense that allowed plenty of unearned runs to spare. The club's ERA dipped below 4.00 for the first time in 1967, placing eighth in the league, thanks in large part to the addition of rookie Tom Seaver. The 1968 Mets improved by more than a run to 2.72 (good for fifth in the league), held opponents to an NL-low .230 batting average, and surpassed 1,000 strikeouts for the first time after never before reaching 900. Seaver was the anchor of the staff, but he was joined by rookies Jerry Koosman and Nolan Ryan.

The 21-year-old Ryan, subject of a *Life* magazine feature before he'd even started 10 major league games, could throw a ball through the wall and seemingly often tried to. He could be unhittable one game and walk the park the next, an inconsistency that haunted his four seasons in New York. He also had blister problems that landed him on the disabled list and kept him from starting after July. Koosman, on the other hand, blistered the opposition. After pitching briefly without a win in 1967, the 25-year-old Koosman tossed shutouts in his first two '68 outings (including the home opener), threw another complete-game victory in his third start, beat the Reds to go 4–0, and rolled to a 12–4 start. He earned the save in the All-Star Game in the first multi-Met Midsummer Classic (Seaver and Grote were also invited to the Houston shindig). Kooz stayed strong, even as the Mets offense, compiling a league-low .228 average, provided no support. Koosman tied Grover Cleveland Alexander's 1911

A Hero Returns
GIL HODGES

Gil Hodges hit the first home run in Mets history. Twice. There was his blast to left field in the first-ever Mets game on April 11, 1962. And then there was the touch-'em-all season of 1969, when Hodges made the previously moribund Mets the first expansion team to win a World Series and perhaps the most unlikely world champion of all time. There was a lot of luck in 1969, but in the words of his first general manager in Brooklyn, Branch Rickey, "Luck is the residue of design."

A powerfully built, slick fielding first baseman, Hodges retired as the all-time right-handed National League home run hitter (topping Mets announcer Ralph Kiner and soon eclipsed by Hank Aaron and Willie Mays). The Mets sent Hodges into his next career by trading him to Washington, for Jimmy Piersall, to manage the expansion Senators in 1963. He did as well as could be expected in Washington, but having wedded a Brooklynite, he never moved from the borough and always longed to return. The Mets engineered another trade in the fall of 1967—this time for Bill Denehy and $100,000—to bring him home.

A Marine sergeant in the Pacific during World War II, Hodges brought a quiet intensity that instilled loyalty in his men. While other players lolled about during the spring training lockout in 1969, his men worked hard at "Camp Seaver" (Tom Terrific was another former Marine). When Hodges told Tug McGraw he

Focus on Sport/Getty Images

thought he'd be better suited as a reliever than a starter, he created a career that lasted long into the 1980s. When Hodges walked out to left field in the middle of a game to remove Cleon Jones after he didn't hustle after a baseball, he sent a message, and the Mets responded by overcoming a 10-game deficit in mid-August. And when he brought a baseball to home plate with shoe polish on it in Game 5 of the 1969 World Series, he got a call reversal that put the Mets on their way to clinching the title. (Jerry Koosman later confessed that he quickly rubbed the ball on his shoe at his manager's request, but such is the respect for the Mets manager that most people still think Kooz is kidding.)

Hodges had suffered a heart attack during his first season as Mets manager and quit his heavy smoking habit, but during the two years of frustrating play that followed the world championship, he took it up again. "Watch the cigarettes" were Joan Hodges' last words to her husband when they parted at the airport a few weeks before his shocking death two days before his 48th birthday.

The Mets wore a black armband in his honor and retired his number 14, but without Gil Hodges the Mets weren't the same organization. Without him, they were no longer whole.

Author's collection

record with seven shutouts. He toyed with 20 wins and a sub-2.00 earned run average before settling for 19 wins and a 2.08 ERA, plus 17 complete games, all of which landed him in the top five in the NL in an extremely stiff year for competition. Seaver was nearly as good, recording five shutouts, posting a 2.20 ERA, setting a club mark with 278 innings, and becoming the first Met to reach 200 strikeouts in a season.

Though no one could imagine what was to come, fans were ecstatic that hometown hero Gil Hodges had returned and guided the Mets to their best season yet. And then they almost lost him.

Recuperation, Preparation

A heart attack is termed "mild" when it happens to someone else. After Gil Hodges said he was feeling ill and was going to lie down during a late September game in Atlanta, Rube Walker, his pitching coach since Washington and a longtime Dodgers teammate, knew something was wrong. As reporter Jack Lang noted, "It was not like Hodges to leave the dugout during a game." Trainer Gus Mauch rode with Hodges to the hospital in a taxi.

Walker managed the Mets the last five games of the year—the Mets finished 2–3 for their first 70-plus win season, avoiding last place for the second time in team history.

Hodges remained in Atlanta in intensive care for weeks with his wife, the former Joan Lombardi, at his side while their four children remained in school in Flatbush. He spent the winter recuperating, mostly in Florida, quit his three-pack-a-day smoking habit, began a low-calorie diet, and save for a conference call or two, was kept away from the press and questions such as "Will you manage the team in 1969?"

Other than twisting his ankle while fishing, Hodges was fully healthy when spring training began in St. Petersburg, but the game was not. The first labor strike in the game's history delayed the opening of spring training, as new commissioner Bowie Kuhn was immediately challenged by the fledgling player's union, which urged its members not to sign their contracts until a dispute over pensions and benefits had been settled. The Mets, unlike some teams, held their own players-only workouts. Led by ex-Marine Seaver, the workouts helped keep the players in shape and ready to go when the two sides reached agreement on a new labor contract at the end of February.

The soon-to-be-legendary 1969 Mets were not considered anything special that spring. They had the usual assortment of kids in camp, some trials worked out (rookie Rod Gaspar filling in for injured Art Shamsky in right field), and others failed (Hodges' attempts to make unwilling Amos Otis into a regular third baseman). The Mets tried to trade for Joe Torre of the Braves (he went to the Cardinals instead), and the lone offseason acquisition to make the team was Rule V pick Wayne Garrett. The Mets prepared for baseball's first year of divisional play, a lowered pitching mound, and a smaller strike zone by going 14–10 in spring training, tied with the 1966 squad for best preseason record to that point in Mets history. Still, most pundits thought the 100–1 Las Vegas odds for this team winning the World Series were pretty accurate.

Seemingly given a foolproof chance of winning on Opening Day for the first time, the Mets played the fool. Facing the expansion Montreal Expos in their first-ever game, Tom Seaver and the bullpen were hit hard in an 11–10 loss at Shea Stadium. Though New York still won the opening series—with Gary Gentry's major league debut coinciding with Tommie Agee's legendary upper deck home run at Shea—the team got off to its usual sagging start. The Mets fell five games under .500 on three occasions over the first seven weeks. They hit the .500 mark on May 21, the latest date the team had ever *not* had a losing record. The club's reaction, as chronicled by beat writer Leonard Koppett, was different: "The players couldn't have cared less. In fact, they were sort of insulted at the idea of being fussed over." The Mets promptly lost five straight.

The top national story in the first three months of 1969 was the Chicago Cubs. A quarter of a century since their last pennant and 61 years removed from their last world championship, Chicago was crazy about its NL club's roster of all-stars, celebrity manager, heel-clicking third baseman, and sizeable lead in the standings. Even after the Mets reeled

The 1969 Mets program celebrated the 100th anniversary of professional baseball. By year's end, Mets fans would have so much more to celebrate. *MVP Books collection*

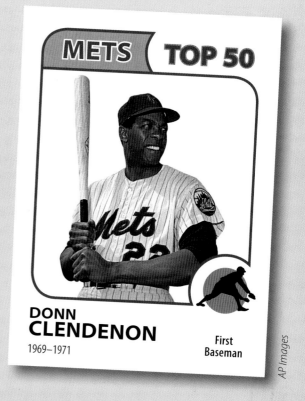

off a record 11-game winning streak at the end of May, it lopped only two games off Chicago's lead. But it did build confidence in the young Mets.

The lead was down to five and half games when the Cubs came to Shea Stadium on July 8. With slugging first baseman Donn Clendenon arriving from Montreal to add power and veteran leadership, Cleon Jones hitting .354, and both the team and Seaver upwards of 10 games over .500, Mets fans were in a frenzy of their own. Writers Paul D. Zimmerman and Dick Schaap were even working on a book about the midseason 1969 Mets, *The Year the Mets Lost Last Place*, chronicling the July series with the Cubs at Shea and at Wrigley. The book would be out by October. The Mets made for a captivating read.

The first game saw the Mets rally for three runs in the ninth on two misplayed flyballs by Cubs center fielder Don Young. The next night, a jam-packed Shea Stadium witnessed Tom Seaver throw his fabled "Imperfect Game," retiring every Cub in order until a one-out single in the ninth by rookie Jimmy Qualls, Chicago's replacement center fielder, ended Seaver's bid for a perfect game. Though the Mets lost the next afternoon, New York was euphoric.

At these dizzying heights, the Mets were pounded by the Expos, 11–4, but they rebounded to sweep a Sunday doubleheader before heading to Wrigley Field for a rematch. Santo's taunt, "Wait until we get them to our park," might have unnerved a team contending for the first time, but

METS TOP 50

DONN CLENDENON
1969–1971

First Baseman

Mets general manager Johnny Murphy sent four prospects to the Montreal Expos for Donn Clendenon at the June 15, 1969, trading deadline. The right-handed slugger homered and drove in nine runs in three games against Pittsburgh, which had been his team until a whirlwind saw the Expos select him in the expansion draft, the Astros trade Rusty Staub for him, and then Clendenon refuse to report to Houston. He stayed an unhappy Expo until Murphy's call.

Donn Charles Clendenon was raised in Atlanta by his mother and stepfather, former Negro Leaguer Nish Williams. A brilliant student and athlete, Clendenon was recruited by the Harlem Globetrotters and Cleveland Browns. He signed with the Pirates out of Morehouse College and put together a few impressive seasons at first base, but his inconsistency and attempts to juggle law school and baseball angered team management.

Though Clendenon brought the power bat that the Mets craved, manager Gil Hodges' platoon system usually had him sit against righties. He hit 12 home runs in 202 at bats in 1969 and did not play in the sweep of the Braves in the NLCS. He feasted on Baltimore's southpaws in the World Series, however, homering three times—the most memorable coming in the sixth inning of the clinching fifth game—and earning World Series MVP honors. Clendenon set a team record with 97 RBI the following year. He tumbled in 1971 and his career ended in St. Louis. Like his father, Clendenon died of leukemia. He was 60 years old.

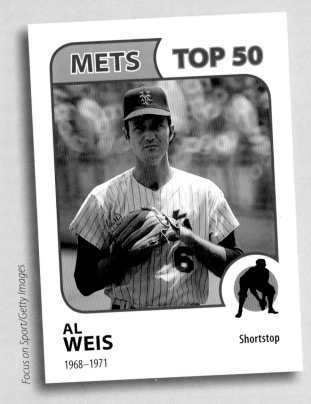

METS **TOP 50**

AL WEIS
1968–1971

Shortstop

Acquired in December 1967 from the White Sox with Tommie Agee, Albert John Weis had missed the second half of the previous season with a cracked kneecap. In his first week as a Met in April 1968, his error ended the longest scoreless game in history. Rather than blame the 24th-inning error on Weis, general manager Johnny Murphy insisted that the error was due to the Astrodome's choppy infield dirt. (A subsequent rule, known as the "Murphy Drag," required that infields be dragged every five innings.)

To try to improve his .172 batting average in '68, Weis decided to stop switch hitting and just bat right-handed. He platooned at second base with Ken Boswell in 1969, but Weis ended up playing more games at shortstop due to Bud Harrelson's military obligations. Weis hit his only two home runs of 1969 in consecutive wins at Wrigley Field in July. He batted just once in the NLCS because of Atlanta's right-handed pitching. Baltimore's two lefty starters provided his chance to be a World Series hero.

Dave McNally elected to pitch to Weis with Game 2 tied in the ninth; his single scored the deciding run. His game-tying home run in the seventh inning of Game 5 was his only home run ever at Shea Stadium. Weis had five hits and four walks, a .455/.563/.727 line for a player with a puny .553 career OPS. He earned the World Series Babe Ruth Award from New York sportswriters and remains the unlikeliest of heroes in Mets lore.

not these Mets. In his first game since imperfection, Seaver allowed just one run in the series opener, but Chicago's Bill Hands made it stand up by blanking New York. In the second game, the Mets swung back—with the lightest stick they had. Al Weis, a New York native but a Chicago resident, earned the ire of his neighbors for decades to come when he launched a three-run homer in the fourth inning of a 5–4 Mets win. Then he hit another the next day as New York won again. Two homers in two days from a player with seven career home runs? And doing it during what everyone was calling the most crucial nine days in Mets history? There's a word for that: Amazin'.

The Drama Builds

The All-Star Game, Chappaquiddick, and Neil Armstrong walking on the moon were merely images on TV compared to the starved Mets fan's obsession with this sudden bounty of hope. And then came the slump. Needing to keep up with the Cubs, the Mets instead went 10–14, losing six straight to Houston, punctuated by Gil Hodges' calm walk past the mound and all the way to left field to remove his best hitter, Cleon Jones, mid-game after the left fielder did not hustle for a ball during a doubleheader blowout loss. The Mets claimed an injury necessitated his removal, but everyone interpreted it as a message. By the time they had finished with the extended Cincinnati, Atlanta, and, ugh, Houston portion of the schedule on August 15, the Mets were 10 games out, their largest deficit of the season.

Destiny began to change the same weekend that the new youth of America converged for "Three Days of Peace and Music" near the upstate town of Woodstock. It was a very wet year in New York—as evidenced by the muddy scenes at Woodstock—and the rainouts that had piled up for the Mets started to pay dividends. Expansion helped, too. The newly created San Diego Padres were named after a minor league

STEALING A DIVISION IN 10 SIMPLE STEPS

AUGUST 19: Mets rookie Gary Gentry and Giants ace Juan Marichal matched zeroes for 10 innings at Shea. Cleon Jones was thrown out at the plate in the bottom of the 12th, but the next inning, Jones—perfectly positioned in a four-man outfield alignment—robbed Willie McCovey of a home run. Tommie Agee cleared the wall in the 14th for the only run of the game. **8 games back.**

AUGUST 30: After Marichal blanked Gentry in the Candlestick rematch, ending the Mets' six-game winning streak, the teams were tied in the bottom of the ninth in the second game of the series. McCovey's one-out double against the shift appeared certain to bring in the winning run, but Rod Gaspar's throw nailed Bob Burda at the plate. When Jerry Grote rolled the ball toward the mound, believing it to be the third out, Donn Clendenon raced over and threw out Big Mac at third. Clendenon's homer the next inning was the difference in the 3–2 win. **4 games back.**

SEPTEMBER 8: Fresh off being swept at home by the Pirates, the Cubs stumbled into Shea leading by a mere two and a half games. Cubs hurler Bill Hands knocked down Tommie Agee leading off the bottom of the first, and Jerry Koosman responded by drilling Ron Santo the following inning. In the sixth, Agee slid home to break a 2–2 tie as catcher Randy Hundley bounced in the air in fury. **1½ games back.**

SEPTEMBER 9: The most famous stray cat in New York history appeared in the first inning. One of Shea's own—black, sinewy, and spooky—strolled in front of the Cubs dugout as Leo Durocher tried not to look. Tom Seaver retired the Cubs in order, and Ken Boswell laced a two-run double in the bottom of the inning to kick off a 7–1 rout of Fergie Jenkins. **½ game back.**

SEPTEMBER 10: A twi-night doubleheader with Montreal after the two-game sweep of the Cubs was just what the Mets needed. The Expos had lost 97 times since opening the season with a win at Shea. The Mets, with 82 wins, were assured of their first winning season ever, and now they had a chance to take over first place. Expo Charlie Wegener and Met Jim McAndrew each pitched 11 innings. Ron Taylor backed up a poor throw to nail a runner at the plate in the top of the 12th, and Boswell's hit just beyond a diving Darrell Sutherland won it in the bottom of the inning. Nolan Ryan's complete-game win in the nightcap made it a clean sweep. A Cubs loss in Philadelphia prompted the scoreboard to crow, "Look Who's No. 1." **1 game ahead.**

SEPTEMBER 12: With Cleon Jones hurt and Art Shamsky sitting in his hotel room because of the Jewish holiday, this doubleheader in Pittsburgh belonged to the pitchers. The notoriously poor-hitting Jerry Koosman helped his own cause by singling in a run in the fifth inning of the first game for the only score of the game, as Kooz held the Pirates to three hits. In the nightcap, right-hander Don Cardwell's two-out hit brought home Bud Harrelson in the second with what turned out to be the only run of that game. **2½ games ahead.**

SEPTEMBER 15: Cardinals lefty Steve Carlton became the first pitcher in history to strike out 19 batters in a game. And he lost. Ron Swoboda, who struck out in his other two times at bat, clubbed a pair of two-strike, two-run homers in St. Louis, and the Mets won, 4–3. **4½ games ahead.**

SEPTEMBER 21: A day after Pittsburgh's Bob Moose threw what would be the last no-hitter ever at Shea Stadium, the Mets played their 22nd and final doubleheader of 1969. Featuring the same two pitchers who drove in the only runs in the twin shutouts nine days earlier at Forbes Field, this time both pitchers went hitless. The Mets won both once again. **4½ games ahead.**

SEPTEMBER 23: With the Cubs losing to Montreal in the afternoon, the Mets took the field against the Cardinals with a magic number of two. Trailing Bob Gibson by a run, Shamsky knocked in the tying run in the eighth. With Gibson still on the hill in the 11th, Harrelson singled home the winning run to put the Mets one win from rapture. **6 games ahead.**

SEPTEMBER 24: Steve Carlton followed up his monumental performance of nine days earlier by striking out just one Met in his final start of the year, which lasted less than an inning. After fanning Jones with two on in the bottom of the first, "Lefty" yielded a three-run homer to Clendenon. He then walked Swoboda, and Ed Charles followed with his final career home run. The rest of the game was about keeping the squirming fans in their seats as Gary Gentry blanked the Cardinals, the preseason favorite to win a third straight pennant. With two on and one out in the ninth, Joe Torre rapped into a 6–4–3 double play, and Shea Stadium exploded as the Mets clinched the first postseason appearance in franchise history. Fans tore the place apart after what was the last regular-season game of the year in Flushing. **6 games ahead.**

SHUTOUT MACHINE

On two occasions during the final month of the 1969 season, the Mets pitching staff shut out the opposition for 36 or more consecutive innings, including five complete-game shutouts. (In the period between the two scoreless-inning streaks, Jerry Koosman and Tom Seaver pitched back-to-back complete-game shutouts in Montreal on September 17 and 18.)

Innings totals shown below count only before or after run scored.

9/10, vs. Montreal (2nd game of doubleheader)*:
Nolan Ryan (W), 7 IP
9/11, vs. Montreal: Gary Gentry (W), 9 IP
9/12, @ Pittsburgh (1st game): Jerry Koosman (W), 9 IP
9/12, @ Pittsburgh (2nd game): Don Cardwell (W), 8 IP;
Tug McGraw (Sv), 1 IP
9/13, @ Pittsburgh: Tom Seaver (W), 2 IP
= 36 consecutive scoreless innings

* The only run scored by Montreal in the second game was unearned. The *earned* run streak extends to 48 innings, including the first game of the doubleheader.

9/23, vs. St. Louis: Jim McAndrew, 2 IP; McGraw (W), 4 IP
9/24, vs. St. Louis: Gentry (W), 9 IP
9/26, @ Philadelphia: Koosman (W), 9 IP
9/27, @ Philadelphia: Seaver (W), 9 IP
9/28, @ Philadelphia: Gentry (W), 5 IP; Ryan, 3 IP;
Ron Taylor (Sv), 1 IP
= 42 consecutive scoreless innings

team and played that way, coming in to the weekend series at Shea with the worst record in baseball at 35–81. The first game between the Mets and the first-year club was rained out. Combined with an earlier rainout in May, that gave the Mets consecutive doubleheaders. New York scored a total of 10 runs in the four games and won them all. The buildup of doubleheaders would be a boon to the pitching-rich Mets, who had adopted a five-man rotation under the guidance of pitching coach Rube Walker. In the nine doubleheaders they played from mid-August on, the Mets went 6–1–2. (The Mets were 11–3–8 in twin bills overall, more than twice the number of sweeps in any other season before or since.)

The dual San Diego sweeps, which left the Mets with a 66–51 record and eight games back in the standings, kicked off a 38–11 finish that included some of the most astonishing events in Mets history (see page 47).

The Mets ended up winning the first National League East title by eight games. They won nine straight after being no-hit at Shea on September 20, and then lost on the final day at Wrigley Field in a game that couldn't have mattered less.

THE UPSIDE-DOWN BASEBALL WORLD OF 1969

NL EAST	W	L	PCT	GB
New York Mets	100	62	.617	—
Chicago Cubs	92	70	.568	8
Pittsburgh Pirates	88	74	.543	12
St. Louis Cardinals	87	75	.537	13
Philadelphia Phillies	63	99	.389	37
Montreal Expos	52	110	.321	48

The Shea scoreboard says it all as the Mets claimed first place in the NL East after defeating the Expos 3–2 in 12 innings on September 10. They did not relinquish the spot through the final three weeks of the season. *Mets Inside Pitch Archive*

Fans go wild on the Shea Stadium field after the Mets clinched the division with a 6–0 win over St. Louis on September 24, 1969. *Herb Scharfman/Sports Illustrated/Getty Images*

While the fans partied outside, the Mets players got a little crazy in the clubhouse after securing the first postseason berth in franchise history. Ron Swoboda, Art Shamsky, and Ken Boswell are all lathered up in celebration. *John Duprey/NY Daily News Archive/Getty Images*

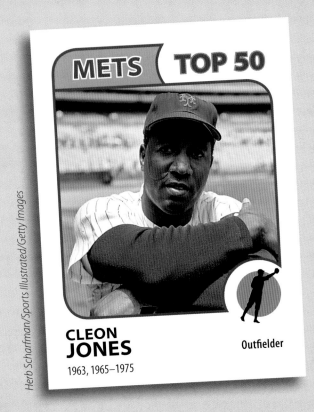

METS   TOP 50

CLEON JONES
1963, 1965–1975

Outfielder

Cleon Jones seemingly had a hand (or, in at least one case, a foot) in every critical moment in the first dozen years of the Mets franchise.

Signed during the team's first season, Cleon Joseph Jones debuted under Casey Stengel as a center fielder in 1963 and then moved to left field in 1968 with the arrival of Tommie Agee, his high school teammate from Mobile, Alabama. Jones had his finest season in 1969, when he was an all-star starter and compiled a .340 average—a mark 37 points higher than any previous Met. A down moment that year proved equally key: When Gil Hodges removed Jones from left field in the middle of a game for not hustling, it seemed to light a fire under the Mets, as they rallied toward the pennant. Jones hit a scorching .429 in the NLCS, and though he hit just .158 in the World Series, he sparked a Game 5 comeback with the famous shoe-polish incident. Jones ended the game and the series with a catch and near genuflection in left field.

An improbable carom found Jones at the center of the "Ball on the Wall" game in late September 1973, which helped catapult the club toward another division crown. He reached base 13 times in that year's World Series, though his team-best five runs scored were not enough to bring the Mets another championship. Jones retired as the franchise leader in several hitting categories (most of which were eventually broken by Ed Kranepool), and in 1991 he became the sixth player inducted into the Mets Hall of Fame.

Oh, Atlanta

The League Championship Series was a new concept in baseball. It had never been tried before, except in a best-of-three tiebreaker format (with the Dodgers taking part in each of the four NL playoff series, losing three of them). This time there was no tie to break, however; the series was to decide whether East or West would represent the National League in the World Series. Never mind that anyone with a map could tell you that both cities were in the East. The Atlanta Braves had won 93 times and had their own divisional race to deal with. As late as September 22, the Braves trailed the Giants by a half game, but Atlanta won six of its last seven to overtake San Francisco for the NL West crown.

The Braves had hit 16 points higher than the Mets on the year (.258 to .242), and with Hank Aaron and Orlando Cepeda in the lineup, they had far more power. The Mets featured one of baseball's most dominant pitching staffs, but Atlanta held its own with knuckleballer Phil Niekro (who finished second to Tom Seaver in wins with 23) and 18-game-winner Ron Reed. Las Vegas installed the Braves as 13–10 favorites despite their 4–8 record against the Mets during the season.

Not only was this the first postseason appearance in Mets history (and the first for the Braves since moving to Atlanta), everything was a first in National League Championship Series history. Tommie Agee's ground out christened the event, and then the firsts started flying. Art Shamsky had

Nolan Ryan gets a hug from catcher Jerry Grote after Ryan pitched the final seven innings in relief to sew up Game 3 of the NLCS and clinch the pennant over Atlanta. *Bill Meurer/NY Daily News Archive/Getty Images*

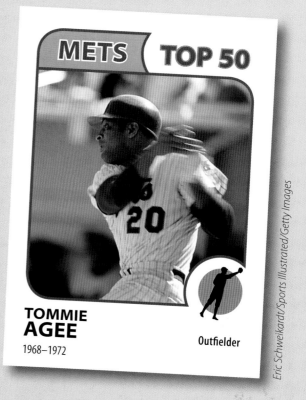

the first hit and scored the first run, on a Jerry Grote single in the second inning. The Braves had some firsts as well—including three straight doubles to take the lead in the third—but Seaver and the Mets had the most important first: the first win in an NLCS. Trailing by a run in the eighth, New York scored five times as the Braves threw the ball all around the field, committing two errors in the frame.

The second game was even uglier, but the Mets won that as well, in an 11–6 slugfest. Koosman was knocked out of the game during Atlanta's five-run fifth and failed to qualify for the win. The Braves had wasted their home-field advantage and headed to New York needing to win or go home for the year. They again got the Mets' starter in trouble yet could do nothing against the bullpen. Nolan Ryan relieved Gary Gentry in the third and threw seven innings of relief to clinch the pennant. To add insult to injury, Wayne Garrett, whom the Mets took from the Braves in the Rule V draft for $25,000 the previous winter, hit the go-ahead home run in the fifth inning.

Once again Shea was torn apart by celebrating fans. Once again they put it all back together just to tear it up one last time.

METS TOP 50

TOMMIE AGEE
1968–1972

Outfielder

Tommie Lee Agee was the center fielder that Gil Hodges wanted, and the one that the manager stuck with despite a horrendous first season in New York. After Hodges pushed for the Mets to acquire Agee—the 1966 AL Rookie of the Year—from the White Sox, the Alabama native bounced back from his .217 outing in 1968 to help make history in 1969.

Agee began the year by hitting the only fair ball into the upper deck in the history of Shea Stadium. He led the Miracle Mets in homers (26), RBI (76), and runs (97). His leadoff home run in Game 3 of the World Series kicked off Agee's day for the ages. His spectacular backhanded catch in the fourth inning ended one Baltimore rally, and his sprawling catch with the bases loaded in the seventh signaled that maybe miracles could come true.

After the Mets won their unlikely World Series, Agee and six other teammates, including left fielder and high school chum Cleon Jones, did a musical review in Las Vegas. Agee had quite an encore in 1970, breaking the club single-season records for runs (107), hits (182), and stolen bases (31) while hitting a career-high .286. He had another solid season in 1971, but knee injuries started slowing him down, and the trade for Willie Mays the following spring marked the end of Agee's time as a Met. He remained in New York as a businessman and died suddenly in 2001. He was elected to the team's Hall of Fame the following year.

A Miraculous Autumn in New York
THE 1969 WORLD SERIES

The heretofore horrible New York Mets had rallied from an August 10-game deficit in the standings, won 100 games, swept the first-ever National League Championship Series, and landed in the 1969 World Series. Was this some sort of a dream?

The Baltimore Orioles, winners of 109 games in 1969, had a staff full of aces in Mike Cuellar, Dave McNally, and Jim Palmer. They had swept through their League Championship Series with ease, and when Don Buford homered to lead off Game 1 of the World Series, and the Orioles knocked around 25-game winner Tom Seaver in a three-run fourth, it appeared that this would be a quick World Series. It was—only in a way that no one envisioned.

The Mets had their own stable full of excellent arms. Everyone knew about Seaver, but Jerry Koosman was no slouch, coming off a 17–9 season with a 2.28 ERA. The cunning Kooz was perfect through six innings in his World Series debut in Game 2, but Baltimore's only two hits of the day tied the game at 1–1 in the seventh. The Mets put two men aboard in the ninth and

First baseman Donn Clendenon did what he was brought to New York to do: deliver clutch hits at crunch time. He hit .357 in the five-games series and belted three homers, including a two-run shot in the clinching game. *Focus On Sport/Getty Images*

Game 3 was all Tommie Agee. After leading off the game for New York with a homer, his two spectacular catches in the field prevented several Baltimore runs. His running catch at the wall squashed an Oriole rally in the fourth. *Frank Hurley/NY Daily News Archive/Getty Images*

MVP Books collection

McNally went after the light-hitting Al Weis with two outs and the even-lighter-hitting Koosman on deck. Weis singled to score Ed Charles. Koosman got the first two outs in the bottom of the ninth before walking the next two and giving way to reliever Ron Taylor. Brooks Robinson, who'd driven in Baltimore's lone run, hit a smash to third base that Charles snagged and threw to first. The series was even at one game a piece.

The first World Series game at Shea Stadium belonged to Tommie Agee. He homered leading off the first inning for the Mets and snuffed two Baltimore rallies with unbelievable—scratch that—amazin' catches. He robbed Elrod Hendricks with a snow-cone grab in front of the 396-foot sign in left-center with two men on in the fourth inning. His belly-flop catch of Paul Blair's bases-loaded drive in the seventh saved at least three runs. Gary Gentry doubled in two runs and threw shutout ball for 6⅔ innings. Nolan Ryan got the save, though it was Agee who saved the day.

The next afternoon was even more surreal. Donn Clendenon's home run in the second held up until the ninth, when the Orioles put men on the corners against Seaver. Brooks Robinson drilled a liner to right field that Ron Swoboda dove for and somehow caught. Frank Robinson tagged up and crossed home plate to tie the game, but the series might have gone very differently had the ball gotten by Swoboda. Seaver was removed in the bottom of the 10th for pinch hitter J. C. Martin with two on and none out. He laid down a bunt that Orioles reliever Pete Richert fielded, but his throw caromed off Martin's wrist and Rod Gaspar scored the winning run. The Orioles argued that Martin was running out of the baseline, but Baltimore wasn't winning any arguments in New York.

After the Orioles took a 3–0 lead the next day on a pair of home runs, an inside pitch seemed to hit Frank Robinson in the sixth. Umpire Lou DiMuro said it hit his bat. The Orioles argued, again to no avail. In the bottom of the inning a McNally pitch landed near Cleon Jones' right foot and bounced into the Mets dugout. Gil Hodges emerged with a ball with shoe polish on it and Jones was sent to first. A minute after the Orioles quit arguing, Clendenon slammed a home run to make it 3–2. Unlikely slugger Al Weis homered the next inning to tie the game, and a Swoboda double gave the Mets the lead in the eighth. Koosman, who had allowed only one hit since surrendering the two homers in the third inning, allowed a leadoff walk in the ninth, but he retired the next two. Davey Johnson's flyball was reeled in by a genuflecting Jones, and the Mets were world champions.

Jerry Koosman leaps into the arms of catcher Jerry Grote after the Mets shocked the world with a four-games-to-one World Series triumph over the Orioles. Amazin'! *Walter Iooss Jr./Sports Illustrated/Getty Images*

THE MIRACLE METS ARE WORLD CHAMPS!

New York Mets 5, Baltimore Orioles 3
World Series Game 5
Thursday, October 16, 1969
at Shea Stadium, Queens, NY

	1	2	3	4	5	6	7	8	9	R	H	E
BAL	0	0	3	0	0	0	0	0	0	3	5	2
NYM	0	0	0	0	0	2	1	2	x	5	7	0

Baltimore Orioles	AB	R	H	RBI
Buford, LF	4	0	0	0
Blair, CF	4	0	0	0
F Robinson, RF	3	1	1	1
Powell, 1B	4	0	1	0
Salmon, PR	0	0	0	0
B Robinson, 3B	4	0	0	0
Johnson, 2b	4	0	1	0
Etchebarren, C	3	0	0	0
Belanger, SS	3	1	1	0
McNally, P	2	1	1	2
Motton, PH	1	0	0	0
Watt, P	0	0	0	0
Totals	32	3	5	3

HR: F Robinson, McNally. **Team LOB:** 3
E: Watt, Powell.

New York Mets	AB	R	H	RBI
Agee, CF	3	0	1	0
Harrelson, SS	4	0	0	0
Jones, LF	3	2	1	0
Clendenon, 1B	3	1	1	2
Swoboda, RF	4	1	2	1
Charles, 3B	4	0	0	0
Grote, C	4	0	0	0
Weis, 2B	4	1	1	1
Koosman, P	3	0	1	0
Totals	32	5	7	4

2B: Swoboda, Koosman, Jones. **HR:** Clendenon, Weis. **HBP:** Jones. **SB:** Agee.
Team LOB: 6.

Pitching Summary

Baltimore Orioles	IP	H	R	ER	BB	SO
McNally	7	5	3	3	2	6
Watt, L (0–1)	1	2	2	1	0	1
Totals	8	7	5	4	2	7

New York Mets	IP	H	R	ER	BB	SO
Koosman, W (2–0)	9	5	3	3	1	5

Umpires: HP Lou DiMuro, 1B Lee Weyer, 2B Hank Soar, 3B Frank Secory, LF Larry Napp, RF Shag Crawford.
Time of Game: 2:14
Attendance: 57,397

The world champion New York Mets were greeted with a tickertape parade through Manhattan after winning the 1969 World Series. *Jack Smith/NY Daily News Archive/Getty Images*

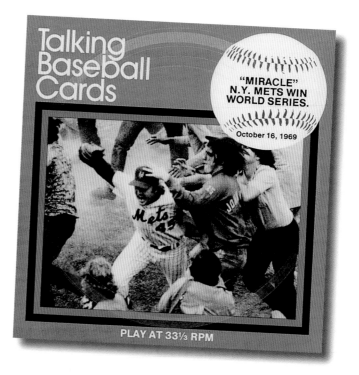

The 1969 World Series was like a dream, an *Alice in Wonderland* upside-down world where nothing was as it was supposed to be. Improbable catches, balls striking players at the most opportune times, a 109-win club looking feeble with bat and glove. While it was a wonderful trip down the rabbit hole for the Mets, it was a bad trip for the Orioles, who talked big before the series only to sound like the lamenting man at the microphone at Woodstock two months earlier: "It's a bummer, please."

Hey, it was the '60s. And what a way for it to go out—with the greatest laughingstock in modern baseball history crowned a champion in the professional game's one hundredth season. The whole thing seemed about as believable as Lewis Carroll's prose. And about as wonderful.

When it was over, the champagne flowed freely, the tickertape reigned down, the hunks of Shea Stadium grass concealed in garages throughout the Tri-State Area seemed forever green, and the singing voices of *The Amazing Mets* (the LP record, that is) rang from the Mets locker room to *The Ed Sullivan Show* to the Las Vegas Strip. The National League's youngest and happiest team would savor its moment, as would the fans who'd run the gamut of emotions with a team that now and forever held a piece of the city's soul.

1960s METS YEAR-BY-YEAR

YEAR	W–L	PCT.	GB	FINISH	
1962	40–120	.250	60.5	10th in 10-team NL	Though an utter failure competitively and critically, the original Mets did all right at the box office. The Mets sold 2,000 season box seats at the Polo Grounds in their inaugural year, more than doubling the highest number of season tickets the Giants enjoyed there.
1963	51–111	.315	48.5	10th	Roger Craig set an NL record with 18 straight losses before Jim Hickman's grand slam in the ninth inning on August 9 at the Polo Grounds broke a 3–3 tie and gave Craig a mark in the win column. Two days earlier, Hickman had become the first Met to hit for the cycle.
1964	53–109	.327	40	10th	After winning both ends of a doubleheader on May 12, 1962, Craig Anderson proceeded to lose his next 16 decisions that year. He lost both of his decisions in 1963 to tie Roger Craig's dubious mark. In 1964 he set the record at 19 in a row by losing his last major league decision.
1965	50–112	.309	47	10th	Cincinnati's Jim Maloney no-hit the Mets for 10 innings before losing on a Johnny Lewis home run in the 11th inning. It was the only win for the Mets over a 15-game span.
1966	66–95	.410	28.5	9th	Besides being the first Mets team not to lose 100 games or finish last, the 1966 Mets were also the first without a 20-game loser. Jack Fisher, who tied a club record with 24 losses in 1965, cut that total by 10 but still led the club in L's.
1967	61–101	.377	40.5	10th	Newcomer Tommy Davis rewrote the club record book during his one year with the Mets, setting the single-season marks for at bats (577), hits (174), and doubles (32). The former two records would be broken by Tommie Agee in 1970; Rusty Staub took over the doubles lead with 36 in 1973.
1968	73–89	.451	24	9th	Despite the team's best record to that point, 1968 wasn't an easy year for Gil Hodges in his first season as Mets manager. It started with the club losing on Opening Day by allowing three runs in the bottom of the ninth inning, and it ended with Hodges having a heart attack.
1969	100–62	.617	–	1st in 6-team NL East	The Mets had been so bad that even after winning 100 games in 1969, their overall winning percentage for the 1960s was .382, with an average record of 62–100. Their record through 1968 was 394–737, a winning percentage of .348, or an average mark of 56–106.

The 1969 New York Mets. *Getty images*

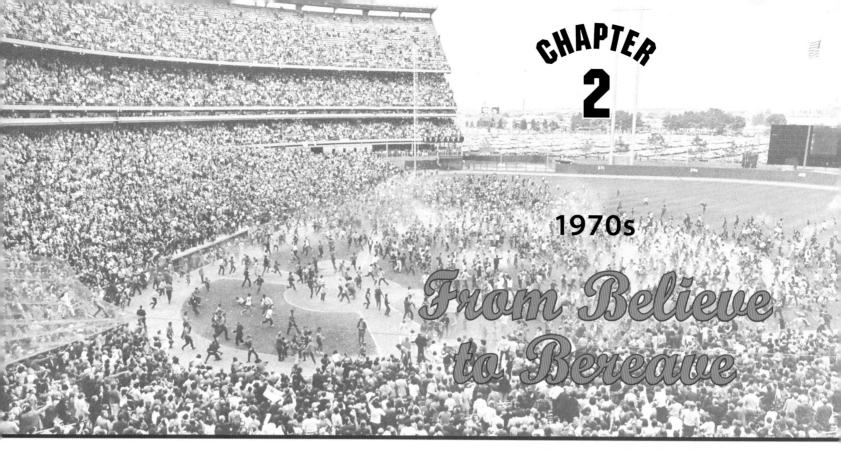

From Believe to Bereave

George Mattson/NY Daily News Archive/Getty Images

Enter Gate D
FIELD LEVEL BOX
251F | 3
BOX | SEAT
48 WEDNESDAY
JULY 10
—1974—
$4.00
RAIN CHECK
ADMIT ONE - Subject to the conditions set forth on the back hereof
SECOND
RAIN CHECK
In the event of a postponement this coupon will admit the holder to the game numbered hereon. Not good if detached from Original Rain Check.
"MR. MET"
48

MVP Books collection

NEW YORK Mets

GO METS! .G.
THE NEWS
NEW YORK'S PICTURE NEWSPAPER

Coming off of one of the most unlikely world championships in baseball history, the 1970 Mets could do no wrong. They couldn't do much right, either.

It was impossible to duplicate all the breaks, calls, and balls that had bounced New York's way a year earlier. The roster returned from its 1969 trip to the moon pretty much intact, with a few exceptions. Backup catcher J. C. Martin—who lives on in Mets annals for a throw that hit his wrist to let the winning run score in Game 4 of the World Series—was traded to the Cubs. The first piece of the '69 club to go, however, was Ed Charles. The veteran third baseman had started four of the five World Series games and memorably danced next to the mound as Jerry Koosman jumped into Jerry Grote's arms moments after the season reached its miraculous conclusion in Game 5. Yet less than two weeks later, Charles was released. The gregarious poet laureate of the Mets joined the team's promotion department before abruptly leaving due to a misunderstanding about moving expenses with general manager Johnny Murphy. By that time, Murphy had already found Charles' replacement at third base.

Murphy traded promising outfielder Amos Otis to the Royals for Joe Foy, who had enjoyed a solid season in Kansas City after clubbing 16 home runs for the 1967 "Impossible Dream" Red Sox. Murphy made a far better deal on December 12, sending two Triple-A players to the Giants for pitcher Ray Sadecki and outfielder Dave Marshall, but that would be his final transaction.

The 61-year-old Murphy suffered a heart attack on December 30, 1969. He died from a second massive heart attack in the hospital two weeks later. A six-time world champion with the Yankees, Murphy went on to run the Red Sox minor league system for 15 years before Boston cleaned house in 1961, and he became one of the Mets' first hires. Murphy rose through the ranks, reeled in Gil Hodges from Washington, and took over as GM after Bing Devine's abrupt departure. In the last year of Murphy's life, he was presented the William J. Slocum Award from the New York baseball writers for "long and meritorious service to baseball," and he was named Executive of the Year by *The Sporting News* for 1969.

After the first heart attack, Murphy was expected to resume his duties within six months, so the Mets assembled a trio to handle the workload temporarily: Jim Thompson, Joe McDonald, and Bob Scheffing. When Murphy died, the Mets named Scheffing, the one man of the triumvirate with major league managing, coaching, and scouting experience, to be the new GM. New York first hired him in 1965 following a meeting in a St. Louis supermarket with Bing Devine. Scheffing's responsibilities as special assignment scout included evaluating the American League and providing information on the Baltimore Orioles prior to the 1969 World Series. He also gave a favorable report on Joe Foy.

A Bronx native who battled weight problems throughout his career, Foy feuded with manager Dick Williams while in Boston. Unhappy with his attitude—not to mention a drunken driving accident—the Red Sox left him available in the 1969 expansion draft. After Foy led the first-year Royals in runs, RBI, and games, the Mets decided he was their future at third base. The return home in 1970 only exacerbated Foy's destructive behavior. His indifferent play and involvement in drugs ruined his brief Mets tenure; the club was only too happy when the Senators claimed him in the Rule V draft. Otis, meanwhile, blossomed in Kansas City and was a key player in the Royals' success in the mid-1970s under Whitey Herzog.

Herzog could have and probably should have taken over as GM after Murphy's death. At age 38, Herzog was nearly two decades younger than Scheffing. The pair had traded jobs after Wes Westrum's resignation in 1967, and Herzog was a more hands-on director of player development than his predecessor. Scheffing initially declined the offer to become general manager in 1970 because the avid golfer had invested heavily in his Arizona home and other real estate ventures. Only after his wife helped change his mind did Scheffing and board chairman M. Donald Grant come to an agreement.

Herzog, on the other hand, breathed the game and had a remarkable eye for talent. He served as Mets third-base coach in 1966 and helped teach Bud Harrelson to switch hit, among his other duties. Late in his one year as coach,

A cornerstone of the Mets for more than a decade, the slick-fielding Bud Harrelson earned back-to-back all-star invitations in 1970 and 1971 and won the only Gold Glove Award of his career in '71. *AP Images*

Herzog opined that "a good third-base coach can win 16 or 17 games a season for his club." The '66 Mets won 16 more games than the '65 version. Herzog believed that baseball men—not Joan Payson's stockbroker—should make baseball decisions. When Grant offered his opinions on personnel issues, Herzog told the chairman he didn't know what he was talking about. Grant did know how to hold a grudge, and Herzog never had a chance to advance in the Mets organization as long as Grant was calling the shots. The future Hall of Famer went elsewhere. There was a lot of that with the Mets in the 1970s.

Treadmill

The Mets held steady in third place with identical 83–79 marks in 1970 and 1971. The record may have been the same, but how the team got there was vastly different.

The 1970 Mets were neck and neck in the NL East race with the Pirates and Cubs through mid-September. New York and Pittsburgh were tied for first on September 14, with Chicago one game back, but from that point the Mets won only 5 of their final 15 games to finish six games out. After losing six of seven to the Pirates over successive September weekends, Gil Hodges summed up the post-Miracle year: "It's been a long, long, long season."

It felt even longer in 1971. The Mets were in first place for the last time on May 26 and started July by going 3–15 to kiss their playoff aspirations goodbye.

Two years removed from their world championship, the Mets were just another team in the NL East. Former World Series MVP Donn Clendenon set a club record with 97 RBI in 1970; a year later he simply looked old and was released after the season. By then, the Mets had parted with several other cogs from 1969, including Rod Gaspar, Ron Swoboda, Al Weis, Art Shamsky, and Ron Taylor.

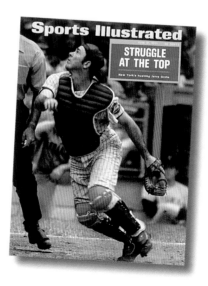

A core member of the 1969 champs, Jerry Grote remained one of the National League's premier catchers in the early 1970s even as the team stumbled. *Tony Triolo/Sports Illustrated/Getty Images*

Tom Seaver receives a peck on the cheek from his wife, Nancy, after "Tom Terrific" set a new major league record by striking out 19 batters in a game, including 10 in a row, on April 23, 1970. *Bruce Bennett/Getty Images*

The youthful core from that '69 team remained intact, however. Jerry Grote was one of the game's best backstops, and Tommie Agee put together two seasons to rival what he had done in 1969, including winning a Gold Glove Award in 1970—the first ever given to a Met. Shortstop Bud Harrelson earned a Gold Glove in '71 to go with successive all-star appearances for the two most productive seasons of his career. Cleon Jones predictably fell from his lofty .340 perch of 1969, but he had his average back up to .319 two years later. And then there was Ed Kranepool, who hit just .170 in 1970 and ended up in the minors for the first time since 1964. Written off yet again despite being just 26 years old, Kranepool batted 110 points higher in '71 and set a career high with 58 RBI while taking back first base.

But in any discussion of the Mets of the early 1970s, the first person to come up was always Tom Seaver. The 26-year-old ace just kept getting better. He did not approach his 25-win total of 1969, but he led the National League in ERA and strikeouts the two years that followed. His 1.76 ERA in 1971 would not be surpassed over a full National League season until Dwight Gooden's 1.53 ERA in 1985. Seaver's 21 complete games and 289 strikeouts in '71 are still franchise records. He won "only" 20 games, yet in nine of his losses or no-decisions, the Mets scored two runs or fewer, and he earned a loss in four one-run contests.

By some measures, 1971 was Seaver's best season, though he finished a distant second in the Cy Young voting to Chicago's Fergie Jenkins, who accumulated 24 wins yet had an ERA a full run higher than Seaver's (though Fergie's

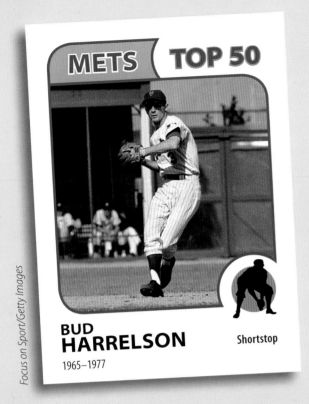

METS TOP 50

BUD HARRELSON
1965–1977

Shortstop

Bud Harrelson was one of the smallest and toughest Mets in history and the infield glue for more than a decade. In 1969, manager Gil Hodges platooned at every infield position except shortstop. The 1973 Mets skittered most of the year until Harrelson returned from injuries.

Derrell McKinley Harrelson was born on the day of the D-Day Invasion in 1944, his father an auto mechanic and his mother a former track standout. Despite weighing under 100 pounds, Bud made all-state in football at Sunset High in Hayward, California; he had a deadly outside shot in basketball and was, not surprisingly, a top defender. Though no schools recruited him for baseball, he earned a hoops scholarship at San Francisco State. When several teams came calling after Harreslon hit .430 in the spring, he chose the Mets. "I figured I could make that club fast," he said.

Harrelson debuted in New York just two years after he signed. He learned to switch-hit and amassed 45 triples and 115 steals as a Met, but fielding was his forte. He had a 54-game errorless streak in 1970 and won the 1971 Gold Glove Award. Harrelson started every postseason game in '69 and '73. Like many other Mets veterans of the era, he was discarded in the late 1970s, finishing his career in Philadelphia and Texas. He served as a Mets coach for seven years and replaced Davey Johnson as manager in 1990. He took the club to second place, but a poor 1991 led to his dismissal. Harrelson later became co-owner of the independent Long Island Ducks.

37 walks in 39 starts were eye popping indeed). Tom even declared himself, well, terrific. "I think I pitched as well as anyone can pitch," Seaver said before the Cy Young votes were counted. "I don't want to sound egocentric, but I think I'm the best pitcher in baseball. I really do."

But Seaver already had a Cy Young Award. The day he picked up his 1969 hardware, April 23, 1970, he tied the then-major league mark with 19 strikeouts and set the all-time mark by fanning 10 in a row en route to a two-hit, 2–1 victory at Shea. That shattered the club mark of 15 strikeouts in a game, set just four days earlier by Nolan Ryan. Ah, Ryan.

Worst Trade Ever

For every eye-popping start by Ryan, there were two head-scratching outings. He recorded complete games in four of his first six starts in 1970, and then had just one more the rest of the year. The '71 season likewise began with promise and ended with him failing to retire a batter in his last start. Seaver, a close friend whose family visited Ryan's Texas ranch that winter, wrote the beleaguered fireballer a long letter after the season telling him not to lose faith. It was the Mets who lost faith.

Though measuring pitch velocity was generally unavailable at the time, many in baseball, including Hodges, ranked Ryan's fastball with that of Gil's former teammate, Sandy Koufax. It was an interesting comparison because, like Koufax, Ryan had major control problems early in his career. A 12th-round pick by the Mets in the first major league draft in 1965, Ryan debuted in New York a year later at age 19. He spent four-plus seasons teasing management, press, and fans with glimpses of brilliance and bouts of utter wildness. For the Mets, 1971 was the last straw. He won six of his first seven decisions and had a stellar 1.08 ERA by Memorial Day; from then on he went 4–13 with a 4.50 ERA. For the year

Mets fans never got a chance to enjoy the power and dominance of Nolan Ryan while he was in New York. With an already solid starting staff, the unreliable Ryan seemed expendable in 1971. *Herb Scharfman/Sports Imagery/ Getty Images*

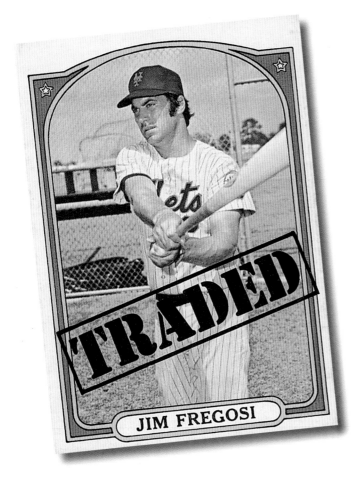

JIM FREGOSI

he walked a staggering 116 batters and hit 15 others in 152 innings. His nine bases on balls—in only five innings—on July 29 broke the club record of eight, which Ryan himself had reached four times previously.

The Mets had reached the end of their rope with Ryan, and the lack of power at third base was likewise driving the front office to distraction. Players acquired to fill that role the last two years had been busts: Joe Foy in 1970 and Bob Aspromonte in 1971. Wayne Garrett, a Rule V pick in '69 who had done the job for the Miracle Mets, picked up the slack for Foy in 1970, but he wasn't any better than Aspromonte the following year. The Mets tried 45 different men at third base over the club's first decade, and they were ready to deal from strength to fill their most glaring weakness.

Ryan should have been a superstar with the Mets, but several factors worked against him. First, he was a slow developer compared to the top three in the rotation—Seaver, Koosman, and Gentry—who had come up from the minors and immediately excelled in the big leagues. Part of the reason was out of his hands.

Due to the Vietnam War and conscription, many young men were required to fulfill military obligations. In 1970, Ryan spent one weekend per month in U.S. Army Reserve training, plus two weeks during the summer.

Though he would later become a physical marvel who still threw bullets well into his 40s, Ryan had a recurring blister problem as a young pitcher. Trainer Gus Mauch had tried to toughen up his skin by dipping his fingers in pickle juice. "I've always hated pickles," Ryan said. "And I couldn't stand the smell of that pickle brine."

The team's way of doing things was a source of frustration for Ryan. "We believe that pitchers need four days of rest between starts," GM Bob Scheffing decreed. "That means a man works every fifth day. But with some guys absent for military drills, and with doubleheaders, we need six starters to maintain the rotation." The end result was less work for the remaining starters, who also had to be on-call to assist the four-man bullpen as needed. The five-man rotation, initiated by pitching coach Rube Walker in 1968, benefited the young staff, but it also irritated those who were consistently skipped. Gary Gentry was even more annoyed—and vocal—than Ryan.

Yet the Mets preferred Gentry over Ryan. "More interest is being shown by other clubs in Gary Gentry than Nolan Ryan," Leonard Koppett noted in the *New York Times* in October 1971. "The first half performance of Ryan [8–4, 2.05 ERA in 12 starts] warrants continued faith in him despite his second-half problems." Jack Lang, beat writer for the *Long Island Press*, stated that "the Angels wanted Gentry in the Jim Fregosi deal. The answer was 'No.'"

Ryan had asked for a trade, mostly because his wife, Ruth, was frightened by New York, and Ryan worried about her when the team was on the road. But in those days, players—especially, young, wild, unestablished pitchers—had no choice but to do what the team told them. The Mets told Ryan to go west.

The Mets traded Ryan and three prospects to the Angels for a third baseman with pop. Jim Fregosi had made the all-star team six times, but as a shortstop. In fact, he had never played a major league game at third base. Fregosi made two errors at his new position in the first intrasquad game and then broke his right thumb fielding fungoes. He was out of action for a month and never caught up. Ryan did, however.

Ryan-for-Fregosi was a watershed moment for the organization. The trade drew some criticism when it was made, but the chorus against the Mets grew and grew—starting with Ryan, who fired back during spring training, "There just wasn't much communication from Hodges and Walker, and it's my feeling that one of the reasons I never achieved anything with the Mets was because I never received any instruction."

Ryan also complained that Walker had a hard time relating to pitchers because he'd been a catcher. Characteristically, Hodges said little about the slight by his former pitcher. But the day the trade was made, the manager didn't mention any regrets. "He could put it together overnight," said Hodges, "but he hasn't done it for us, and the Angels wanted him. I would not hesitate making a trade for somebody who might help us right now, and Fregosi is such a guy."

By the end of March 1972, Fregosi was still unable to throw, Jerry Koosman's left arm hadn't been the same since the 1969 World Series, and the other pitchers the team was counting on to mature and fill out the rotation had not. Instead, rookies John Milner and Jon Matlack were winning jobs in spring training that had previously been held by established players.

On April 1 the first mass strike in baseball history brought baseball to a standstill. The next afternoon, the Mets' world came crashing down.

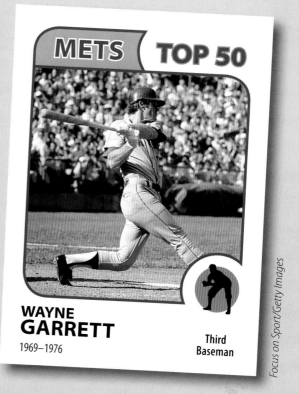

METS TOP 50

WAYNE
GARRETT
1969–1976

Third
Baseman

Focus on Sport/Getty Images

With a little more faith in Wayne Garrett, the Mets may have kept Amos Otis in center field and Nolan Ryan on the mound. As it happened, they traded both to try to shore up third base, yet Garrett wound up playing more games at the position than any Met until Howard Johnson surpassed his 709 games in 1991.

Ronald Wayne Garrett came from a ball-playing family in Florida. Brothers Adrian and James were already in the Braves system when Milwaukee drafted Wayne out of high school in the sixth round in 1965. The Mets needed infield depth heading into 1969 because of Bud Harrelson's knee surgery, so they took the redhead in the Rule V draft. Required to stay in the majors all season, the youngest player on the '69 club won the lefty platoon at third base and also started 34 times at second. He hit .218 with just one home run during the season, but his homer in Game 3 of the NLCS helped secure the pennant.

Blessed with a good eye and decent speed, Garrett batted leadoff for the "Ya Gotta Believe" Mets of 1973 and clubbed 16 home runs, plus two more in the World Series. Despite Garrett playing in a team-high 151 games in 1974, the Mets traded for another veteran third baseman: Joe Torre. Garrett responded with his best average yet in 1975 (.266), then New York made another rotten deal involving a third baseman in 1976 when they sent Garrett to Montreal.

DECEMBERS TO DISMEMBER

The Mets spent the first half of the 1960s drowning in their own incompetence. By the end of the decade, though, the front office looked brilliant as the Mets put together the unlikeliest of world championship clubs in 1969. And then it all fell apart in the 1970s.

Though the Mets pulled off a few shrewd trades during the '70s, the decade really came down to five December deals, made in conjunction with the winter meetings, that cost the Mets dearly. The first trade, pulled off while 1969 tickertape was still floating around Manhattan, was the unraveling of what could have been a decade of dominance for the Mets.

December 3, 1969

Amos Otis and Bob Johnson to the Royals for Joe Foy

The first major gaffe was pulled off in the final weeks of general manager Johnny Murphy's life. Otis immediately became an all-star and the kind of center fielder the Mets spent the rest of the decade unsuccessfully trying to find. The troubled Foy lasted less than a year as a Met. They continued their fruitless quest for a third baseman, which led to …

December 10, 1971

Nolan Ryan, Leroy Stanton, Don Rose, and Frank Estrada to the Angels for Jim Fregosi

Angels GM Harry Dalton said Ryan had "the best arm in the National League and, at 24, is just coming into his own." Meanwhile, Mets GM Bob Scheffing wondered, "How long can you wait?" Apparently one more year would have done the trick. Despite walking the most batters in baseball (157) in 1972, Ryan won 19 games for the worst offensive team in the majors and led the American League with nine shutouts and 329 K's. The trade grew exponentially worse as Ryan's career continued … for 21 more years.

December 3, 1974

Tug McGraw, Don Hahn, and Dave Schneck to the Phillies for John Stearns, Del Unser, and Mac Scarce

The toughest trade of this quintet to judge because the Mets received catcher John Stearns, who became a four-time all-star, but Philadelphia quickly leapfrogged New York in the NL East with the acquisition of the southpaw with the unhittable screwball. Mets leads weren't nearly as safe as they'd been with the animated McGraw, who had helped the Mets nail down two unlikely pennants and made New York believe.

DEC. 12 SPORTS EXTRA 1975
LOLICH COMES TO METS IN 4-MAN SWAP
PITCHER MICKEY LOLICH

DEC. 12 SPORTS EXTRA 1975
LE GRAND ORANGE GOES TO MOTOR CITY
OUTFIELD RUSTY STAUB

MVP Books collection

December 12, 1975

Rusty Staub and Bill Laxton to the Tigers for Mickey Lolich and Billy Baldwin

After Staub has his most productive season in New York, piling up a club record 105 RBI, the Mets sent the 29-year-old outfielder to Detroit for the over-the-hill and obese Lolich. Staub, who was voted as a starter in the 1976 All-Star Game, hit .299 with 15 homers and 96 RBI that season and was even better in the two years that followed. Lolich quit New York after an 8–13 season. Rusty did return in 1981 as a pinch-hitting specialist, but that doesn't make up for the disastrous deal that dispatched him in 1975.

December 8, 1977

Jon Matlack to the Texas Rangers and John Milner to the Pittsburgh Pirates for Willie Montanez from the Atlanta Braves and Tom Grieve and Ken Henderson from the Texas Rangers

It was a bit mind boggling how the Mets lost arguably their top starting pitcher and top slugger while getting only Tom Grieve, Ken Henderson, and Willie Montanez in return. Pittsburgh and Texas, meanwhile, ended up getting all-stars Bert Byleven and Al Oliver, respectively. Grieve, a former first-round pick who previously hit 20 homers with the Rangers, was lucky to crack 20 *hits* over a full season with the Mets. Ken Henderson, New York's Opening Day right fielder in 1978, was an experienced switch hitter with pop, but he spent just seven days with the club before being traded to Cincinnati for reliever Dale Murray.

"Just This Side of Worship"

A devout Catholic, Gil Hodges attended Mass on Easter Sunday, April 2, 1972. He saw Expos outfielder Rusty Staub at St. Anne's Church in West Palm Beach, and the two talked for several minutes. Hodges, the consummate professional, never let on that the Mets had just worked out a trade for Staub at Hodges' urging. The deal was done, with shortstop Tim Foli going to Montreal, but the teams held off on making an announcement because of the strike.

Hodges and coaches Eddie Yost, Rube Walker, and Joe Pignatano—who had been together since Hodges managed the Senators—had completed 27 holes of golf and were standing in the parking lot of the Ramada Inn discussing what time to meet for dinner when Hodges suddenly fell straight back and hit his head on the pavement. He never regained consciousness. Two days shy of his 48th birthday, Hodges had died of a massive heart attack.

M. Donald Grant and general manager Bob Scheffing hastily arranged to meet with coach Yogi Berra. Twice passed over as manager of the club, Yogi was now asked to take over in the most trying of circumstances. After taking some time to consider it and talk with the other coaches, Berra accepted. Again, the Mets delayed the announcement.

"To people connected to the Mets," Leonard Koppett later wrote, "feelings towards Hodges were just this side of worship....The organization felt unreserved love, from Mrs. Payson and Grant down." Yet the way the team handled one of the most emotional moments in club history was indicative of how things would go in the post-Gil world.

Even as the Mets dismissed reporter queries, saying they could not begin to consider a new manager in the hours

immediately after Hodges' death, the club was doing just the opposite. The team also failed to cancel their Opening Day game, scheduled in Pittsburgh for the same day as Hodges' funeral. The Yankees, who flew north with the Mets on the same plane that carried Hodges' body, had canceled their opener in New York because of the funeral. The Mets accused the American League club of "upstaging" them. Tom Seaver, who was extremely close to Hodges, said there was "no way" he would pitch in Pittsburgh instead of paying his respects. "I doubt there is a man on the club who would play."

The team was spared further indignity when the strike canceled the game, but in the words of *New York Times* writer Joe Durso, they "turn[ed] tragedy into tactlessness" by telling reporters at the funeral that they would hold a news conference at 4 p.m. that afternoon. Although the Mets made the announcements about Berra and Staub in a low-key manner, Durso warned, "No amount of success on the field can completely repair the air of innocence that fascinated their fans during the 10 merely nerve-racking years that preceded this one."

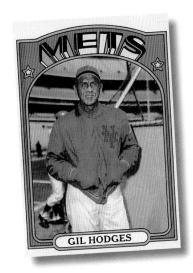

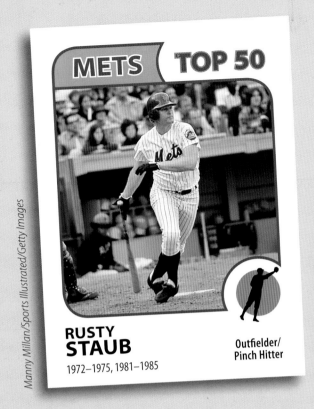

METS TOP 50

RUSTY STAUB
1972–1975, 1981–1985

Outfielder/
Pinch Hitter

New Mets manager Yogi Berra surveys the scene prior to the 1972 season opener against the Pirates. New York got off to a hot start under Berra, winning 8 of their first 10 games and rolling to a 25–7 record with an 11-game win streak in May. *John Iacono/Sports Illustrated/Getty Images*

Making Rusty Staub a Met was Gil Hodges' final baseball decision, and although Hodges didn't get to see it, Staub was an integral part of Yogi Berra's pennant-winning club of 1973. His numbers that season were unspectacular, but nothing could stop him in October... except the wall at Shea Stadium. After homering three times against the Reds in the NLCS, he collided while making a sensational catch in Game 4. He still batted .423 and played in all seven World Series games despite shoulder pain that forced him to throw underhand.

Daniel Joseph Staub grew up in New Orleans, where he learned to both cook and hit. He debuted at age 19 with expansion Houston, then was an original Expo in 1969 and became Montreal's first baseball star. In 1975, "Le Grand Orange" became the first Met to surpass 100 RBI in a season, and that December he was traded to the Tigers, for whom he was an all-star in 1976.

Staub returned to New York in 1981 as a player–coach, but he gave up his coaching role to focus on helping the team with his bat off the bench. His 77 pinch hits are second to teammate Ed Kranepool's 90, and Staub tied major league records with eight straight pinch hits and 25 pinch RBI in 1983. Overall, Staub had 2,716 hits when he retired as a Met at age 41. The one-time announcer, chef, and humanitarian joined Bud Harrelson as the first players inducted into the Mets Hall of Fame in 1986.

A New Order

By trading away Ryan and three promising youngsters—former first-round picks Ken Singleton and Tim Foli and highly regarded Mike Jorgensen—for two veteran hitters, the Mets were clearly making a run at the Pirates, the defending world champions and the class of the National League East. The Mets hadn't totally given up the farm, but they pretty much told director of player development Whitey Herzog, who opposed both trades, what they thought of his opinion.

Though newspaper speculation during the Mets media blackout had included Herzog—as well as Rube Walker—as possible managerial candidates, it was Yogi's team from almost the moment Hodges was pronounced dead. (Herzog would be hired to manage the Texas Rangers a year later.) The Mets front office could now act more independently of the manager than had previously been the case. Hodges had influenced personnel decisions since almost the day he was hired in 1967, starting with center fielder Tommie Agee.

MVP Books collection

Agee was hitting .291 with 13 RBI in 21 games in 1972 as the first-place Mets enjoyed their best start to that point in franchise history. Then came the third blockbuster trade in six months: Willie Mays was coming back to New York.

The Say Hey Kid was no kid, having just passed his 41st birthday, and was coming off his worst season in 20 years when San Francisco finally said "yes" to Joan Payson and New York. The city's unswerving love for Mays was akin to Brooklyn's worship of Gil Hodges, Duke Snider, Jackie Robinson, and *The Boys of Summer* (Roger Kahn's popular book by that name was in its first printing in the spring of 1972). Unlike those Brooklyn stars of yore, many of whom

had been retired for a decade, Mays was still playing, even if his odometer was about to roll over.

Payson had been the lone dissenting vote in the decision to move the Giants to San Francisco in 1957, and she had tried, in vain, to swap her 10 percent share of the team to bring Mays back to New York in 1962. A decade later, it cost the Mets prospect Charlie Williams and $50,000, plus an assurance to Giants owner Charles Stoneham that Mays would be taken care of by the Mets after his playing days. "Shea Hey," as the papers chimed, debuted as a Met on Mother's Day, the ideal present for the mother of the Mets. In the game—against the Giants, no less—Mays snapped a

Willie Mays made a big splash in his Mets debut, belting the game-winning homer against his former team on May 14, 1972. *Paul DeMaria/ NY Daily News Archive/Getty Images*

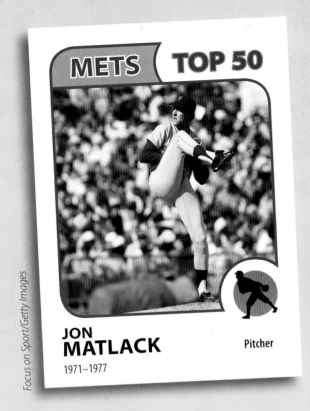

METS TOP 50

JON MATLACK

Pitcher

1971–1977

Even pitching behind Tom Seaver and Jerry Koosman in a stellar rotation, Jon Matlack made plenty of headlines. He was the National League Rookie of the Year in 1972, tossed a two-hit shutout in the 1973 NLCS, led the league in shutouts in 1974 and 1976, and earned the win and co-MVP honors in the 1975 All-Star Game.

Jonathon Trumpbour Matlack was the fourth overall pick in the 1972 draft after posting a 22–1 high school record in West Chester, Pennsylvania. The tall lefty made the final cut in 1972 just days before Gil Hodges died. Matlack won 15 games as a rookie and placed fourth in the league with a 2.32 ERA.

A line drive fractured Matlack's skull in May 1973, but that July he threw a one-hitter, and in October he started three World Series games. In 1974 he had nearly as many shutouts (7) as home runs allowed (8). Through five full seasons with New York, Matlack had a 2.90 ERA and 60 complete games, but the team's failure to improve its lineup through free agency pitted him against management. After a tumultuous 7–15 season in 1977, the Mets traded Matlack and fellow '72 rookie John Milner in a four-team deal. Matlack had a 2.27 ERA his first year with the Rangers, but the Texas offense and front office weren't much more helpful than New York's. He had a 125–126 career mark despite a 3.18 ERA. Matlack became a scout with the Tigers and served as Detroit's pitching coach in 1996.

tie with a home run. He reached base in each of his first 20 games in a Mets uniform and batted .311 with a .921 POS during that stretch.

If batting Mays leadoff seemed to defy time, putting him at first base seemed more a concession to his age. Yet he found himself in center field more and more, with Agee playing left field for the first time as a Met. A fractured bone in Staub's right hand, courtesy of a pitch from Atlanta's George Stone, broke the continuity in the lineup. After Rusty, the injuries seemed to multiply—Jones, Harrelson, Fregosi, and Agee all missed time in 1972—and following a 47–33 start to the season, the Mets went 36–40 the rest of the way. On the bright side, they got more than they expected out of Milner, who led the club with 17 home runs and finished third in the National League Rookie of the Year voting. Matlack finished first, thanks to his 15–10 record and 2.32 ERA.

The 1972 Mets managed to finish 10 games over .500 despite scoring 50 fewer runs than they allowed and batting an NL-low .225. Considering New York had gotten off to the best start in club history and stood 19 games over .500 when June began, finishing a distant third wasn't what most fans had in mind. Even with three home games cut from the schedule because of the strike, the Mets still drew two million for the fourth straight year—a number they would not reach again until 1985.

Before the 1972 season even ended, there was talk of wholesale changes to shake up a team that had seemingly become too comfortable under the more relaxed reigns of Yogi Berra. Rumors floated once more of Joe Torre coming to New York, and of Jerry Grote going to Atlanta for Felix Millan. The Mets did get the Braves second baseman, plus southpaw George Stone, but for the more reasonable price of Gary Gentry and Danny Frisella. The September 15 headline in the *New York Times*, "Mets Dismantling Due," proved premature. These Mets had one more trick up their sleeve.

Rookie John Milner (second from left) filled in admirably for manager Yogi Berra in 1972 while veteran stars Cleon Jones (left) and Rusty Staub (right) battled injuries. *Marty Lederhandler/AP Images*

Ya Gotta Believe!

The biggest problem the Mets had entering the spring of 1973 was that even with Willie Mays—oh, irony of ironies—the Mets had no center fielder. Tommie Agee's ailing knees, steep decline in offensive production, and perhaps most surprisingly, poor defense had made it clear that he was no longer the answer in center, and Agee was traded to Houston in the offseason. New York opened 1973 with the 42-year-old Mays in center, hoping he had something left. He went on the disabled list early in the season, and seven other Mets started games in center field in 1973, including left fielder Cleon Jones, infielder Teddy Martinez, and reserve Rich Chiles, who came from Houston for Agee and batted .120.

The Mets settled on Don Hahn, the return from Montreal in the 1971 trade for Ron Swoboda and a career .236 hitter. Hahn was a decent fielder, though his most memorable moment may have been a frightening on-field collision with fellow outfielder and quirky character George "The Stork" Theodore. As Theodore and Hahn gave chase to a flyball off the bat of Atlanta's Ralph Garr, the two collided at the warning track. Hahn got to his knees to try to retrieve the ball but collapsed as Garr circled the bases. The Stork was carried off the field on a stretcher with a broken hip. He did not play again until September, when he appeared in one game.

It was a painful year all around for the Mets. Six players (including Theodore) had been injured by pitched balls in the first two months of the season—thankfully, no one was hurt when Tom Seaver and Bob Gibson got into a "beanball war" in St. Louis in April—and Bud Harrelson was knocked flat at second base by Cincinnati's Bill Plummer, breaking a bone in his left hand. And there was Jon Matlack taking a line drive to the head.

Matlack was holding a 3–1 lead and had the bases loaded with two outs in the seventh on May 8 when Atlanta's Marty Perez rocketed a liner that grazed the pitcher's glove and struck him square in the forehead. Matlack went down and the ball caromed into the Mets dugout for a double. The smallest night crowd to that point in Shea Stadium history (6,840) squirmed as Matlack was carried off the field. By the time he got to Roosevelt Hospital, Matlack was the game's losing pitcher. Insult on top of injury, that's how the first three quarters of the year went.

The closest Yogi Berra got to a vote of confidence was a *New York Post* poll, which picked Bob Scheffing and M. Donald Grant ahead of Yogi as members of Mets management most deserving of termination. Grant's attempt to motivate the ballplayers with a clubhouse speech ended with Tug McGraw's repeated shouts of "Ya Gotta Believe!"—though intended to mock Grant, McGraw's catchphrase proved to be the team's rallying cry in 1973.

With just 42 games left to play, the Mets stood at 53–66, good for last place and seven and a half games out. Starting with a 12–1 drubbing of the Reds at Shea on August 18, the Mets kicked off a furious finish akin to their 1969 charge past the Cubs. New York closed the season with a 29–13 flourish, a .683 percentage that was tops in the league down the stretch. How did everything turn around so suddenly?

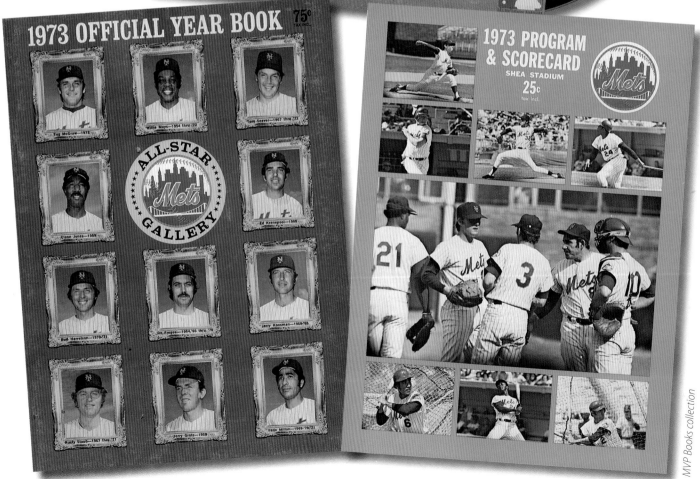

Leaving

The Mets had seen enough of Jim Fregosi by July and finally decided they could live with Wayne Garrett at third base. Red had the most productive year of his career, belting 17 home runs and leading the lead-footed club with his six stolen bases. The Mets sold Fregosi to Texas, which was managed by former Mets farm director Whitey Herzog, who had advised New York against the Ryan-for-Fregosi trade.

Lineup

It took most of the season, but the Mets finally got healthy. Cleon Jones and Jerry Grote returned after missing considerable time with wrist injuries, while Bud Harrelson had recovered from breaks to both his hand and sternum. The Mets entered mid-August with the fewest runs scored in the NL, but they suddenly found those timely hits that had been their hallmark in 1969. And like '69, their pitching down the stretch was outstanding.

Lefties

Jerry Koosman had endured injuries and inconsistency since his spectacular '69. After being named the NL's Pitcher of the Month in April 1973, he lost eight of nine starts heading into August 19. The Reds scored an unearned run in the fifth inning that game, but Kooz did not permit another run for a still-standing club record of 31⅔ consecutive scoreless innings. Even after the streak ended, Kooz didn't allow an earned run in his final two starts.

Jon Matlack, who returned to the mound just 11 days after the line drive fractured his skull, struggled through the end of July with a 7–14 record. The 23-year-old southpaw then won seven of his next eight decisions.

George Stone, acquired from the Braves, won his last eight decisions, including five straight starts during New York's September push.

Tug McGraw was as important as any member of the team during the six-week run from last to first. His "Ya Gotta Believe" rally cry was great for morale, but his screwball made believers of everybody. What had been an abysmal season transformed into his most memorable one. In his last 41 innings, McGraw saved 12 games, went 4–0, and had a 0.88 ERA. To top it off, his wife Phyllis had a baby during that stretch.

Ray Sadecki was the least pivotal member of this southpaw quintet, but he had two key moments in September extra-inning affairs. After McGraw tired during his sixth inning of relief on September 7, Sadecki came in with the bases loaded, one out, and a two-run lead over Montreal in the 15th. He got out of the jam to complete a doubleheader sweep. Sadecki was also the beneficiary of the most fabled carom in Mets history.

Luck

A home-and-home, five-game series in late September with first-place Pittsburgh began with the Pirates taking the opener at Three Rivers Stadium. The Mets were in fourth place at the time, but just three and a half games back. Trailing the next night, 4–1, New York scored five times in the top of the ninth for the win. Moving on to Shea, Stone beat the Bucs on Wednesday, and suddenly the Mets were a game and a half out. The Pirates took the lead in the top of the ninth inning in the fourth game, but in the bottom half, Mets catcher Duffy Dyer, who had gone almost a month without a hit, stroked a two-out double to tie the game. With Sadecki in his fourth inning of relief in the 13th, rookie Dave Augustine slammed a pitch to deep left off the top of the wall. Rather than bouncing into the bullpen for a home run, the ball deflected to Cleon Jones, who threw to Wayne Garrett, who gunned it on a hop to rookie catcher Ron Hodges, who slapped the tag on Richie Zisk at the plate. Hodges then singled in the winning run in the bottom of the inning.

METS | **TOP 50**

TUG McGRAW
1965–1967, 1969–1974

Pitcher

No Met has ever been as associated with a playoff team as Tug McGraw was with the 1973 squad. His mantra of "Ya Gotta Believe" got the team and the city to indeed believe.

A free spirit from Northern California, Frank Edwin McGraw earned his nickname while still nursing—and tugging. The southpaw was signed by the Mets at the insistence of his brother, Hank, a highly regarded catcher in the Mets system whose outspokenness kept him stuck in the minors. Tug began his major league career at age 20 under Casey Stengel, handing Sandy Koufax his first loss against the Mets after the Hall of Fame lefty went 13–0 in his career against the expansion club. Inconsistency and injuries kept Tug bouncing between New York and the minors, and it was on a golf course where he learned the pitch that would keep him pitching until he was 40.

Veteran Ralph Terry showed McGraw the screwball, a pitch many old timers frowned on because of the pressure it put on the arm. Gil Hodges, however, approved of the pitch and made McGraw a reliever in 1969. Sharing the bullpen burden with righty Ron Taylor, McGraw had a 0.84 ERA in the second half as the Mets rallied for the National League East title. He pitched in the NLCS, but the Mets starters were so dominant against Baltimore that McGraw did not appear in the World Series.

Tug had back-to-back 1.70 ERA seasons and earned the win in the 1972 All-Star Game, but 1973 looked to be a disaster. He had a 6.20 ERA in July while losing his first six decisions.

TUG MCGRAW

Born: August 30, 1944, in Martinez, CA
Died: January 5, 2004
Signed by New York Mets, 1964
Mets Debut: April 18, 1965
Bats: Right. **Throws:** Left

New York Mets Pitching Record

YEAR	W–L	ERA	G	IP	SV
1965	2–7	3.32	37	97.2	1
1966	2–9	5.34	15	62.1	0
1967	0–3	7.79	4	17.1	0
1968	did not play				
1969	9–3	2.24	42	100.1	12
1970	4–6	3.28	57	90.2	10
1971	11–4	1.70	51	111.0	8
1972	8–6	1.70	54	106.0	27
1973	5–6	3.87	60	118.2	25
1974	6–11	4.16	41	88.2	3
Mets Totals	47–55	3.17	361	792.2	86
MLB Totals	96–92	3.14	824	1514.2	180

When he finally won a game on August 22, the Mets also began their move out of last place. McGraw started saying "Ya Gotta Believe" after having lunch with a motivational speaker. He blurted the phrase repeatedly during a team clubhouse meeting with M. Donald Grant. The curmudgeonly chairman of the board was insulted at the time, but Grant had no problem with it when McGraw was screaming it in the champagne-soaked clubhouse several weeks later.

McGraw pitched in the last two games of the upset win over the Reds for the pennant, getting the last out and getting out of Shea Stadium with his life when fans engulfed the field. He pitched six innings in relief to earn the win in Game 2 of the World Series in Oakland and tossed 13⅔ innings in the seven-game loss while fanning 14 batters. McGraw felt the pain the following year. The Mets tried everything, including making him a starter, to get him on track in 1974. The only thing they didn't try was listening to his complaints about his shoulder. Instead they traded him to the Phillies, who were unaware of the problem. A simple operation corrected it, and McGraw pitched for another decade, appearing in five postseasons. He was on the mound for the first world championship in Phillies history in 1980.

Affable, lovable, a Mets Hall of Famer, and the father of country singer Tim McGraw, Tug McGraw succumbed to brain cancer at age 59 in 2004. Instead of a black armband, Mets uniform sleeves that year bore Tug's motto: "Ya Gotta Believe."

Focus on Sport/Getty Images

Willie Mays, playing in his final major league season, enjoys a champagne shower after the Mets defeated the Chicago Cubs 6–4 to clinch the NL East on September 30, 1973. *AP Images*

Seeing Is Believing

"The Ball on the Wall Game," as the remarkable 13-inning win over the Pirates came to be known, was the tipping point for the franchise and the faithful. After only three crowds of 40,000 at Shea Stadium all season, 51,381 turned out on Friday, September 21, for the fifth game of the week against Pittsburgh. The Mets, who had been as many as 12½ games out in July and residing in last place almost all summer, had Tom Seaver on the mound with a chance to move into first place. Cleon Jones and Jerry Grote each had two-run doubles in the first inning as the Mets beat the Bucs for the fourth straight night.

With the NL East very tight and very mediocre in 1973, the late September seven-game winning streak put the Mets ahead by a game and a half. Willie Mays, who had recently announced his retirement, made a heartfelt speech in the regular-season finale at Shea. Willie said, "It's time to say goodbye to America." A sign in the stands said, "We who are about to cry salute you."

After three days of rain, the Mets started a doubleheader at 11 a.m. at Wrigley Field on Sunday, September 30. The Cubs scratched out the opening game's only run in the eighth inning to hand Matlack his first loss since August 13. Chicago kicked the ball around in the second game and

Koosman's win clinched at least a tie for the division title. With the Cubs now eliminated, Pittsburgh and St. Louis were still alive. Though the Cards' season was complete, the Pirates had to play a makeup game on Monday afternoon. If they won and the Cubs took both games of the doubleheader with the Mets, it would present the first three-way tie in history. With Seaver on the mound, there was no need for contingencies. Tug McGraw, who hadn't pitched in five days, closed the door while allowing just one hit in three innings, and that base runner was erased in the ninth when John Milner grabbed Glenn Beckert's soft liner and then stepped on first base to end the game. The Mets were division champions with the worst record ever to that point for a postseason club: 82–79.

When word came to the clubhouse that the now meaningless second game of the makeup doubleheader was cancelled, the celebration began in earnest. Seaver, who won 19 times despite shoulder problems, put the comeback in perspective. "Nothing will ever be like 1969; we were all so young then," he said in the champagne-soaked visitor's clubhouse. "We still have to win a playoff and a World Series to match 1969. But in a way this was more earned."

Yogi's words from that summer live on for every underdog that still has one out left: "It ain't over till it's over."

The Big Red One and Done

Many assumed that the pennant was effectively decided before the teams even took the field. The Cincinnati Reds had won 99 games, the most in baseball in 1973, and they'd secured pennants in two of the previous three seasons. When Seaver lost the NLCS opener on a Johnny Bench game-ending home run, the smart money said this was the end of the line for the little-engine-that-could Mets. No one told Jon Matlack.

Just like in the 1969 World Series, when Seaver lost the first game to a heavily favored club on the road, it was a second-year southpaw who came to the rescue. To accommodate football, Game 2 of the 1973 NLCS was a 4 p.m. start, as it had been the day before when Seaver fanned an NLCS record 13 in the Cincinnati twilight. Matlack struck out nine and allowed just two hits. The Mets broke open a 1–0 game with four runs in the top of the ninth.

In an interview early in the series, Bud Harrelson had compared Cincinnati's hitting to his own—and even though Harrelson had notched a career-high mark of .258 that year, it was not meant as a compliment. Already on edge, the Reds were incensed. Joe Morgan approached Harrelson before

Game 3, warning him that Pete Rose, in particular, was angry. Rusty Staub home runs in the first and second innings helped stake the Mets to a 9–2 lead and didn't improve Rose's mood. When the Mets turned a 3–6–3 double play in the top of the fifth, Rose slid hard into second base. "I'll be honest, I was trying to knock [Harrelson] into left field," said Rose. The displeased Harrelson got in his assailant's face. Not a good idea.

Rose, carrying about 50 pounds on Harrelson, quickly had the shortstop on the ground. Third baseman Wayne Garrett jumped on Rose to try to pull him off as reinforcements arrived from the dugouts and bullpens. Little-used Met Buzz Capra—who was about the same size as Harrelson—exchanged haymakers with strapping Reds wildman Pedro Borbon.

"I was standing there watching and trying to break things up and then—pow!—someone belted me one," Capra told the Associated Press after the game. "I looked around and there was Borbon at my elbow. I thought he did it and I let him have one. Pretty soon both of us were swinging at each other." Borbon then put on a hat he thought was his—a blue one, a teammate pointed out—and the reliever tore it with his teeth.

After Bud Harrelson unadvisedly retaliated for the hard slide from Pete Rose in Game 3, he quickly found himself on the ground beneath the beefier Rose. It didn't take long for the benches and bullpens to empty, making for an all-out brawl.

Marty Lederhandler/AP Images

Though no one was ejected, the five-minute main event was the most memorable brawl in Shea Stadium history, including the three prizefights held at the ballpark in the mid-1960s. The scene got even more out of control when Rose went to take his position in left field the next inning.

The Columbus Day crowd hurled cups and other garbage at Rose throughout the bottom of the fifth. Shortly after a whiskey bottle whizzed by his head, Rose left his post for the dugout, and Reds manager Sparky Anderson pulled the rest of his team off the field. National League president Chub Feeney asked Yogi Berra and Willie Mays to try to settle down the fans, or risk a forfeit if the situation continued. Rusty Staub, Cleon Jones, and Tom Seaver joined the peace delegation and soothed the rowdies in the left field stands. The game went on and Jerry Koosman tossed the third straight complete game of the series for the Mets, now one victory from the pennant.

Rose made sure things would not go so easily for New York. After Tony Perez homered off George Stone to tie Game 4 in the seventh, Tug McGraw pitched four and one-third scoreless innings of relief before leaving for a pinch hitter in the 11th. His replacement, Harry Parker, gave up the tiebreaking homer the next inning to Rose. Borbon retired the Mets in order in the 12th to earn the save.

The Mets had blown a chance to clinch, dropping their second 2–1 decision in the series on a last-inning home run. New York managed just three hits in each of the losses, but the Mets put together three hits in the opening inning of Game 5 at Shea. They scored two on a single by Ed Kranepool, the replacement for Rusty Staub, who injured his shoulder making a superb catch the previous day. The Reds tied it against Seaver, but Cleon Jones doubled in a run in the fifth. Mays, making his first appearance in the series and batting for the first time in a month, knocked in a run, as did Hahn and Harrelson. The rowdiness that had

Harold Harris/AP Images

Bill Meurer/NY Daily News Archive/Getty Images

The rowdiness of the fans and the series as a whole spilled onto the Shea Stadium field after the Mets clinched the pennant with a 7–2 win in the NLCS finale on October 10, 1973. Thirty people were treated at the stadium's first aid station and five had to be taken to the hospital. *Dan Farrell/NY Daily News Archive/Getty Images*

permeated since the Rose–Harrelson brawl intensified as the game drew toward a close. The wooden barrier for the temporary seats along the first-base line gave way as fans crowded near the field after the Mets went up 7–2. Seaver ran out of gas in the ninth, exiting two outs shy of New York's fourth complete game in the best-of-five NLCS. The game was halted so the Cincinnati contingent in the stands, jostled and harassed in the crush of fans surging forward in anticipation of the last out, could exit through the Reds dugout for safety.

As Tug McGraw caught the toss from John Milner for the final out, the field was instantly awash in people. Rose, on the bases at the time, made like a running back and blasted his way through the melee. Mays, recipient of several ovations during the game, fought his way from center field to the Mets bullpen, fending off a fan trying to steal his hat. "It's the only cap I have right now and it's sort of good luck to me," Mays said in the jubilant clubhouse. "I realized he just wanted a souvenir. But if he had asked me, I would have given him my shirt." The 340 police officers and security guards on the premises were no match for the thousands of riotous fans. It wasn't pretty, but nothing about the 1973 season was a study in beauty—especially the World Series.

Mustaches Trump Miracles
THE 1973 WORLD SERIES

Felix Millan made an error that cost the Mets the opener of the 1973 World Series. The next day he was in the same spot in the lineup. Mike Andrews, Oakland's third second baseman of Game 2, made errors on consecutive plays in the 12th inning that allowed New York to even the series with a 10–7 win, the most runs ever scored by a Mets team in World Series play. The next day Andrews was mysteriously pronounced injured.

Oakland owner Charlie Finley, who'd paid bonuses to his players to grow mustaches in one of his countless stunts, tried to pull a fast one. He claimed Andrews had an injured shoulder and replaced him on the roster with minor leaguer Manny Trillo. No one bought it. Commissioner Bowie Kuhn ordered Andrews back on the A's roster.

The first World Series night games ever played in New York City were frigid, and the home field was surprisingly unfamiliar at a crucial moment. Center fielder Don Hahn misplayed a flyball by Sal Bando, leading to a double, because he wasn't sure where

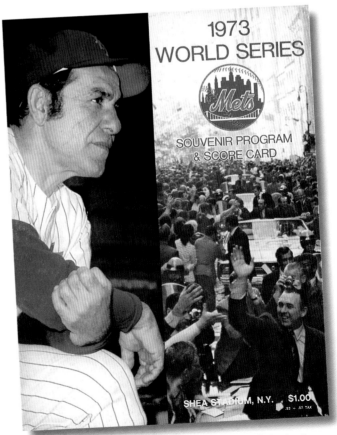

1973 WORLD SERIES
SOUVENIR PROGRAM & SCORE CARD
SHEA STADIUM, N.Y. $1.00

Author's collection

Felix Millan's error in the third inning of the 1973 World Series opener led to two Oakland runs and set the precedent for a sloppy series by both teams. *Jerry Cooke/Sports Illustrated/Getty Images*

Willie Mays pleads in vain with umpire Augie Donatelli after teammate Bud Harrelson was called out at home in the 10th inning of a tied Game 2. Oakland went on to win in 12 innings. This was one of several breaks that didn't go New York's way in the taut seven-game series. *Jerry Cooke/Sports Illustrated/Getty Images*

the warning track was. Since the infield had been shredded by marauding fans after the NLCS victory, grass had been taken from the outfield for the repair job, and the warning track was made larger. Bando ended up scoring in what concluded as a one-run loss for New York.

Wayne Garrett had gotten things off to a good start in Game 3 with a leadoff homer, and a wild pitch plus an error by Catfish Hunter had the Mets leading 2–0 after the first. Despite putting runners on base in all but one inning, the Mets scored no more. After Hahn's misplay led to Bando's run in the top of the sixth, Oakland tied it in the eighth against Tom Seaver. A passed ball in the 11th set up Bert Campaneris' go-ahead RBI.

Game 4 was all Jon Matlack (eight innings, one unearned run) and Rusty Staub (four hits, five RBI), but the most poignant moment came when Mike Andrews pinch hit in the eighth inning and received a standing ovation at Shea.

The next night Jerry Koosman and Tug McGraw combined on a three-hit shutout. If not for an error here, a passed ball there, the 1973 Mets might have enjoyed a champion-ship celebration like they'd enjoyed following Game 5 in 1969. Instead, the Mets took a plane to Oakland needing one win in the last two games.

Though the years have dulled the perception that the series was sloppy—*Sports Illustrated* dubbed it "Buffoonery Rampant"—a decision that received

minor scrutiny at the time has since grown in importance in New York. Needing one victory for the championship, Mets manager Yogi Berra chose Tom Seaver on short rest to start Game 6 over fully rested George Stone, who was coming off the season of his life and had saved Game 2. Berra went with the best pitcher in the league and the man who had clinched both the division title and pennant. This time Seaver lost a 3–1 game. Series MVP Reggie Jackson gave the hindsight patrol a morsel to chew on: "This was not Tom Seaver on ability, but Tom Seaver on heart."

The Swingin' A's, who had sent 218 men to the plate without landing a ball over the fence, put Game 7 away with third-inning home runs by Campaneris and Jackson against Matlack. Oakland pitcher Ken Holtzman, who hadn't batted all year because of the new designated hitter rule, got the decisive rally started with a double—just as he had done with a home run in Game 1. (Only Met Ken Boswell, three for three as a pinch hitter, had a higher series average than Holtzman's .667.)

Reliever Darold Knowles got the last out while becoming the first pitcher to appear in seven games in one World Series. Garrett's pop-up set off a celebration punctured by Oakland manager Dick Williams' locker room resignation while holding the trophy. For a team that would win three straight World Series and five consecutive division titles in the 1970s, the A's sure knew how to spoil a party.

MVP Books collection

False Hopes

Following the wonderful run to come within one game of a world championship in 1973, the Mets failed to make any significant upgrades in 1974. The offense stagnated while the pitchers suffered from the lack of support. Matlack, who led the National League with seven shutouts and finished third with a 2.41 ERA, was 6–15 in games in which he allowed the opposition to score. Koosman had his highest win total (15) since 1969, but George Stone (2–7) struggled with injuries and inconsistency. Harry Parker (4–12) was bad as both a starter and reliever. For Seaver, coming off his second Cy Young Award, the 1974 season truly was a pain in the butt.

Seaver endured back problems for most of the year, with the pain centered in his buttocks, and he shut himself down for the season. M. Donald Grant suggested a specialist, and after a couple of treatments, Seaver took the mound again. He was brilliant, fanning 14 Phillies and tying the major league record with his seventh-straight 200-K season, though he lost the game, 2–1. Unfortunately for Seaver and the Mets, it was the final weekend of the season. Seaver missed the all-star team for the first time in his career, registering his worst numbers to that point: 11–11 and 3.20 ERA, which translated into a 20 percent pay cut (to $136,000).

Still, for much of the year, the 1974 team seemed to be on a parallel trajectory with the 1973 pennant winners. A four-game winning streak had the fifth-place Mets just eight and a half games out on August 16—one spot higher in the standings and just one game behind where they'd been exactly a year earlier. They then roared into September 1974 with 10 wins in 11 games, but the rest of the division did not budge this time. The Pirates held on for the NL East title while the Mets fell apart. New York ended the year with a 6–17 slide, including a 25-inning loss to the Cardinals at Shea Stadium that was the longest game played to completion in NL history, with the final pitch coming at 3:13 a.m. Right fielder Dave Schneck set a dubious Mets record by going 0 for 11 at the plate, although he did rob 20-year-old Cardinal callup Keith Hernandez of a potential game-winning homer in the 12th. Home plate umpire Ed Sudol, who ejected Yogi Berra at 1:30 a.m., had also worked the 23-inning game at Shea in 1964 and the 24-inning Mets game in Houston in 1968. (Also Mets losses, of course.)

Joe McDonald, who took over for retiring Bob Scheffing as general manager in 1975, put his stamp on the team immediately. Duffy Dyer and Ken Boswell—both vets of '69 and '73—were dispatched in trades a week apart in October. Earlier that month, after years of rumors of Joe Torre coming to New York, the Mets finally got him, giving up pitcher Ray Sadecki and minor leaguer Tommy Moore to St. Louis. But Sadecki was not the most significant lefty the Mets sent packing that offseason.

After exceeding 50 appearances and 100 innings in four of the previous five seasons, Tug McGraw seemed worn down in 1974, as reflected by his 6–11 mark and 4.15 ERA. Complaints about his shoulder led the Mets to try him as a starter, which McGraw later understood was just to showcase him to other teams. The Phillies were impressed enough to send the second overall pick in the 1973 draft—catcher John Stearns—plus center fielder Del Unser and lefty reliever Mac Scarce; the Phillies also received Don Hahn and Dave Schneck. After the shock wore off, the ever-optimistic McGraw looked at the bright side. "The Phillies are ripe for a pennant," he noted.

McGraw's departure left Ed Kranepool and Cleon Jones as the only remaining Mets who dated back to the Casey Stengel regime (not counting Bob L. Miller, who went 1–12 for the original Mets, reappeared in the last week of the '73 season, and was on the roster again in 1974). The last original Met who had never left the organization, Kranepool set a

The fans started to get a little punchy by the 21st inning of the Mets' 25-inning marathon against the Cardinals on September 12, 1974. This dance routine kicked in at about 1:50 a.m. *Ron Frehm/AP Images*

major league record in 1974 with a .486 average as a pinch hitter (17 for 35). Jones' time, however, was nearing its end.

Jones had surgery to repair torn cartilage in his left knee after the season. Appearing at spring training of 1975 in a knee brace, he was asked about the February purchase of Dave Kingman from San Francisco for $150,000. "How's he going to play every day?," Jones replied. "Maybe the Mets think I need help, but I don't."

The injury kept Jones in Florida after the Mets headed north, but the pain was just starting. Jones was arrested for indecent exposure with a young woman in a van parked on a street in St. Petersburg. The club summoned Jones back to New York to "keep him under constant medical supervision," according to McDonald. It also put Jones in proximity of M. Donald Grant for a tongue lashing—in front of the press and his wife. When asked why the player was fined $2,000 despite the charges being dropped, Grant responded, "It was bad for baseball's image. It was in the newspapers." Jones signed a statement apologizing for his "behavior in St. Petersburg."

Jones rejoined the team in late May. With Kingman launching titanic home runs and Kranepool batting .382, it was hard to find a place for Jones (or John Milner, for that matter). After sitting for a week, Jones was called on to pinch hit on July 18 and lined out softly. He threw his helmet and bat and refused to take the field as directed by his manager. This is where Yogi Berra, derided in the press and by his players for being too lenient, took a stand and refused to play Jones.

Why had Jones defied his manager? Because his leg wasn't taped. On nights he was in the starting lineup, he had his tender leg taped, but he didn't have it done when he was sitting on the bench, because the tight bandage made his leg swell. The stubborn Jones did not tell his manager, and his manager drew a line in the sand, which the Mets hierarchy soon stuck their head in.

After Jones vetoed two proposed trades, the Mets board suspended him. The MLB Players Association filed a grievance, and the team finally acceded to the outfielder's wishes by granting him his unconditional release. Jones did not play again in the majors that year, and he spent less than a month with the White Sox in 1976 before being released for good.

The 1975 season didn't go well in New York, with or without Cleon. In mid-June, the Mets had been nip and tuck with the Pirates for first place. A month later they were 10½ games out. Despite a rare surplus of offensive talent,

Broadcast Legends
LINDSEY, MURPH, AND RALPH

It took a skilled voice to make the 1962 Mets sound like a wise investment of one's time. The team was blessed with three such voices, and fans of the fledgling franchise quickly came to trust them like three lovable uncles that you could spend all summer with.

Bob Murphy made the new club official on April 11, 1962: "Well, we are about to be witnesses to history in the making right here in St. Louis as the New York Mets become a reality."

Lindsey Nelson was the first hire, giving up *Game of the Week* to be in on the ground floor of a new venture in New York. His honeyed Tennessee voice established the tempo of playing it straight. No "we" or "c'mon, get a hit" was uttered in the Mets booth, a standard upheld by every Mets announcer since. California-raised Ralph Kiner had been both a minor league executive and major league announcer, not to mention the lone ballplayer in the group—a seven-time National League home run champ and Hall of Famer. Oklahoma-born Murphy, a former Red Sox and Orioles announcer, was the least known of the trio when he was hired in 1962. As coverage changed from Channel 9 to cable for most games, Murph could be found every night on the radio "painting the word picture."

After 17 years together, the longest teaming by any announcing trio in history, Nelson broke up the act when he packed up his gaudy sports jackets for San Francisco after the 1978 season. Kiner had a chance to go to the Dodgers, and Murphy was no favorite of board chairman M. Donald Grant, who actually thought the inventor of "The Happy Recap" too critical of the last-place club. Grant was the one who wound up getting booted.

Kiner remained on the TV crew for decades, serving as announcer and host of *Kiner's Korner* until 1995. No post-game show has better captured the thrill of players and managers in studio dressed in soiled uniforms, telling stories, and paying deference to the Hall of Fame slugger. Cooperstown also acknowledged Nelson and Murphy, bestowing the Ford Frick Award to each in 1988 and 1994, respectively. The Mets inducted the trio into the team's Hall of Fame in 1984.

Murph's calls live on, even for people too young to have heard them live. Lenny Dykstra's ninth-inning home run in the 1986 NLCS at Shea: "It's fairly deep. . . . It's way back, by the wall. . . . A home run! A home run!" Mookie Wilson's fateful groundball two weeks later in the World Series: "And a ground ball trickling. . . . It's a fair ball. It gets by Buckner! Rounding third is Knight. . . . The Mets will win the ballgame. . . . They win! They win!" And culminating with the final pitch by Jesse Orosco: "The dream has come true. The Mets have won the World Series, coming from behind to win the seventh game." Not a "we" to be heard.

But we loved 'em. Fans mourned Nelson's death in 1995 and many came to St. Patrick's Cathedral to pay their respects to Murphy in 2004, just a year after he retired. Kiner maintained a limited schedule into his mid-80s, telling stories of the old days to a new crowd.

---

the Mets lacked timely hitting. And without Tug McGraw, they had plenty of trouble closing out games.

Rookie Rick Baldwin was handed much of the responsibility and ended up blowing more saves (seven) than McGraw did in his worst full season in New York (six, in 1974). It didn't help that McGraw returned to his dominant form in Philadelphia after an operation to clear up a problem in his shoulder (a procedure the Mets didn't consider). McGraw pitched for another decade as a Phillie, nailing down more saves against the Mets (22) than any other team. Tug's torment of his old team began in his first appearance in a road uniform at Shea on June 29, 1975. He tossed three perfect innings for a save in the opener of a doubleheader and then pitched four innings of one-hit relief to earn the win in the nightcap in 12 innings—after Baldwin had blown a save in the ninth.

New York spent most of the year trying different arms in late-inning situations, including Bob Apodaca, Ken Sanders, and Tom Hall, among others. Skip Lockwood, a former infielder converted to reliever, made his Mets debut on August 7 and went on to become the team's most reliable arm out of the bullpen in the post-Tug 1970s. Lockwood didn't do Yogi much good, however. The manager was fired that same night.

Though Berra had won his battle with Jones, he lost the war. The Mets went on a 12–5 run after Jones defied his manager, but that hot streak ended on August 3 with a doubleheader sweep at the hands of the Pirates. When the third-place Mets were shut out at home by identical 7–0 scores in a doubleheader against last-place Montreal, Yogi Berra became the first manager to be fired by both the Yankees and the Mets.

The choice for Berra's replacement was not exactly a headline grabber: Roy McMillan, the bespectacled coach and former shortstop under Casey Stengel. Grant called McMillan "another Gil Hodges" because of his quiet demeanor. Too quiet, as it turned out. McMillan was uncomfortable as a leader, and the Mets did not follow him.

The Mets did find lightning in a bottle during the short reign of Roy. A minor deal that sent Ted Martinez to St. Louis for shortstop Jack Heidemann also brought the Mets a minor league outfielder named Mike Vail. He hit .342 at Triple-A Tidewater and the Mets had nothing to lose by calling him up. Vail debuted as a pinch hitter in Houston on August 18 and singled. Ten days later, he was batting .480 and was in the midst of a 23-game hitting steak, tying the National League rookie record and Cleon Jones' club mark. The streak ended in an 18-inning win on September 16 in which Vail had eight plate appearances.

Tom Seaver, however, won just twice in the final three weeks of what was one of his finest seasons. Despite the lack of offensive support and a weak bullpen, Seaver put together streaks of eight and seven wins, highlighted by his Labor Day blanking of the Pirates that netted his 20th victory and established a major league record of eight straight seasons with at least 200 strikeouts. His most aggravating start also came in September, when his fifth legitimate try at a no-hitter went by the wayside with two outs in the ninth at Wrigley Field. Joe Wallis, an obscure rookie outfielder, singled to right on a hanging curve. Even if he'd retired Wallis, Seaver wouldn't have gotten the no-hitter or even the win because

It's the bottom of the ninth, and Tom Seaver has not allowed a hit against Chicago on September 24, 1975. The batter, Joe Wallis, is about to spoil that no-hitter. Even though Seaver shut the Cubs out through 10 innings, his own team failed to score as well. Reliever Skip Lockwood eventually lost the game in the 11th. *Charles Kelly/AP Images*

the Mets couldn't score. New York lost in 11 innings when Lockwood walked in the winning run. Still, Seaver led the league with 22 wins and 243 strikeouts to join Sandy Koufax as a three-time Cy Young winner.

Seaver's resurgence, Vail's streak, Staub's becoming the first Met to surpass 100 RBI, and Kingman's breaking the club home run mark (36) took people's minds off how mediocre the team had been in 1975. They managed a tie for third place, their fourth finish in that spot since 1969. Frustrating as it was, fans would soon look back on these as happy days.

1 The Sign Man was a fixture at Shea Stadium for nearly two decades. Banners were a big part of the Mets fan identity from the club's earliest days, but Karl Ehrhardt took it to another level, offering a vast array of block-letter messages to fit almost any situation on the field. *AP Images*

2 After a big offensive season in 1975, the Mets were looking to Mike Vail, Ed Kranepool, and Joe Torre to keep the bats hot in '76. While Vail was a non-factor, Torre and Kranepool led the squad with averages of .306 and .292, respectively. *Focus on Sport/Getty Images*

3 Tom Seaver shows off his hardware after winning Cy Young Award number three in 1975—becoming the first right-handed pitcher to win that many Cy Youngs. *Larry C. Morris/New York Times Co./ Getty Images*

4 One-year-old Bobby Apodaca, son of Mets reliever Bob Apodaca (34), wasn't part of the team's youth movement in the mid-1970s, but he did make an appearance at Family Day at Shea on July 19, 1975. *AP Images*

5 Ken Boswell was a veteran of both Mets pennant winners in 1969 and 1973—and he batted .421 in the two postseasons—but after the 1974 season, the 28-year-old infielder was traded to Houston for Bob Gallagher, who played in just 33 games for New York. *Focus on Sport/Getty Images*

6 Nino Espinosa won only 25 games for the Mets in two full and three partial seasons, but his sizeable afro was noteworthy even for the time. He did lead the staff in wins in 1977 and 1978, but with just 10 and 11 victories, respectively, for some poor clubs. *Jacob Kanarek/Metsintheseventies.com*

Maligned as it was through the years, Shea Stadium was the place to be in the mid-1970s. It already served as home to the Mets and Jets, but with a major renovation underway at Yankee Stadium in the Bronx, the Yankees arrived with their belongings in 1974. The football Giants made it a quartet in 1975.

From April to October 1975 the only time Shea went more than two days without a game was in late September, when rains cancelled four days' worth of baseball games. The last day that the Yankees served as hosts at Shea (other than a one-game emergency 21 years later) was for a doubleheader against the Orioles on September 28. The Yankees had the best record of any of the Shea teams in 1975, winning 83 games (43 at Shea) to the Mets' 82 (42 at home). Over their two-year life in Flushing, the Yankees went 172–150 overall (90–69 at Shea) before moving back to the rebuilt Yankee Stadium.

Both the Yankees and Mets fired managers in the same August week in 1975; the Jets followed suit in November. The Jets were the tail enders of '75, going 3–11 with a 1–6 mark at home. Because of the double-duty schedule, the Dallas Cowboys, St. Louis Cardinals, and Baltimore Colts all won more games at Shea than the Jets in 1975. The Giants, who played the previous year at Yale Bowl, had to jump into the crowded house in Flushing as free dates arose; they twice played early season Saturday games at Shea. After a 5–9 season under Bill Arnsparger (2–5 at Shea), the Giants moved to the Meadowlands in 1976, marking three seasons in three different stadiums in three states.

All in all, Shea Stadium had 3.7 million fans pass through its turnstiles in 1975. The Mets drew 1.7 million, almost 500,000 more than the Yankees. The Jets and Giants each averaged 51,000 per game. Any lingering newness to the 11-year-old Shea Stadium rubbed off for good in 1975, but during a fiscal crisis and stadium shortage in New York, Shea acted like a family taking in the neighbors during an emergency.

Mickey Moose and Killer Kong

The 1975 team scored more runs (646) than any previous Mets incarnation except for 1970, and the team batting average surpassed .250 for the first time ever in '75. It wasn't quite on par with NL powers like Cincinnati's Big Red Machine or Pittsburgh's Lumber Company, but given their pitcher-friendly ballpark and pitching-dominated ballclub, there was reason to hope that New York could narrow the gap. And then that notion went right out the window.

Rusty Staub, an RBI machine for a team not known for scoring runs, was sent to Detroit in December 1975 for pitcher Mickey Lolich, a 207-game winner for the Tigers. The Mets, who had been critical of Staub when he put on weight after an injury two years earlier, said nothing of Lolich's heft, generously listed in the yearbook at 215 pounds. And as much as Mets fans didn't want Staub to leave, Lolich didn't want to come. As a 10-and-5 man (one of the motivations for trading Staub was to keep him from reaching that status), Lolich could refuse any trade. The Mets persisted, though, with Joe McDonald, Bob Scheffing, and M. Donald Grant spending hours on the phone with Lolich at the winter meetings as the trading deadline approached.

The Mets had three starting pitchers that any team would envy, but the team's failures had a lot to do with the back of the rotation, where rookies Randy Tate and Hank Webb proved to not be major league caliber, George Stone was too frail, and Craig Swan was too inexperienced and coming off elbow tendonitis. The last two spots in the rotation went 16–27 with 17 no decisions in 1975.

Now the Mets banished a corner outfielder for the second time in five months and neither the back of the rotation nor the lineup was any better for it. The 35-year-old southpaw with the oversized uniform (size 48) and contract ($125,000 annually) to go with unorthodox methods (treating his arm with scalding water in the shower) went 8–13 in 1976 and pitched the fewest innings (192⅔) since his rookie year of 1963. Fortunately, the team's one, two, and three starters held their own. Koosman had his first 20-win season, Matlack won 17, and though Seaver's victory total dipped to 14, the triumvirate tossed 49 complete games, 14 shutouts, and 780⅓ innings with a cumulative 2.75 ERA.

Mike Vail, whose emergence at the end of 1975 convinced the Mets brass that he could replace Staub, could not. After being sent home from winter ball in Venezuela because of a sore left knee, he dislocated a bone in his right foot three months later playing pickup basketball. He did not return until mid-June and batted just .217.

The '76 Mets donned striped pillbox hats for holiday games to mark both the country's bicentennial and the 100th year of the National League. They also wore a black armband all season to honor matriarch Joan Payson and

MVP Books collection

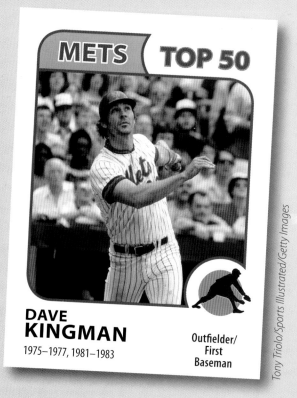

METS TOP 50

DAVE KINGMAN
1975–1977, 1981–1983

Outfielder/
First
Baseman

Tony Triolo/Sports Illustrated/Getty Images

patriarch Casey Stengel, who had died within a week of each other the previous October. It seemed like the offense was in mourning as well. With Staub and Vail already out of the picture, another two capable, if slumping, bats were discarded in June when Del Unser and Wayne Garrett were sent to Montreal for Pepe Manguel and Jim Dwyer, neither of whom played for the Mets beyond that season. John Milner resumed regular duty and responded with a career-high 78 RBI and 15 home runs, including three grand slams. Felix Millan, who had set the club record with 191 hits a year earlier, was solid again in the two-hole and remained one of the most reliable hit-and-run men in the game (19 strikeouts in 587 plate appearances), but neither Felix the Cat nor any other infield kittens provided much power. That came from one animal: Kong.

Dave Kingman's massive swings and sky-high flies were legendary. Sky King could hit the ball out of any park—when he hit it. Kingman fanned 153 times in 1975 and posted another 135 strikeouts in '76, while walking a scant 62 times over those two seasons and hitting a composite .235. He was a home run hitter, pure and simple. But those home runs went a long, long way.

Dave Kingman launched home runs with a ferocity and frequency never before seen at Shea Stadium. He swung—and missed—epically, shattering Mets home runs records with a reign of power. He was often moody with the media and angry at management, but the fans loved Kong.

David Arthur Kingman could also pitch, going 11–4 with a 1.38 ERA for USC in 1969 before converting to first base. In 1970, he was the first overall pick by San Francisco. Five years later, with the Giants in need of cash and the Mets desperately seeking power, Kong changed coasts.

He landed in New York with a bang, homering in his first game as a Met. That July he collected a club-record 13 home runs and went on to set the team season mark with 36 long balls. In 1976, he had 30 homers by the midseason break and was on pace to top the NL single-season record until torn ligaments in his thumb sidelined him for a month. He broke his own club record with 37 homers but finished second again to league-leader Mike Schmidt.

Kingman wanted a long-term contract and money like Reggie Jackson got; instead he and Tom Seaver were traded the same night in 1977. Sky King returned from the Cubs in 1981 and finally won a home run title as a Met in 1982. He was released after the 1983 season and ended his career with three years as Oakland's DH. He retired with career 442 clouts, 154 as a Met.

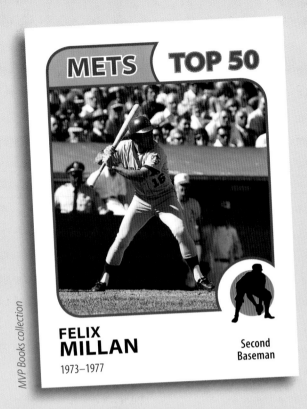

MVP Books collection

METS TOP 50

FELIX
MILLAN
1973–1977

Second
Baseman

Jerry Koosman is congratulated by teammates after the lefty struck out 13 Cardinals batters and earned his 20th win of the season on September 16, 1976. *Richard Drew/AP Images*

Gary Gentry (retained by the Mets instead of Nolan Ryan in 1971) was traded in 1972 to the Braves with reliever Danny Frisella for second baseman Felix Millan and lefty pitcher George Stone. In a decade of regrettable Mets trades, this was one steal of a deal.

Millan, who had hit .333 for Atlanta in the 1969 NLCS against New York, provided consistency at second base, something the Mets had not gotten from Ken Boswell in his five years as the primary pivotman. A two-time Gold Glove winner in Atlanta, Millan made just nine errors in a career-high 830 chances in 1973, although his miscue in Game 1 of the World Series led to the go-ahead run.

Felix the Cat's distinctive style of choking up high on the bat made him nearly impossible to strike out, yet it also severely limited his power (eight homers in five years with the Mets). In 1975 he became the first Met to play all 162 games and set a club record for hits (191) that stood for 21 years. His 37 doubles in '75 were not surpassed until 1989 (by Howard Johnson). Millan had four hits in a game three times in one week that July, including one game in which Joe Torre erased him each time by grounding into four double plays. An ill-advised punch to Pirate catcher Ed Ott in 1977 led to a career-ending injury when he was slammed to the Pittsburgh Astroturf in retaliation. He played in Japan but never again in the United States.

By the 1976 All-Star break, Kingman had 30 homers, putting him on pace to challenge Hack Wilson's National League single-season record of 56. Kingman was voted the NL's starting right fielder for the All-Star Game, joining all-star repeaters Seaver and Matlack. He launched a tape-measure shot at Shea in the first game after the break and then hit another three days later to give him 32, but when he tore ligaments in his thumb diving for (and missing) a flyball, Kingman's chase of Hack Wilson, Roger Maris, Babe Ruth, and everyone else was done. He couldn't even fend off Philadelphia's Mike Schmidt, who won the NL crown by one (38–37). The race with Schmidt's team wasn't nearly as close. The Mets never got within 10 games of the division-leading Phillies after June 5.

Joe Frazier, the first Mets manager ever promoted from the minor leagues, did about as well as could be expected in 1976, leading the club to its second-highest win total in history to that point (86–76). A winner of five championships in the minors, Frazier was essentially unknown to M. Donald Grant when general manager Joe McDonald proposed him as the team's skipper. Most fans and members of the media were likewise unfamiliar with this Joe Frazier—the world knew the heavyweight boxer of the same name who'd lost the "Thrilla in Manila" to Muhammad Ali just days before the Mets named their new manager. The pecan farmer from North Carolina suddenly pushed into the New York spotlight was met with a persistent refrain: "Joe who?" And the new Joe could have been veteran infielder Joe Torre, who led the team with a .306 average in 1976. Though the Mets acted quickly after the '75 season to replace Roy McMillan (who remained with the team as a coach), they did consider Torre to be managerial material. "When he quits playing," Grant said in October 1975, "we will try to help him as a manager." A year and a half later, all sides were ready.

Nearing the End of the Line

The Mets had enjoyed winning records in eight of the previous nine seasons heading into 1977. They had a three-time Cy Young winner leading the staff, a former Rookie of the Year spinning shutouts, and a former World Series hero coming off a 20-win season. New York was also strong up the middle, with former Gold Glovers at second base and shortstop and first-round picks with tremendous upside behind the plate and in center field. And they had a slugger who could launch home runs with any player in baseball. So what went wrong? Everything.

The first free-agent draft was held in November 1976, and the Mets were a noticeable no-show. The team desperately needed a hitter in the middle of the lineup, and many thought outfielder Gary Matthews would be an optimal fit. The Mets made a token offer that paled next to the five-year, $1.2 million deal lavished on him by Ted Turner's Braves. Given that Matthews had hit 20 homers for the Giants in 1976, what was Kingman, who had walloped 36 and 37 dingers in the previous two years, worth? The Mets' offer of a $200,000 annual salary was repeatedly turned down by Kingman. He was thinking more along the lines of the $2.9 million for five years that Reggie Jackson received across town.

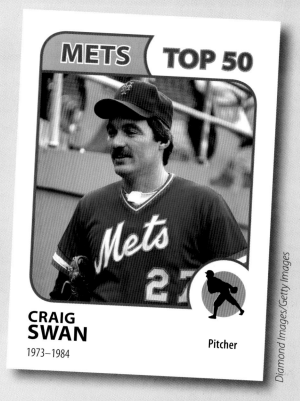

METS TOP 50

CRAIG SWAN
1973–1984

Pitcher

Craig Swan came up as a Met during the mid-1970s and was on his last legs just when the Mets turned it around in the mid-1980s. The measuring stick for pitchers of his day—wins—were few and far between for both Swannie and his club. In 1978 he became the first Met besides Tom Seaver to win an ERA crown (2.43), but with a mere 9–6 record for a 96-loss club, he did not get a single Cy Young vote. Never mind that his 1.071 walks plus hits per inning were good enough for second-best in the league.

Craig Steven Swan was drafted by the Cardinals out of high school in Long Beach, California, but he opted to play for powerhouse Arizona State University. After allowing just one run in 18 innings in the 1972 College World Series, he was selected by the Mets in the third round of the draft. He was the fifth starter behind Seaver, Koosman, Matlack, and Lolich in 1976; a year later, Swan had more wins than Koosman or Matlack, and Seaver and Lolich were gone.

New Mets ownership saw Swan's value and gave him a five-year, $3.1 million deal in 1980 that made him the highest paid Met at the time, but he was plagued by arm and shoulder troubles. He finished second in the 1982 NL Comeback Player of the Year voting after an 11–7 mark and 3.35 ERA. Swan was released in 1984, clearing the way for the younger Mets arms.

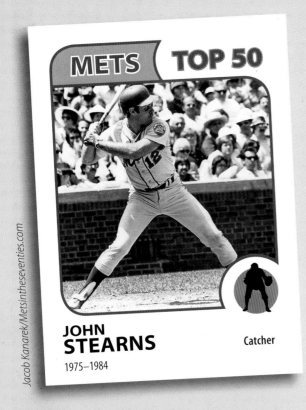

METS TOP 50

JOHN STEARNS
1975–1984

Catcher

John Hardin Stearns earned the nickname "Bad Dude" as a two-sport star at the University of Colorado. The son of a CU football player, Stearns set the school's career interceptions mark (16), and as a catcher for the baseball team, he won a Big Eight batting title as a sophomore and led the NCAA in home runs a year later. The Phillies made Stearns the second overall draft pick in the 1973 draft.

After appearing in one game for Philadelphia in 1974, Stearns came to the Mets that December in the Tug McGraw deal. He sat behind Jerry Grote for close to two seasons before earning the first of four all-star berths in 1977. Stearns set a major league record with 25 steals by a catcher a year later. During a June 1978 game against Pittsburgh, with the Mets up by a run in the ninth, he received a throw to the plate and then received the 235-pound Dave Parker running from third. Stearns withstood the collision and preserved the win for New York; Parker walked away with a black eye, a broken cheekbone, and needing stitches. "That was like the Pennsylvania Railroad colliding with the B&O," said Pirates manager Chuck Tanner.

Injuries would catch up to Stearns, but he batted .284 over his last three years as a regular. He later coached and scouted for the Mets. Wired for sound on TV during the 2000 NLCS, a key hit by Mike Piazza had him loudly repeating, "The monster is out of the cage." Bad Dude ought to know.

Seaver, Matlack, and Koosman looked at the princely sum the Yankees gave talented but oft-injured Don Gullett (an average of $330,000 for six years) and wondered what kind of salary they might command. Seaver had pressed for a multiyear contract after completing his third Cy Young season in 1975, and during the following spring training he hammered out a three-year deal with an annual base salary of $225,000, plus incentives. For the first time, M. Donald Grant was personally involved in negotiating a contract, at Seaver's request. The pitcher's feelings about those negotiations soon began to fester, however, as he watched the first class of free agents suddenly make him underpaid in his field. And the team's top star wasn't afraid to share his views on labor relations and free agency, which did not sit well with old guard chairman M. Donald Grant.

"From the time I signed my last contract," Seaver later said, "feelings between me and Mr. Grant have been unbearable. The reason for all this fuss and furor goes back to that day."

For his part, Grant resented the new rules and the players who pursued their newfound rights, but Grant mostly resented that the public and the press sided with "The Franchise." More than once Grant told reporters, "Mrs. Payson and I are the franchise." He ran the Mets for 17 years and simply never got it.

Matlack was also outspoken about the team's lack of support—both offensive and financial. Grant's cryptic reply to charges that the Mets were cheapskates was foreboding: "People write us and say you're losing your audience. Hell, we lost it last year when the Yankees got their $100 million stadium and then jumped out on top. We knew we were bound to lose that way."

The Mets would soon be losing in every way. They won three of four games to start the season and then dropped 29 of their next 41, costing Joe Frazier his job. The manager's small-town demeanor and minor league pedigree did not

jibe with a veteran-laden club bristling about management's penurious methods.

Joe Torre knew all about the changing scenery in the sport. He'd been traded twice, served as a player rep in the union, and enjoyed major league success as a batting champion, MVP, and nine-time all-star. The Mets had never promoted a player to manage, but they secretly summoned Torre from Philadelphia on an off day in May to discuss the possibility. A week later the job was his.

Players arriving at the ballpark on May 31 found no manager, and they finally got a clue when Torre emerged in a suit heading to a press conference 90 minutes before the game. "It's the start of another outstanding career for him," Seaver said at Torre's appointment.

"I don't know how it will work, managing my former teammates," Torre told the press. "Maybe some of the excuses won't work now. But May is a little early for a team to quit." The Mets waited until June.

"The Midnight Massacre"

New York snapped a six-game losing streak in Torre's managing debut and won 11 of the first 16 games under the new skipper. The only player-manager in team history, Torre went hitless plus a walk in his two appearances in the dual role before retiring as a player. He certainly handled his personnel better than his predecessor had. Torre took former all-star catcher Jerry Grote off third base, moved Lenny Randle (acquired after he punched his manager in Texas) from second to third, and put Felix Millan back in the lineup at second base. After myriad different lineups under Frazier, Torre established continuity.

The Mets pulled within 10 games of .500 and inched closer to fifth place. Seaver was his old dominant self with a 7–3 mark, five complete games, and three shutouts, including his fifth career one-hitter. But he remained unhappy with his salary, Grant, and the resulting snipes in the press by *Daily News* columnist Dick Young. One of the original

Yet everything changed on the morning of the June 15 trade deadline when Young blasted Seaver and his family in the pages of the *Daily News*. "Nolan Ryan is getting more now than Seaver," penned Young, "and that galls Tom because Nancy Seaver and Ruth Ryan are very friendly and Tom Seaver long has treated Nolan Ryan like a little brother."

That single sentence ended the Seaver era in New York. True, Ryan was making $75,000 more than Seaver, but the idea that his family could be dragged into this unseemly business was the last straw for Seaver. He called Arthur Richman, the Mets public relations director, yelling "Get me out of here!"

Before Seaver and de Roulet had come to their (brief) agreement on an extension, the *New York Times* postulated that a trade with the Reds could net Doug Flynn, Ken Griffey, and Rawley Eastwick for Seaver. When the actual trade brought back Flynn, Pat Zachry, Steve Henderson, and Dan Norman, the *Times* commented that the return value was "surprisingly low." Zachry was a mid-rotation pitcher and the 1976 co-Rookie of the Year, but the other three stood little chance of breaking into Cincinnati's lineup.

That trade at least brought back more value than the deal that sent the disgruntled Kingman to San Diego for Bobby Valentine and Paul Siebert, completed the same day. A third deadline swap landed Joel Youngblood from St. Louis for utility infielder Mike Phillips—a pure baseball deal, and a pretty good one for the Mets. Put all the deals together, though, and you have the "Midnight Massacre."

The back-page headline of the *Daily News* the next day brought a thud to the heart of every Mets fan: "Mets Deal Stars: Seaver to Reds, Kingman to S.D." Underneath a photo of Seaver, his hat turned backwards, the caption read, "His Wish Is M. Don Granted."

The out-of-town reaction to the trade was equally unkind. "This has to be one of the biggest steals since the

"New Breed" in 1962, Young was now fully in the camp of M. Donald Grant, who happened to employ Young's son-in-law. Jack Lang, hired that year by the *Daily News* after the *Long Island Press* folded, also dated back to the team's early days and was Seaver's confidante. Young and Lang went toe-to-toe on the *News*' "battle page," with the pro and con Seaver commentary running side by side. The phones in the Mets offices, meanwhile, were ringing off the hook—screaming, insisting, and begging to keep Seaver.

A trade of the team's most recognizable star seemed inevitable, but on Lang's recommendation, Seaver went over Grant's head to team president Lorinda de Roulet. The two came to an understanding on a three-year extension for $1 million.

The announcement that Tom Seaver was being traded to the Reds was a very emotional moment for the future Hall of Famer who had gotten his start with the organization a decade earlier. Although he had his run-ins with team management, there was no love lost between Tom Terrific and Mets fans. *Carl T. Gossett Jr./New York Times Co./Getty Images*

Babe Ruth trade [to the Yankees in 1920]," said Dodgers second baseman Davey Lopes. "A trade is supposed to help both clubs. But I don't think the Mets are as good a club as they were before. I can't see how they improved their club one iota."

The post-trade postmortem at Shea Stadium was an open wound for all to see. Seaver, in three-piece suit, answered the media's questions matter-of-factly as the cameras rolled and clicked. Then he started talking about the fans, who had always adored him and had basked him with a two-minute ovation in his last home start when he passed Sandy Koufax on the career strikeout list (in an 8–0 shutout against the Reds and Pat Zachry). Seaver's head went down and his hands covered his eyes as he recalled the last moment at Shea. He could not go on.

In August, when Seaver pitched against his old club for the first time—beating Jerry Koosman before a full house at Shea to complete a four-game Reds sweep—a TV special about Seaver's arrival in Cincinnati was shown in New York. A boy of perhaps 12, standing outside the home of the two-time defending world champion Reds, was asked which team Seaver had come from. "The Yankees?" he replied. Ugh.

Life Goes On—Unfortunately

Koosman went from 20 wins to 20 losses in one year. The three Mets who tied for the club home run lead in 1977—John Stearns, John Milner, and Steve Henderson—combined to finish one homer shy of Kingman's 1976 total, with 12 apiece. The 98 losses were the most by the club in a decade, and the team was almost unrecognizable. Grote was sent to the Dodgers before the season ended. Matlack and Milner departed in a four-team deal involving the Braves, Pirates, and Rangers. Bud Harrelson was traded to the Phillies in spring training. Koosman and Kranepool were the only Mets left who'd played in the 1969 World Series—or the 1973 series, for that matter.

The 1978 Mets were a collection of players who were supposed to be good at some point yet never quite got there. Tom Hausman, a minor league pitcher with the Brewers, was the first Mets free agent signee, penned for three years and $175,000 (total). The Mets also signed Elliott Maddox, a versatile infielder/outfielder who had

I WAS A BELIEVER BUT NOW WE'VE LOST SEAVER

MVP Books collection

METS TOP 50

LEE MAZZILLI

1976–1981, 1986–1989

Outfielder/
First
Baseman

When the Mets were at their nadir in the late 1970s, at least they had Lee Mazzilli's good looks. "Lee Mazzilli Poster Day" accentuated the Brooklyn boy's tight pants and winning smile despite his club's losing ways. The switch-hitting "Italian Stallion" was selected for the 1979 All-Star Game, during which he hit a game-tying homer and later walked with the bases loaded to bring in the winning run.

Lee Louis Mazzilli, the son of welterweight boxer Libero Mazzilli, specialized in basket catches and could hit and throw both ways. A first-round pick in 1973, he homered in his second at bat in the majors in September 1976. The rookie played more games and caught more balls than any National League center fielder in 1977. He averaged 16 homers, 73 RBI, and 32 steals the next three years for a club devoid of power.

Traded just before the 1982 season—for minor leaguers Ron Darling and Walt Terrell—Maz had little success out of a Mets uniform. The last-place Pirates cut him in 1986, and Mazzilli rejoined the Mets. He was now a bench player, but this was no longer the lousy Mets of his youth. His pinch hits started rallies in Games 6 and 7 of the World Series. Maz batted .306 in 1987 and ended his career in the postseason with the 1989 Blue Jays. He managed in the minors; coached at Yankee Stadium for Joe Torre, his former Mets skipper; managed the Orioles in 2004 and 2005; and served as a Mets TV studio analyst.

once sued the Yankees, the Mets (as lessees), and the city because he injured his knee on the soggy outfield turf at Shea Stadium while playing for the Yankees in 1975. He lost.

The only two 1978 starters from the previous year's Opening Day lineup were Lee Mazzilli and John Stearns. With Felix Millan's major league career ended by a bodyslam from powerful Pirate Ed Ott, Doug Flynn became the everyday second baseman—.191 average as a Met in 1977 be damned. The new first baseman and cleanup hitter was Willie Montanez, New York's big payoff in the 10-player deal that sent away Milner and Matlack.

The flashy Montanez provided comic relief and spurts of power. He stutter-stepped around the bases 17 times and knocked in 96 runs for a team that was next to last in batting and slugging. New York made it easier to hit home runs in 1978, cutting the distance down the lines at Shea Stadium from 341 to 338 feet so umpires could better determine if a ball cleared the fence or hit the wall behind it. The Mets still hit two fewer home runs than the year before—just 86 homers in all.

Koosman fell to 3–15 despite a 3.75 ERA. Pat Zachry won 10 of his first 13 decisions and was named to the all-star team, but his season came to an abrupt end when, after allowing a single to Pete Rose, Zachry kicked the dugout step and broke his foot. Even with the National League ERA leader (Craig Swan, 2.43) and a catcher who broke a 75-year-old mark for stolen bases at his position (Stearns, 25), the Mets barely surpassed one million in attendance, just like they barely avoided 100 losses.

It was obvious that 1979 would not be much more pleasant, but at least Lorinda de Roulet and her father, Charles Shipman Payson, ensured that the person running things would not be M. Donald Grant. Grant was voted out as board chair in November 1978.

Pete Rose was the club's major target in the free-agent market, but he flatly declined all three offers from Flushing.

1970s METS YEAR-BY-YEAR

YEAR	W–L	PCT.	GB	FINISH	
1970	83–79	.512	6	3rd in 6-team NL East	Gil Hodges was the first Met to manage an all-star team. No Mets were voted to start, but he named Tom Seaver the starting pitcher. Seaver tossed three shutout innings while reserve Bud Harrelson had two hits. The NL won when Pete Rose barreled over Ray Fosse in the 12th inning.
1971	83–79	.512	14	3rd (t)	Same finish as 1970, but the Mets were no match for the eventual world champion Pirates. Though their team batting average was the same as in '70 (.249), the Mets scored 107 fewer runs. The staff allowed 80 fewer runs than the year prior and had fewer saves and complete games.
1972	83–73	.532	13 ½	3rd	Despite six games cut from the schedule due to a strike, the team's 41 saves set a Mets record that lasted until 1984. Tug McGraw set an individual club mark with 27, and five other pitchers, including starters Jerry Koosman and Jim McAndrew, saved at least one game.
1973	82–79	.509	–	1st	The club's worst winning percentage since 1968, yet the Mets take the pennant! The Mets did nothing for almost five months—playing .395 ball for May, June, and July—but got hot at the right moment, surged to the top in a mediocre division, and nearly stole a championship from Oakland.
1974	71–91	.438	17	5th	Though Mets attendance (1.72 million) was down for the fifth straight year, the tenant Yankees had their highest gate (1.27 million) since 1964, the year of their last pennant. The Yanks and defending NL champion Mets charged the same $4 price for box seats; $2.50 for upper reserved.
1975	82–80	.506	10 ½	3rd (t)	Jon Matlack became the fourth Mets pitcher since 1967 to get a win or a save in an All-Star Game, joining Tom Seaver (1967 save), Jerry Koosman (1968 save), and Tug McGraw (1972 win). Matlack shared game MVP honors with Cub Bill Madlock in the only voting tie in the award's history.
1976	86–76	.531	15	3rd	Jerry Koosman won all five starts in May and lost his first five in June. He had a 9–6 record and 4.00 ERA at the All-Star break but was unstoppable from then on, going 12-4 with 14 complete games and a 1.64 ERA for his first 20-win season and only one as a Met.
1977	64–98	.395	37	6th	Jerry Koosman got the other end of the stick in 1977. Kooz rhymed with lose 20 times—despite a respectable 3.49 ERA. He was the last Met to lose 20 and the last major leaguer to go from 20 wins to 20 losses in one year.
1978	66–96	.407	24	6th	The Mets were in fourth place and just six games out on June 7 despite allowing the most runs in the NL to that point. The pitching improved a few notches, but the team's standing did not. The Mets went 40–66 and finished with the worst record in the National League.
1979	63–99	.389	35	6th	Three-of-a-kind brutal seasons in a row. Craig Swan, often plagued by poor support, wound up winning 14 games, the most victories by a Met between 1976 and 1984. His 10 complete games and 251 ⅓ innings were likewise the most in that span.

"It was clear that teams like the Mets would have to put up a very staggering amount," said GM Joe McDonald, who was authorized to go only as high as $2 million for three years. "And we can't ask our fans or our sponsors to bear that."

The inexorable pull to rock bottom was complete in 1979. The Mets settled into last place in the first week of May and never budged. Shea saw its lowest attendance ever for a full year (788,905). It took a season-ending six-game winning streak to avoid a 100th loss. The Mets finally put Jerry Koosman out of his misery and traded him to his hometown Twins (for whom he won 20 games in 1979). They dealt Nino Espinosa for a third baseman who vociferously hated everything about being a Met (Richie Hebner), and they swapped shortstops with Pittsburgh: Tim Foli for Frank Taveras. The Mets also had a former Shea hot dog vendor (Ed Glynn) in the bullpen, and they had Mettle the Mule.

The mule had been given to Joan Payson by a neighbor, and now the de Roulet women—Lorinda, the widow of the former ambassador to Jamaica, and daughters Bebe and Whitney—brought the mule to Shea, where it lived in a stall under the stands behind home plate. Before every game, Bebe or an employee rode Mettle around the warning track from a small carriage. The de Roulets tried hard, but no one was buying. The team didn't draw 30,000 to a game all year and barely cracked 10,000 for the home opener. One of the largest crowds was at the last home game of the year—completing an 0–9 final homestand—as fans said goodbye to this lousy team and, it so happened, Payson ownership.

Ten years earlier the Mets had entered the new decade seemingly without a care in the world. Now they stumbled into 1980 in search of a new owner, a new identity, and a new direction. They had to start somewhere. But at least they had nowhere to go but up.

The Magic Really Is Back

John Roca/NY Daily News Archive/Getty Images

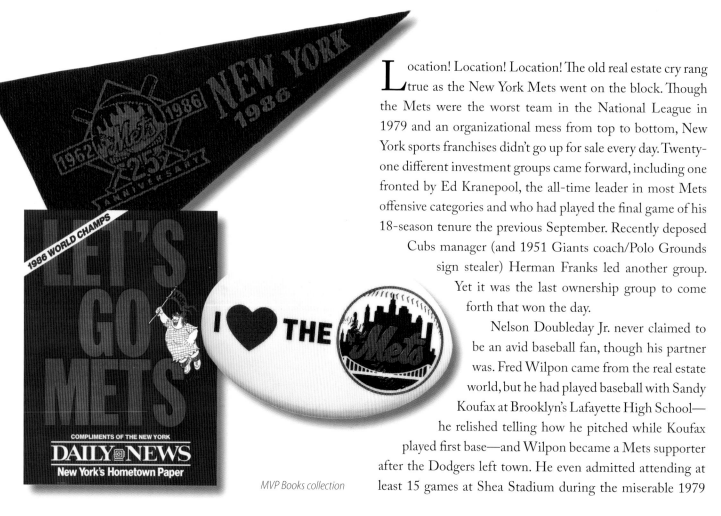

MVP Books collection

Location! Location! Location! The old real estate cry rang true as the New York Mets went on the block. Though the Mets were the worst team in the National League in 1979 and an organizational mess from top to bottom, New York sports franchises didn't go up for sale every day. Twenty-one different investment groups came forward, including one fronted by Ed Kranepool, the all-time leader in most Mets offensive categories and who had played the final game of his 18-season tenure the previous September. Recently deposed Cubs manager (and 1951 Giants coach/Polo Grounds sign stealer) Herman Franks led another group. Yet it was the last ownership group to come forth that won the day.

Nelson Doubleday Jr. never claimed to be an avid baseball fan, though his partner was. Fred Wilpon came from the real estate world, but he had played baseball with Sandy Koufax at Brooklyn's Lafayette High School—he relished telling how he pitched while Koufax played first base—and Wilpon became a Mets supporter after the Dodgers left town. He even admitted attending at least 15 games at Shea Stadium during the miserable 1979

season, a feat that probably should have knocked a little off the record $21.1 million price tag for the team. The Oyster Bay–raised Doubleday was in publishing; his grandfather started the publishing house bearing the family name, and Rudyard Kipling's immortal *Just So Stories* had been written for his father when he was a boy.

After nearly two decades of the Paysons running the team, the sale to Doubleday was a complete break from the past. Almost.

The Mets kept Joe Torre as manager despite a winning percentage of just .404 (178–263). General manager Joe McDonald was not as fortunate. An employee of the team since its inception, he remained with the Mets even as they looked for his replacement. Tal Smith, executive vice president of the Astros, was on the team's radar, but Houston owner John McMullen refused the Mets permission to talk to Smith because two years remained on his contract. One available name had a familiar ring to it: Whitey Herzog.

Herzog had been the Mets' director of personnel when the team transformed from laughingstock to champion in 1969, but he left the organization in 1972 and embarked on a successful managing career. Kansas City fired Herzog the previous October despite a winning record and three division titles. "He's one hell of a baseball man," Wilpon said of Herzog. "But we're not thinking of him as a possible general manager and he knows it. If we hire him, it would be something where he has an outstanding track record: the development of talent." Overlooked by the Mets for promotion after the deaths of Johnny Murphy in 1969 and Gil Hodges in 1972, Herzog was passed over a third time. The Mets offered Herzog his old Mets post as director of personnel, but he declined. The Cardinals hired Herzog as manager in June, and by the following season he held the GM job as well—the lone man in baseball handling such

dual roles. Herzog hired Joe McDonald as his executive assistant in St. Louis.

The Mets, meanwhile, were now run by Frank Cashen, hired as the sixth GM in club history just as the team was about to embark on spring training in 1980. The father of seven children, Cashen was the architect of the great Baltimore teams that reached the postseason six times between 1966 and 1974, winning four pennants and two World Series. His most trying moment, ironically, had come at the hands of the Mets, who defeated his heavily favored Orioles in the 1969 World Series. A one-time sportswriter with a penchant for bowties, Cashen had moved on to the commissioner's office following a change of ownership in Baltimore. Commissioner Bowie Kuhn himself lobbied for Cashen to be named general manager in New York.

Cashen was the ideal man to run the Mets. And that first season, with little time to prepare and next to nothing to trade with, the club rolled into the season without much in the way of hitters or pitchers, but it certainly had one memorable pitch.

"The Magic Is Back"

Previous Mets mottos had grown organically or appeared spontaneously. "Let's Go Mets!" emerged as the throaty cry from the stands in 1962 and still remains the de facto in-stadium refrain. "Amazin'" came from the mouth of Casey Stengel, "Miracle Mets" was alliteration and circumstantial wish fulfillment at its finest, and "Ya Gotta Believe" was a trite phrase turned into citywide rallying cry by Tug McGraw. As the 1980s rolled around, the Mets had one of the top advertising men in the business, Jerry Della Femina, working on something big.

"We're looking to Mets with a star quality, like Lee Mazzilli," said Della Femina. "We believe that he's the big glamour player in this town in the mold of Joe DiMaggio, Mickey Mantle, people like that."

The Mets drew 12,000 in the first game of the new regime. While the Cubs floundered in the soupy outfield grass on Opening Day, right fielder Joel Youngblood snagged a ball off the bat of Larry Biittner that seemed headed for the bullpen. The Mets batted around in the sixth inning that afternoon, with pitcher Craig Swan producing the only hit with men in scoring position. The Opening Day magic was short-lived,

but the slogan "The Magic Is Back" was emblazoned on the outside of the stadium, heard on radio commercials, and seen in newspaper ads. Della Femina got his point across in Mets country, but his comments about the neighborhood around Yankee Stadium being unsafe cost the Mets a $5,000 fine from the commissioner's office.

With the Mets in last place and eight games under .500 as Memorial Day approached, the team suddenly found a little luck—or was it magic?—that had been missing since 1973 or so. Unexpected things were happening in Flushing as the summer of 1980 approached. And it wasn't just the mid-game prize of the night awarded as "This Magic Moment" by Jay and the Americans blared on the improved sound system.

The Mets embarked on a 12–6 run, punctuated by sweeping the Dodgers out of first place at Shea. The last-place Giants then skunked New York on Friday the 13th. When San Francisco knocked out Pete Falcone in the second inning the next night, it looked like the team's luck had returned to its previous state. The score was 6–2 and the Mets were down to their last out in the ninth when Mazzilli singled in a run. The unwalkable Frank Taveras walked, and Claudell Washington, who had been acquired a week earlier from the White Sox for a minor leaguer, singled Mazzilli home for another run. With the tying runs on base, San Francisco brought in starter Allen Ripley to pitch to Steve Henderson. Hendu was then among the league leaders in batting at .341, but the club's cleanup hitter had not hit a home run in 11 months, and he had struck out three times that night. A Ripley fastball under his chin sent him sprawling backward. "I try to keep my temper," Henderson said after the game. "But when someone does something like that to me, throwing too close, I sort of turn into a monster." The newfound hulk drilled an outside pitch "deeeep to right field" to use Bob Murphy's lexicon. The

Steve Henderson (5) led the Mets in batting in 1980—albeit with a relatively paltry .290 mark— and also crossed the plate 75 times for a team that finished third from the bottom in runs scored in the National League.
Jacob Kanarek/Metsintheseventies.com

ball cleared the fence into the bullpen, and the Mets had a 7–6 win.

To the world at large, this was no big deal (Bobby Murcer pulled the same trick that night for the Yankees in Oakland), but given a spark of hope, Mets fans were moved to flock to Shea Stadium the next afternoon, Father's Day, in such numbers that thousands were turned away. With the Mets' luck, the club was in the process of replacing 6,000 old wooden seats with new plastic ones. The Mets hadn't seen a crowd like that Sunday's 44,910 in almost three years. Who thought they could cause a sudden box-office rush? Fred Wilpon admitted as much as he issued a formal apology, though he saw the silver lining: "Two months ago I never anticipated that we'd get the public's attention to that degree."

The Mets lost their next seven, but they embarked on a 14–7 run that began when Washington homered three times at Dodger Stadium to tie the club record shared by Jim Hickman (1965) and Dave Kingman (1976). Washington's achievement in itself was shocking because the 1980 lineup lacked power on an epic scale—more representative of the club was Doug Flynn's mark of three triples on August 5. The 1980 Mets set team records at the time for highest batting average (.257) and stolen bases (158), but they were last in the majors in home runs and established a dubious club record for fewest long balls. Though New York had a .500 record in mid-July and was within three and a half games

of first place in a tight NL East, the real race was in the *Daily News*, where each day the Mets battled the home run pace of Roger Maris' then-record 61 homers. Though playoff contention faded to memory during a late summer slide of 19 losses in 20 games—and the one win was protested by the Giants—the home run battle with Maris came down to the last weekend of the year. The first career home run by call-up Hubie Brooks left the 1980 Mets and the 1961 Maris tied at 61 homers, but the team edged out the Cubs to avoid the basement for the first time in three years. It wasn't magic, but it was something.

Strike Out

The first three months of the 1981 season were consumed by talk of the impending strike and the rest of the year was spent cleaning up the mess it left. The Mets, however, remained close enough in the free-for-all, post-strike split season to take orders for playoff tickets.

The club added pop to a punchless lineup when Rusty Staub, 37, and Dave Kingman, 32, returned from exile. Rusty was a free agent and Kong came back in a $100,000 transaction that sent Steve Henderson to the Cubs, making "Steve Wonder" part of trades for both Seaver and Kingman. A year after the colored panels were removed from Shea Stadium's exterior, a top hat in center field became the ballpark's new signature feature. Each time a Met homered,

a giant apple featuring the words "Mets Magic" appeared from a nine-foot-tall hat in center field. Signs in the parking lot warned fans they were entering a "Kingman Fallout Zone," and distance markers were placed in outlying areas seemingly accessible only to Kong. When it came to home runs, the Mets were aiming for quality over quantity. The pitching had neither.

With Craig Swan, signed to a five-year contract, enduring pain in his shoulder, the Mets shipped out flashes-in-the-pan Mark Bomback (a 9–3 start but a 1–5 finish in 1980) and John Pacella. They let reliable Ray Burris leave for Montreal as a free agent and acquired arm-weary former Cy Young winner Randy Jones in the Pacella trade to add veteran presence to a rotation rounded out by Mike Scott, Greg Harris, and Ed Lynch. UCLA stud Tim Leary made the team after one superb minor league season, thanks to lobbying by Joe Torre. Leary started the third game of the year and threw two hitless innings before his elbow stiffened in the cold and damp April weather at Wrigley Field. "We don't think it's serious," said Torre, who would not be in New York when Leary finally made his Shea Stadium debut two years later.

The crème de bullpen was the combination of Neil Allen and hard-throwing second-year man Jeff Reardon. Trading from one of their few areas of strength, the Mets sent Reardon (plus Seaver-trade washout Dan Norman) to Montreal for outfielder Ellis Valentine. Reardon would be on the mound at Shea that October when the Expos clinched the only postseason berth of their existence; Valentine was a shell of his former power-hitting self following a beaning and personal issues. The trade grew worse as time wore on and Reardon racked up save after save.

Though baseball's tenuous peace had been tested for more than a decade with brief work stoppages, the 1981 showdown between owners and players over free agent compensation resulted in a two-month strike, devastating fans who had never known a summer without daily doses of baseball. Yet at the same time it also wiped away another long, hopeless summer at Shea. The Mets were 17 games under .500 and 15 games out on June 11 when Cincinnati's Tom Seaver, who would lead the NL with 14 wins, defeated Pat Zachry, who would lead the league with 14 losses. All on-field irony was lost as the major leagues closed up shop around the same time many schools let out for the summer.

When the players returned in August, Joel Youngblood was a Mets all-star. Injured but leading the league in hitting at .359 when the lights went out on the season, he was in Cleveland for the rescheduled Sunday night All-Star Game. Youngblood re-injured his knee in a post-strike exhibition against Toronto; he would try to play through the pain, but Youngblood and his .350 average were done for the year by the first post-strike weekend. The Mets went to Wrigley Field for Opening Day for the second time in 1981—and won again. The Mets, in fact, won the first three official second-half games and contended in the tight NL East.

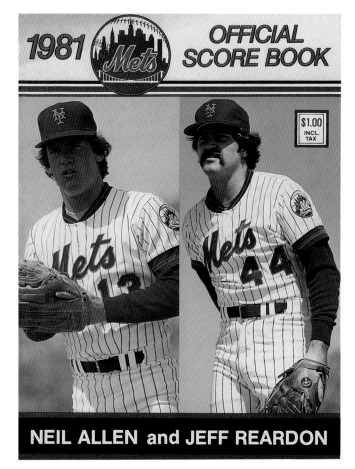

1981 **OFFICIAL SCORE BOOK**

$1.00 INCL. TAX

NEIL ALLEN and JEFF REARDON

Neil Allen and Jeff Reardon were expected to be a formidable bullpen tandem in 1981, but Reardon was traded away that May. Allen later became expendable with the emergence of Jesse Orosco as the team's closer.
Author's collection

As Mets kept getting hurt after the long midseason layoff, Torre tried everything and everyone. Most of Triple-A Tidewater was pitching in Flushing. The Mets even dug up iconoclast, kinesiologist, and union activist Mike Marshall, who once pitched in 106 games in a season but hadn't thrown in the major leagues in a year. Marshall, Terry Leach, Ray Searage—anyone who could pitch was thrown out there.

Dave Kingman carried the team with five homers and a staggering—for Kong—.314 average over a two-week span and then endured the coldest stretch of his hot-and-cold career. Ellis Valentine, batting under .200, was benched. Meanwhile, base-stealer Mookie Wilson, who hit in 15 of his first 16 post-strike games, and Hubie Brooks, who had a .307 average, emerged as rookie heroes. They had debuted at the end of the 1980 season, and now a year later they were so immersed in the Mets order—Wilson leadoff and Brooks

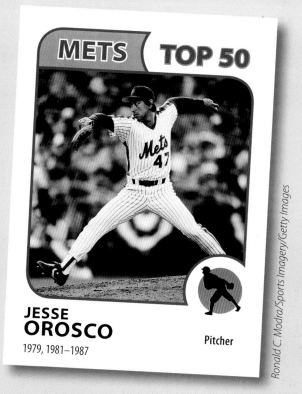

METS **TOP 50**

JESSE OROSCO
1979, 1981–1987

Pitcher

Ronald C. Modra/Sports Imagery/Getty Images

Jesse Orosco first joined the Mets in 1979 and worked his way to become a left-handed relief specialist. His continuing development freed up New York to trade Neil Allen—for Keith Hernandez—in 1983, and Orosco was magnificent that year: 13–7, 62 games, 84 strikeouts, and a 1.47 ERA. He placed third in the Cy Young Award voting, the closest a Met had gotten to the award since Jerry Koosman's second-place finish in 1976.

Jesse Russell Orosco is forever linked with Koosman for other reasons, too. Kooz threatened to retire in 1979 if he wasn't traded to his hometown Twins from Mets purgatory. Orosco, a Santa Barbara native, had been drafted a year earlier by Minnesota; Twins owner Calvin Griffith, oblivious to the young lefty's existence, blundered into trading him for Koosman. By 1986 Orosco was a two-time all-star who owned the Mets career saves mark. Like Koosman in 1969, Orosco was on the Shea Stadium mound when his team clinched the World Series in 1986.

Orosco's three NLCS wins that year are also part of Mets lore. He staggered through the last three innings of Game 6 to lock up the pennant, lending credence to his nickname of "Messy Jesse." He saved 108 games in eight seasons as a Met and blew 36 chances. In his other 18 years of major league service—which kept him busy until age 46 and allowed him to set an all-time mark with 1,252 appearances—he saved 36 and blew 40.

METS TOP 50

MOOKIE WILSON
1980–1989

Outfielder

New York appeared to have solved its perennial need for an anchor at third base as Hubie Brooks blossomed in his first full season, leading the team with a .307 average and 21 doubles. He and Mookie Wilson became anchors in the lineup for several years as well. *Bruce Bennett/Getty Images*

It says a lot about a franchise's history when the Mets' most famous batted ball was a slow grounder to first base, but Mookie Wilson always made grounders exciting. Twice in four days during the otherwise miserable 1983 season, he scored from second base on infield outs to win games in the team's final at bat. Until Jose Reyes came along, Wilson was the all-time Mets leader in steals and triples.

As a child, William Heyward Wilson couldn't say "milk," but his ensuing nickname made sure he never got booed at Shea Stadium. Good day or bad, he was always greeted the same when he stepped to the plate: "MOOOOOOKKKK!!!"

The 1980 arrival of Mookie Wilson and Hubie Brooks was an early sign that the dark ages at Shea would soon end. Despite being a renowned hacker (just 240 walks in 1,116 Mets games), Wilson's ability to fight off pitches is what extended his fabled at-bat against Bob Stanley in the 10th inning of Game 6 of the 1986 World Series. His flexibility helped him leap out of the way of Stanley's errant palmball, which allowed Kevin Mitchell to score the tying run. Mook took care of the rest with his dribbling groundball on the ninth pitch of his at bat.

After finishing his playing career with Toronto, Wilson returned to New York as the Mets' first base coach, and he went on to manage in the farm system, first at Kingsport (2003–2004) and then for the Brooklyn Cyclones (2005).

in the three hole—that broadcaster Ralph Kiner frequently transposed their names. It was easy to confuse Hubie Wilson and Mookie Brooks on September 20 because they each had four hits. In that game, the Mets somehow had outhit the Cardinals 20–8 and still trailed by a run with two outs and nobody on in the bottom of the ninth with Mets scourge Bruce Sutter on the mound. Frank Taveras doubled and up stepped Wilson. He had botched a flyball in the top of the inning to give St. Louis the lead, but Mook changed the storyline by slamming a drive into the New York bullpen. The Mets, seemingly out of contention after being swept in St. Louis the previous weekend, returned the favor at Shea. The Mets stood two and a half games out with less than two weeks left in the season.

It didn't last. The Mets went 4–8 (with one tie thrown in) to finish the second half at 24–28. On the season's final day, the manager and his staff were let go. Torre had been with the team since October 1974, immediately hopping on

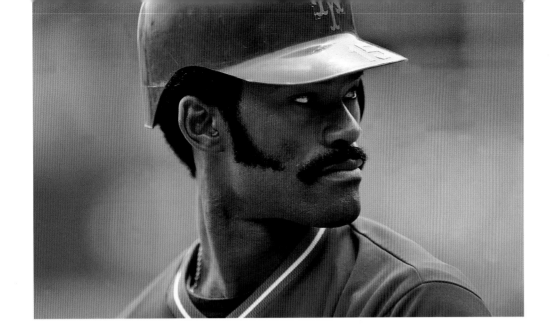

a plane for the club's '74 exhibition series in Japan, and he'd remained faithful to the organization. His 286–420 mark as a manager was far from great, but so was the talent he had to work with. His firing also meant the end for pitching coaches Rube Walker (he of the five-man rotation innovation) and Bob Gibson (he of the intimidating 1.12 ERA in 1968), plus bullpen coach Joe Pignatano (he of the bullpen tomato garden). They joined the manager in 1982 in Atlanta, where the Braves set a record by winning the first 13 games of the season and squeaked out Torre's first postseason appearance as manager.

By George, They Haven't Got It

Phase three of the not-so-new-anymore ownership regime involved importing yet more slugging to Shea Stadium. First, the Mets brought in George Bamberger to manage the club, one of many hires from Frank Cashen's Baltimore days. The Staten Island native had been Earl Weaver's pitching coach with the Orioles. As a manager he had helped the previously moribund Brewers reach new heights of respectability, but Bamberger had a heart attack in the winter of 1980 and retired that September.

Another George came to Flushing in a trade for practically nothing—unless you count the $10 million for five years showered upon arrival. Former all-star George Foster collected at least 20 homers and 90 RBI in each of his last six seasons in Cincinnati, including the abbreviated strike season. He was the 1977 NL MVP for his 52 homers and 149 RBI, and he finished in the top six in the voting three other times. With Foster in the middle of the lineup

A TALE OF TWO CITIES . . . IN ONE DAY

Joel Youngblood never really found a position in his nearly six years with the Mets, but he did find himself in the record books. On August 4, 1982, Youngblood became the first player in history to have a hit in two different cities in the same day. And let it be noted, both hits came against future Hall of Famers.

Youngblood began that Wednesday batting third and playing center field for the Mets in a Wrigley Field matinee. His two-run single off Fergie Jenkins in the top of third inning broke a 1–1 tie. In the Cubs' third, Youngblood caught a flyball to end the inning and, it turned out, his Mets career. Upon reaching the dugout, Youngblood learned that he'd been traded to the Montreal Expos. He went into the clubhouse, made plane reservations, and left for the airport to fly to Philadelphia, where the Expos were facing Steve Carlton in a night game. "It's funny, I left there in the third and got here in the third," Youngblood said that evening.

Expos manager Jim Fanning inserted Youngblood into right field in the sixth inning with Montreal ahead, 3–2. The first-place Phillies took the lead that inning, but the historic moment came in the seventh when Youngblood beat out an infield hit in his only at bat of the night. That was one busy Wednesday.

As an epilogue to this story, the Mets received Tom Gorman as the player to be named later from Montreal for Youngblood. The left-hander may not have come close to Youngblood's singular—doubular?—accomplishment, but in 1985 he did take the loss in the greatest Mets whipping of all time (a 26–7 loss in Philly) and then got the win in a high-scoring marathon against Atlanta (a 16–13 win in 19 innings) just over three weeks later.

It was a grand homecoming for franchise favorite Tom Seaver, who struck out five batters in six shutout innings on Opening Day 1983. Seaver got a no-decision, but the Mets won the game, 2–0. *John Iacono/Sports Illustrated/Getty Images*

and Dave Kingman behind him, this duo would surely eclipse the club's piddly 1980 total of 61 homers.

The pair actually knocked 50 balls over the fences in 1982, 37 of those came from Kingman's bat—making him the first Met ever to lead the NL in home runs. Kong also set a personal high with 156 strikeouts while batting .204 (not a career-low for Kong). Foster whiffed 123 times, drove in 70 runs, and batted .247. Ellis Valentine hit .288 but slugged only .407 with eight homers, and the Mets were as thankful to be rid of him after the season as the Expos had been a year and half earlier.

Still, the Mets stood in third place on June 20 with a 34–30 record, just three games out of first. From that point on they went 31–67, by far the worst in baseball. After losing three out of four at home against Montreal in late June, New York dropped five games in three days in Philadelphia. Mets scholars had to scramble for the record books as the club dropped 15 straight in August (two shy of the 1962 mark), including the first 0–9 road trip in club history. They suffered injuries all over the diamond, but the most painful was Neil Allen's stomach disorder that sapped his strength and in turn undermined the Mets bullpen.

The Mets called on one more George to see if he could help in 1983: George Thomas Seaver.

"And Now Pitching, Number 41..."

The Midnight Massacre of June 1977 ended in Hawaii. Five and a half years after the Seaver trade became a demarcation line in franchise history, general manager Frank Cashen painted over it at the winter meetings in Honolulu. Cashen had been inquiring about Seaver for two years, to no avail. Now the championship club Seaver had come to in Cincinnati was a faded, punchless mess that lost more games than the Mets in 1982. Seaver was on the block, and Cashen was on the clock.

Seaver wanted to be closer to his family in Connecticut, where they had remained after the 1977 trade. His veteran status allowed him to select his destination, and Seaver gave the Reds a list of four teams: the Mets, Yankees, Phillies, and Red Sox. He had suffered from the flu early in 1982 and missed the last six weeks of the season due to hip and shoulder problems. A year removed from a 14–2 season that could have netted him another Cy Young (if Fernandomania in Los Angeles hadn't bewitched voters), Seaver tumbled to 5–13 with a 5.50 ERA in 1982. Despite age and injury, Tom Seaver was not simply a crowd pleaser nearing the end of his career. Cashen believed he could still contribute on the mound while also providing veteran leadership for the young staff.

A TROPHY FIT FOR A MAYOR

On April 21, 1983, just over 20,000 New York baseball fans convened at Shea Stadium to watch the two hometown teams compete in what would be the last Mayor's Trophy Game. The Yankees won, giving them a 10–8–1 advantage in the long-running exhibition series.

When the expansion Mets arrived in New York in 1962, making it a multi-team town once again, Mayor Robert Wagner announced that an annual exhibition game would be held between the Mets and Yankees starting in 1963 to benefit the New York City sandlot baseball fund. (The Yankees, Giants, and Dodgers had participated in a Mayor's Trophy Series in 1946–55 and 1957.)

The first reincarnation of the Mayor's Trophy Game in 1963 was rained out. The rescheduled game was part of a Yankees day–night doubleheader against 10th-place teams. On Thursday, June 20, 1963, the Yankees played Gil Hodges' Washington Senators in the afternoon and then hosted Casey Stengel's Mets in the exhibition at night. The Yankees won the game that mattered, but you couldn't tell Casey Stengel that the second game was just a charity case.

Stengel took any game against the Yankees personally, as the team had fired him, despite a league-record 10 pennants, because they deemed ol' Case too old. Mets general manager George Weiss had also once gotten the boot from the Yankees, and he was only too happy to uncork champagne when the Mets won the first spring training game in Florida between the clubs in 1962.

The June 1963 game at Yankee Stadium was even more serious because of where it was held, with New Yorkers in attendance as well as Yankees management. Mets fans took it seriously, too, making up the majority of the 50,742 fans at the game. Not taking any chances, Stengel tabbed Jay Hook, one of his top pitchers, to get the start, and then he replaced him in the sixth with another starter, Carl Willey.

According to Leonard Koppett of the *New York Times*, Mets fans "cheered frantically," as their team's 6–2 win in the exhibition was "far more exciting to them than any of the real World Series triumphs that Yankees fans take almost for granted." Even more importantly, the game raised $120,486.26 for New York's sandlot ballplayers, which went a long way in an era when a bat cost $3 and the finest mitt went for $20.

The series had its ups and downs over 20 years under four mayors (Robert Wagner, John Lindsay, Abe Beame, and Ed Koch—for those keeping score). Scheduling conflicts became more difficult to deal with, as did shifting priorities for both ownerships. After more than 700,000 fans helped raise some

New York City mayor Edward Koch (second from right) poses with Mets management following the Mets' 4–1 win over the Yankees on May 27, 1982. With "hizzoner" are manager George Bamberger, chairman of the board Nelson Doubleday, and team president Fred Wilpon. *Ray Stubblebine/AP Images*

$2 million for local youth baseball, the series was halted after the 1983 tilt. A Mets–Yankees exhibition was revived in the early 1990s for the weekend before Opening Day, but it lacked the intensity of the original and was discontinued. The next incarnation would count, with official interleague play beginning in 1997.

Mayor's Trophy Game Results

DATE	SCORE	SITE	ATTENDANCE
June 20, 1963	Mets 6, Yankees 2	Yankee Stadium	50,742
August 24, 1964	Yankees 6, Mets 4	Shea Stadium	55,396
May 3, 1965	Mets 2, Yankees 1 (10 inn.)	Yankee Stadium	23,556
June 27, 1966	Yankees 5, Mets 2	Shea Stadium	56,367
July 12, 1967	Mets 4, Yankees 0	Yankee Stadium	31,852
May 28, 1968	Mets 4, Yankees 3	Shea Stadium	35,198
September 29, 1969	Mets 7, Yankees 6	Shea Stadium	32,720
August 17, 1970	Yankees 9, Mets 4	Yankee Stadium	43,987
September 9, 1971	Yankees 2, Mets 1	Shea Stadium	48,872
August 24, 1972	Yankees 2, Mets 1	Yankee Stadium	53,949
May 10, 1973	Mets 8, Yankees 4	Shea Stadium	39,915
May 31, 1974	Yankees 9, Mets 4	Shea Stadium	35,894
May 16, 1975	Yankees 9, Mets 4	Shea Stadium	26,427
June 15, 1976	Yankees 8, Mets 4	Yankee Stadium	36,361
June 23, 1977	Mets 6, Yankees 4	Shea Stadium	15,510
April 27, 1978	Yankees 4, Mets 3 (13 inn.)	Yankee Stadium	9,792
April 16, 1979	Mets 1, Yankees 1 (5 inn., rain)	Shea Stadium	13,719
1980 & 1981	no game scheduled		
May 27, 1982	Mets 4, Yankees 1	Yankee Stadium	41,614
April 21, 1983	Yankees 4, Mets 1	Shea Stadium	20,471

Special 16 page 10th anniversary feature–"1973: That Championship Season."

The deal hung in the air for a week before it was finally consummated. Foisting Charlie Puleo, Lloyd McClendon, and Jason Felice on the Reds for Seaver couldn't make up for the measly return the Mets had received from Cincinnati in 1977, but a few days before Christmas 1982, at 38 years old and 36 wins shy of 300, Seaver was a present Mets fans could not wait to open.

A strained left thigh left doubts as to whether Seaver could pitch on Opening Day against the Phillies. Come April 5, Seaver was ready, and so was Shea Stadium. The raucous crowd of 51,054 was the largest for an Opening Day since Gil Hodges' return to New York in 1968. As Seaver made his way from the bullpen to the mound, public address announcer Jack Franchetti announced, "And now pitching, number 41. . . ." He didn't need to complete the announcement. The people knew who was back, and they voiced their appreciation—loudly.

Seaver opened the game by fanning Pete Rose (now a Phillie), and the place went wild. He struck out Rose again in his final inning, having to depart after the sixth because of thigh stiffness. Rookie Doug Sisk got the win with three scoreless innings of relief. The game continued two strange patterns of success for the Mets: a 32–27 all-time record against four-time Cy Young winner Steve Carlton and nine straight Opening Day wins, tying the record set by the St. Louis Browns—"another team that started faster than it closed," observed Joseph Durso in the *New York Times.*

Success in 1983 would not be found on the field—the Mets finished last for the fifth time since 1977—but the season was spent assembling pieces for the future. Cashen cleared room for Seaver on the roster by shipping out Pat Zachry, the last remaining Met from the 1977 trade that banished Seaver. The club also sent Mike Scott to Houston for outfielder Danny Heep. They acquired Boston's Mike Torrez, a pitcher nearly a decade older than Scott and remembered in New York for clinching the 1977 World Series for the Yankees and a year later, as a Red Sox, serving up the home run to Bucky Dent that clinched another postseason appearance for the Yanks. All Torrez would be remembered for in Mets annals was setting the club mark for bases on balls in a game (10) and finishing three walks shy of Nolan Ryan's single-season team record from 1971. Torrez led the league in walks (113), earned runs allowed (108), and losses (17). With pitching like that and the lowest batting average in the National League, it was the kind of club that could make a manager quit.

George Bamberger—who'd contemplated leaving after his first season in New York, who'd quit on Milwaukee because of health problems, and who'd admitted accepting the job in the first place as a favor to old friend Frank Cashen—was done with New York. With his club mired in last place at 16–30, and fresh off a 14-inning loss at Dodger Stadium, Bambi left the team. "I probably suffered enough," he said.

Cashen's first choice for a replacement was Earl Weaver, recently retired in Baltimore. Weaver turned him down, so Cashen went with coach Frank Howard, a gentle giant with 382 career home runs as one of the most feared sluggers of the 1960s. The Mets felt they had one of the great sluggers for the 1980s in Darryl Strawberry, the top overall pick in the 1980 draft, Cashen's first with the Mets. Now age 21, the strapping lefty was called up in mid-May, along with the accolades and monikers that had followed him since he

A nattily dressed Darryl Strawberry shows off his Rookie of the Year plaque to all-time legends Willie Mays and Tom Seaver in January 1984. The Mets rising star earned 88 percent of the votes from the Baseball Writers' Association of America. *AP Images*

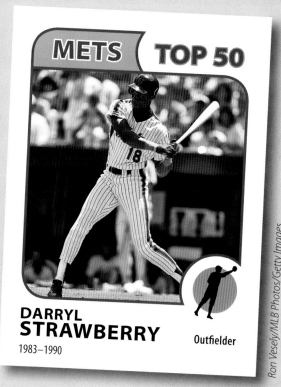

METS **TOP 50**

DARRYL STRAWBERRY
1983–1990

Outfielder

Ron Vesely/MLB Photos/Getty Images

starred at Los Angeles' Crenshaw High School. His most memorable nickname was the "black Ted Williams." Hitting coach Jim Frey served as a father figure to this young man who had grown up with little direction. Frey likened his position as "a horse trainer looking at Man O'War as a two-year-old." Raw, unpolished, and prone to strikeouts, Strawberry still hit 26 home runs, drove in 74 runs, and stole 19 bases to run away with Rookie of the Year honors.

But even the arrival of the team's top prospect was not the most significant event of 1983. Keith Hernandez—the 1979 batting champ and co-MVP, winner of five consecutive Gold Gloves at first base, and hero of Game 7 of the previous year's World Series—was suddenly a Met. Neil Allen, the troubled reliever sent from New York to St. Louis, was surprised that the Cardinals wanted him at such a cost. "I've been traded for somebody who's somebody," Allen said. "They'll remember this trade years from now and they'll say, 'Who was Keith Hernandez traded for?' I'm honored."

The player Allen was traded for had a far different reaction. The Mets had been a bottom-feeding franchise during most of the 29-year-old first baseman's career. His first comment to the New York reporters who would soon be eating out of his hand was that he was not shocked at being traded, "Just shocked at being traded to the Mets."

Hernandez was a star in St. Louis, the number three hitter for the defending world champions, but he had run

Selected with the first overall pick of the first draft after Mets ownership changed hands in 1980, Darryl Strawberry was seen as a franchise savior from his first day as a professional. Darryl Eugene Strawberry arrived on cue in New York in 1983, slugging 26 home runs and winning the Rookie of the Year Award. He reached that same home run total and knocked in 97 runs in 1984 and made the first of his seven all-star appearances as a Met.

In 1988 Straw led the league in homers (39) and slugging (.585) and was among the leaders in runs scored and driven in, with 101 apiece; he was one steal shy of his second 30–30 season. He finished second in the MVP race that year and placed third in 1990. Strawberry left with the all-time Mets records for runs (662), RBI (733), and home runs both by a Met (252) and at Shea Stadium (127).

Raised in a working-class neighborhood in Los Angeles, the lefty with the perfect swing and loping stride was susceptible to every temptation thrown at him off the field. Injuries and drug addiction put his career in limbo. He spent time with the Dodgers and Giants before having to prove himself with the independent St. Paul Saints. He joined the Yankees in August 1995 and played parts of five seasons in the Bronx. A survivor of cancer as well as his own personal demons, Strawberry rejoined the Mets in the SNY studio and as a special ambassador for the club.

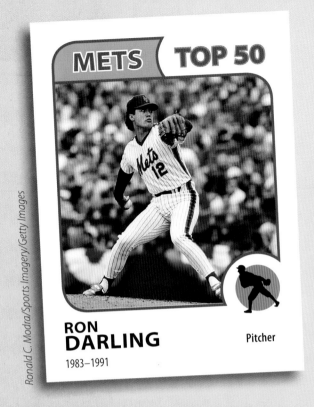

METS — TOP 50

RON DARLING
1983–1991

Pitcher

Known to a new generation as the voice of the Mets, Ron Darling was once the future of the Mets. Acquired from the Rangers with Walt Terrell for Lee Mazzilli in a Texas-sized heist on April 1, 1982, Darling started 33 games as a rookie in 1984, had 12 wins and a 3.81 ERA, and was completely ignored because of the breakthrough season by fellow rookie Dwight Gooden.

Ronald Maurice Darling was born in Honolulu, grew up near Boston, and attended Yale, where he threw an 11-inning no-hitter that he lost in the 12th in a duel with Frank Viola of St. John's University. He later married a model, landed on the cover of GQ, and was dubbed "Mr. Perfect," even if he led the league in walks in 1985 and errors in 1986. He did win a Gold Glove in 1989 and had a masterful pickoff move.

Darling was an all-star in 1985 with a 16–6 record and 2.90 ERA, and he won 15 in 1986 as the Mets won a league-best 26 of his starts. He started three World Series games, winning Game 4 at Fenway Park. Darling did not fare as well in his Game 7 showdowns: the Mets rallied to win in '86 but he lost to the Dodgers in the '88 NLCS. Traded to Montreal in 1991, he was flipped to Oakland, where he won 15 the following year. He retired in 1995 and worked his way up the broadcast ladder, landing in 2006 at SNY with Gary Cohen and ex-teammate Keith Hernandez.

afoul of his manager. Cocaine was a problem in the major leagues in the early 1980s and Hernandez was caught up in it, something he initially refuted but later corroborated when summoned to testify at the Pittsburgh drug trials in 1985. He had quit the drug on his own, but the manager had made up his mind. Whitey Herzog instructed St. Louis general manager Joe McDonald (the former Mets GM) to trade Hernandez promptly. Decades later, many still contend that this was the best deal the Mets ever made. The Cardinals, who were in first place the day of the trade, played 10 games under .500 from that point on and finished fourth.

The Mets put together a 46–57 record after Hernandez arrived, but the direction was more important than the results. Jesse Orosco took over full-time closer duties and had the finest year of a career that lasted another 20. The lefty represented the Mets in the All-Star Game, put together a streak of 27⅔ scoreless innings, and earned four wins in one week in August—including two in one day. The second of Orosco's triumphs on that day came after Pittsburgh's Jose DeLeon had held the Mets hitless until Hubie Brooks singled with one out in the ninth.

The game was scoreless as Mike Torrez threw 11 shutout innings and Orosco escaped a jam in the 12th. In a play set up beforehand via hand signals with third-base coach Bobby Valentine, Mookie Wilson, who was on second base with one out, came around to score the only run of the game on a slow infield groundball. The Pirates got the force at second base, but Wilson never hesitated and ran all the way around to slide in ahead of the tag. He pulled off the same play on another infield grounder three nights later to beat Montreal, and Orosco got another run-off win. Orosco's team-leading 13 victories to go with his 17 saves gave him a direct hand in 44 percent of the team's wins. With a stunning 1.47 ERA in 110 relief innings, Orosco placed third in the Cy Young voting.

It wasn't just Mookie and Jesse giving Mets fans a glimpse of late-inning excitement. Rusty Staub tied the all-time mark with 25 pinch-hit RBI, and his 24 hits off the bench was one shy of the single-season record. He tied a major league mark with eight consecutive pinch hits in midseason and ended the year in Le Grand Orange fashion, cracking a two-run double with two outs in the ninth to bring in the tying and winning runs in a season-ending doubleheader sweep of Montreal. The Mets may have finished with the worst record in the NL, but the club wouldn't finish last again for a decade. The patience of these long-suffering fans would be rewarded with the greatest period of prosperity the club has ever experienced. Now that's magic.

Is There a Doctor in the House?

Mets fans were stunned. Mets brass, too. How could they lose Tom Seaver? Again!

While blame for the first banishment of Seaver could fall squarely on M. Donald Grant (and his accomplice Dick Young), the second loss of "The Franchise" had its roots in the horrific baseball strike two summers earlier. One of the reasons for the 1981 strike was that the owners wanted some form of compensation for teams losing free agents. Clubs could now select from a pool of players left unprotected by any team. The Mets protected 26 men, but not Seaver. The White Sox, entitled to a pick for losing pitcher Dennis Lamp to free agency, replaced him on the roster with Seaver on January 20, 1984.

Outgoing commissioner Bowie Kuhn twice tried to talk the White Sox out of taking Seaver, now 39 years old and 27 wins shy of 300. Though he'd sought the trade to New York the previous year so that he could be closer to his family, Seaver decided to head to the defending AL West champs. The Mets' feelings on the matter were summed up by owner Nelson Doubleday: "The White Sox did us dirty."

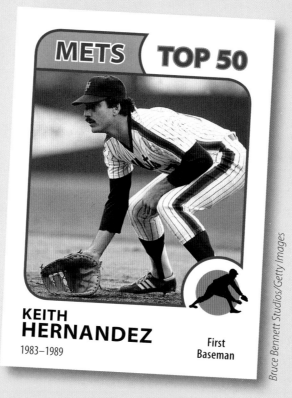

METS TOP 50

KEITH HERNANDEZ
1983–1989

First Baseman

The fortunes of the Mets changed forever on June 15, 1983, when they acquired Keith Hernandez from St. Louis for Neil Allen and Rick Ownbey. A batting champ and co-MVP in 1979, Hernandez was a field general and the best defensive first baseman in the majors.

He handled the press well and showed the young Mets the major league ropes. They grew into all-stars around him. He commented early in 1986, "There's a feeling that even if we're three runs down, we know we're going to come back." The Mets were down by three in the sixth inning of Game 7 of the World Series when Mex's two-run single off Bruce Hurst started the comeback that netted a championship trophy.

In 1987, Hernandez was named the first captain in Mets history; Gary Carter shared the honor the following year. Because of injuries, Hernandez played more than 100 games just four times as a Met, but he remains among the club's all-time leaders in on-base percentage, walks, RBI, multi-hit games, and total bases. His .297 average is third best in club history, and only David Wright hit higher than Hernandez's .301 mark at Shea Stadium. Hernandez's 11 Gold Gloves are more than any first baseman in baseball history.

His post-baseball career included a fabled appearance on *Seinfeld* and many commercials. His current perch in the SNY television booth with Gary Cohen and former teammate Ron Darling keeps Keith in the Mets conversation on a nightly basis.

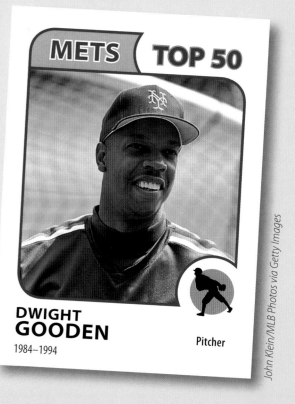

METS TOP 50

DWIGHT GOODEN
1984–1994

Pitcher

In May 1986, with the Mets already on their way to running away with the division title, Dave Anderson of the *New York Times* reflected on the team's two youngest and brightest stars: "Dwight Gooden and Darryl Strawberry—seldom has any baseball team had two dominating players who were so good so young. And each appears capable of remaining a dominating player for the next 15 years, if not longer." By 2001 Gooden's career was over, but the demons that cut short his success did not stop.

The Mets selected Dwight Eugene Gooden with the fifth pick of the 1982 draft, and just two years later he was among the most dominant pitchers in the major leagues—and he was only 19 years old. He set the major league mark for rookies with 276 strikeouts in 1984 and had back-to-back 16-K games in September. Gooden's sizzling fastball and knee-buckling curve made previously dormant Shea Stadium a rollicking place during his starts, complete with a fan-maintained "K" corner that tracked Doctor K's strike zone operations. Gooden provided the Mets their second consecutive Rookie of the Year (Strawberry won in 1983). Doc claimed 23 of 24 first-place votes. He didn't miss any votes in winning the Cy Young Award in 1985.

Gooden's Triple Crown pitching season—24-4, 1.53 ERA, 268 K's, plus a NL-best 16 complete games and 276⅔ innings—not only rates as the top year in Mets history, it was arguably

DWIGHT GOODEN

Born: November 16, 1964, in Tampa, FL
Signed by New York Mets, 1982
Mets Debut: April 7, 1984
Bats: Right. **Throws:** Right

New York Mets Pitching Record

YEAR	W–L	ERA	G	IP	SO
1984	17–9	2.60	31	218.0	276
1985	24–4	1.53	35	276.2	268
1986	17–6	2.84	33	250.0	200
1987	15–7	3.21	25	179.2	148
1988	18–9	3.19	34	248.1	175
1989	9–4	2.89	19	118.1	101
1990	19–7	3.83	34	232.2	223
1991	13–7	3.60	27	190.0	150
1992	10–13	3.67	31	206.0	145
1993	12–15	3.45	29	208.2	149
1994	3–4	6.31	7	41.1	40
Mets Totals	157–85	3.10	305	2169.2	1875
MLB Totals	194–112	3.51	430	2800.2	2293

the best year by any pitcher between Bob Gibson's legendary 1968 and Pedro Martinez's remarkable 1999. That's the kind of historical company Gooden kept until he tested positive for cocaine on April 1, 1987. From that point on, he was still the staff ace despite injuries and diminished effectiveness.

Gooden got the Opening Day assignment eight times as a Met, and he started and lost two All-Star Games, including the 1988 contest against future teammate Frank Viola. Gooden nearly joined Viola as a 20-game winner in 1990. He finished fourth in the Cy Young voting with a 19–7 mark in what would be Doc's fourth and final 200-strikeout season. Still, in 11 seasons with the Mets, Gooden compiled enough wins (157) and strikeouts (1,875) to stand second to Tom Seaver in both team categories; his 1985 marks for ERA and shutouts (8) are unmatched in franchise history. Testing positive for cocaine in 1994, weeks before the players' strike, brought an end to his Mets career and put him on the suspended list through 1995.

Like Strawberry, Gooden found new life on the Yankees, for whom he pitched in 1996, 1997, and part of 2000. He hurled a no-hitter in the Bronx in 1996 and winning 24 times with the Yanks. In between his Bronx stints, he bounced around with three other teams, including the Devil Rays of his native Tampa. Gooden was inducted into the Mets Hall of Fame in 2010.

Ronald C. Modra/Sports Imagery/Getty Images

MVP Books collection

So instead of Tom Seaver pitching his 12th Opening Day as a Met, Mike Torrez was knocked out in the second inning of an 8–1 loss in Cincinnati, the club's first defeat on Opening Day since 1974. But unlike Mets teams of the previous decade that specialized in starting the season with a win and quickly settling into a routine of defeat, the 1984 Mets won the next two games behind rookie Ron Darling and second-year starter Walt Terrell, both taken from Texas in a deal for Lee Mazzilli two Aprils earlier. And then on the season's first Saturday, New York unleashed Dwight Gooden on an unsuspecting league.

The second overall pick in the 1981 draft, Gooden turned 19 in November 1983 and turned heads during spring training 1984. Cashen, who had overseen the development of many outstanding young pitchers in Baltimore, still felt the sting from Tim Leary's elbow injury after then-manager Joe Torre talked him into bringing the prospect north in 1981. Now Davey Johnson, a rookie manager whose playing career Cashen had also launched in Baltimore, pushed to get the phenom on his pitching staff. In his only full year in the minors, Gooden had been *Baseball America*'s Minor League Player of the Year with a 19–4 record and a staggering 300

strikeouts in 191 innings at Class-A Lynchburg—plus two more wins for Triple-A Tidewater in the playoffs. Gooden proved unflappable; he beat the Yankees in front of a full house in Fort Lauderdale in a late March exhibition start, a test to see if he could handle pressure. "Dwight Gooden does not have as good physical equipment as Tim Leary had in 1981," Cashen conceded, "but he's a different kind of person. Adversity rolls off his back easier."

Johnson, Cashen, and new pitching coach Mel Stottlemyre maneuvered the rotation so that Gooden's first regular-season outing would be at the climate-controlled Astrodome in Houston. Gooden said he threw as hard as he'd thrown in his life against the Astros, fanning five in five innings and getting the win. His next start was at Wrigley Field (the place that had been Leary's undoing in his 1981 debut), but the only thing injured was Gooden's pride in his first career defeat. He followed with two solid outings against Montreal, displaying mound aptitude in addition to his explosive fastball and knee-buckling curve. Gooden really made his mark on May 11 at Dodger Stadium. He fanned 11 in a four-hit shutout against Fernando Valenzuela, a game that also pushed the Mets into first place.

All-stars Darryl Strawberry, Dwight Gooden, Jesse Orosco, and Keith Hernandez check out the All-Star Game program in the locker room at Shea in July 1984. Orosco didn't see any action in the midsummer classic, but rookie Gooden struck out three and allowed only one hit in his two innings of work.
Richard Drew/AP Images

The Mets stumbled after a good start in California, and they headed into the ninth inning of the final game of the trip having dropped three straight. Darryl Strawberry, benched that day because of a recent slump, was summoned to face San Diego's Rich Gossage with New York down by a run. Strawberry delivered his first career pinch hit to tie the game. After escaping a jam from the mound in the bottom of the ninth, Jesse Orosco led off the 10th by hitting a flyball that Tony Gwynn botched in center field. Orosco made it to third base, scored on a sacrifice fly, and then set down the Padres in the bottom of the inning to secure the win.

Fans started a "K Korner" in Shea's previously vacant left-field upper deck to honor Gooden, by then known as "Doctor K" and shortened to "Doc." Mets fans, unaccustomed to attending games much less cheering, quickly embraced the team's long-awaited successes. Curtain calls brought heroes out of the dugout after home runs as well as lesser hits. "The Wave" arrived in New York "like acid rain defoliating the countryside," to use the words of *New York Times* columnist George Vecsey. Having crested at a University of Michigan football game the previous fall and gaining speed at Tiger Stadium in the spring, The Wave crashed ashore at Shea—by Vecsey's reckoning—during Doc Gooden's 2–1 loss to the Expos on June 22. The heavily promoted Flip Flop Night coincided with the ending of Hubie Brooks'

club-record 24-game hitting streak, so fans showered the field with shower shoes in tribute during his final at bat. It marked not only an end to Hubie's streak, but to shoe-related giveaways as well.

The Mets stayed hot, and the fans responded. Shea Stadium had the second-biggest attendance jump in the National League through the first half of the season, and the first-place Mets drew nearly 50,000 fans on the Sunday before the All-Star break to see ex-Red Bruce Berenyi put the finishing touches on a five-game sweep of Cincinnati. The 29-year-old Berenyi, acquired in June, was now the senior member of the staff, with veterans Craig Swan, Dick Tidrow, and Mike Torrez all set adrift during the season. It was no longer about catchy phrases or ad campaigns (like "Catch a Rising Star"); the team that fans had long been hoping for had finally arrived in the flesh at Shea Stadium.

An unprecedented four Mets headed to the All-Star Game in San Francisco: Gooden, Hernandez, Strawberry, and Orosco. Though Strawberry, who had a single and a stolen base in the game, was the first Met voted to start an All-Star Game since Dave Kingman in 1976, he was not the top Mets story. Gooden blew away American League hitters in his two innings, combining with Valenzuela to fan six straight and set a new all-star mark. The whole nation got to see what had fans at Shea jumping out of their seats and calling players back on the field for one more bow.

By the time the Mets returned from an 8–3 road trip on July 23, they were two and a half games ahead in the NL East. The Mets won back-to-back nights against the Cardinals in extra innings, beating familiar face Neil Allen both nights, the second on Hernandez's game-winning single against the man he was traded for. The next day the Mets got the third win in as many starts from rookie Sid Fernandez, stolen from the Dodgers by Frank Cashen the previous winter. Shea was at a fever pitch on Friday night when the second-place Cubs came to town. Gooden walked seven but fanned eight in a 2–1 win in front of a packed house, giving New York a four and a half–game lead in the standings.

The next day, in a nationally televised contest, the Mets tied the game in the seventh on a dropped flyball, chasing the Cubs' recently acquired ace, Rick Sutcliffe. The Cubs then mauled the Mets for eight runs in the eighth for the victory. The loss brought an end to New York's seven-game winning streak and started a seven-game skid. The Mets endured another six-game losing streak, including four straight at riotous Wrigley, but from August 11 forward they won as many games as any team in the National League.

The Mets finished the year with 90 victories overall and 48 at home—both totals marking the most by any Mets team since 1969. Chicago, however, comfortably secured its first postseason appearance since 1945, aided by their 12–6 record in head-to-head match-ups with New York. The other difference in '84 was Chicago's red-bearded ace, who went 16–1 after being acquired in June. Sutcliffe beat out Doctor K for the Cy Young Award, although Gooden did run away with the Rookie of the Year Award, the second in a row by a Met. Cubs second baseman Ryne Sandberg finished ahead of Hernandez (.311, 15 homers, 94 RBI, 97 walks) in the MVP balloting.

METS **TOP 50**

SID FERNANDEZ
1984–1993

Pitcher

Sid Fernandez didn't make the 1986 World Series pitching rotation, but he came in from the bullpen to rescue the Mets. Despite going 16–6, placing fourth in the league with 200 strikeouts, and striking out the side in the All-Star Game, Fernandez was bypassed in favor of Ron Darling, Dwight Gooden, and Bobby Ojeda. When Darling faltered in the fourth inning of Game 7, Fernandez came in and threw 2⅓ scoreless innings as the Mets rallied to beat the Red Sox. Boston manager John McNamara summed it up after the game, "Fernandez shut the door on us."

Charles Sidney Fernandez was drafted by the Dodgers in the third round in 1981, but after two appearances and six innings pitched in 1983, the Dodgers parted with him (and Ross Jones) for Bob Bailor and Carlos Diaz that winter. It was a heist worthy of *Hawaii 5-0*, the Honolulu native's favorite TV show and the theme song that played before his starts at Shea Stadium. To further acknowledge his love for the 50th state, El Sid wore number 50.

Three times between 1985 and 1990, Fernandez led the league in fewest hits allowed per nine innings, and he ranks third in major league history behind only Nolan Ryan and Sandy Koufax at 6.85. Fernandez is fourth in team history in strikeouts and starts. He battled weight and wildness, but few hitters relished facing the southpaw's slingshot delivery. After a decade as a Met and stints in Baltimore, Philadelphia, and Houston, he returned to Hawaii and became involved in youth sports.

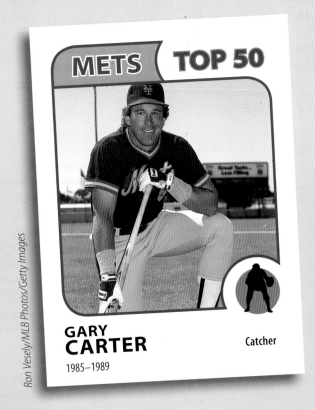

Ron Vesely/MLB Photos/Getty Images

METS TOP 50

GARY CARTER
1985–1989

Catcher

Gary Carter's arrival in New York signaled the shift from surprise contender to perennial power. A seven-time all-star in Montreal, Carter was the best catcher in the National League when the Mets swapped Hubie Brooks, Mike Fitzgerald, and two prized prospects for him in December 1984. With Carter batting cleanup and handling the talented but young Mets pitching staff, the championship he craved was within reach.

It seems fitting that spiritual and fair-haired Gary Edmund Carter should come out of Sunny Hills High School in California. What is surprising is that he spent much of his first two seasons in Montreal in right field before new manager Dick Williams put an end to that.

Carter came through for the Mets from day one. He homered to win his first game in New York and went on to become the first Met to hit 30 homers and drive in 100 runs in the same season. He snapped a horrific postseason slump to win Game 5 of the 1986 NLCS, homered twice in a World Series game, and most famously began the two-out rally in the 10th inning with the Mets on the verge of elimination in Game 6 of the '86 World Series. After going homerless for almost two months, he finally hit his 300th career home run in 1988. Carter, along with co-captain Keith Hernandez, left for free agency after the 1989 season. The only 1986 Met elected to Cooperstown (though with an Expos hat on his Hall of Fame plaque), Carter managed in the Mets farm system in 2005 and 2006.

The Mets had to be content with the franchise's remarkable 22-game turnaround and their wunderkind ace, who set the major league record with 276 strikeouts as a rookie, including 16-strikeout performances in consecutive outings in September. Those two masterpieces were preceded by an 11-strikeout performance against the Cubs in which the only hit was a slow roller by Keith Moreland.

New York had been especially resilient in tight games in 1984, going 29–20 in one-run contests and 11–1 in extra innings. The letdown of finishing in second place was a new kind of disappointment for Mets fans, although the second-place blues was not an uncommon affliction over the next several seasons.

New Kid in Town

The prospects that the Mets had been accumulating since Frank Cashen took over were now represented at every position except for first, third, and left field. Third base was intended for Ray Knight, a late-season acquisition in 1984 whose arrival from Houston pushed Hubie Brooks to shortstop, where he'd played only three innings previously. The Mets added more depth at the hot corner by sending pitcher Walt Terrell to Detroit for reserve Howard Johnson in December. And then came the trade nobody saw coming.

All-star Gary Carter, a cleanup hitter and Gold Glove catcher, arrived from Montreal. Unlike most previous four-for-one Mets deals (see Nolan Ryan 1971 and Tom Seaver 1977), this deal was among the finest in franchise history. The main piece shipped out was Brooks, 28 years old and coming off his best season since his rookie year. While Brooks would drive in 100 runs in 1985 as Montreal's shortstop, he did not have anywhere near the impact of Carter—nicknamed "Kid" and endowed with a level of enthusiasm not appreciated by all in the cynical 1980s. Catcher Mike Fitzgerald, outfielder Herm Winningham, and pitcher Floyd Youmans, Gooden's

buddy growing up in Tampa, were also sent to the Expos in the deal. Carter's predecessor in New York and successor in Montreal, Fitzgerald homered in his first major league at bat in 1983 but hit only two homers in 112 games in '84. Carter hit more than that in his first week as a Met.

Dwight Gooden, age 20, was the youngest Opening Day starter of the twentieth century, although he didn't get the win to kick off what would be the most dominant individual season in Mets history. Davey Johnson removed Gooden with a three-run lead in the sixth, but St. Louis tied the game in the ninth when reliever Doug Sisk walked Jack Clark with two outs and the bases loaded. Carter's New York career began with him getting drilled on the left elbow by Joaquin Andujar in the first inning, and he was hit again by Bill Campbell in the eighth. Facing ex-Met Neil Allen in the 10th, Carter drove a line drive into the left-field bullpen for the game-winning homer. Those December headlines proclaiming the "Yankification of the Mets" in reference to Carter's $1.8 million salary were rendered meaningless as Shea Stadium shook on April 9, 1985—and not from the 40-degree temperature. The Mets went on to win all five games of the opening homestand and started the year 8–1.

The Mets won an epic 18-inning affair with the Pirates and had a run of three straight shutouts in mid-May. That was also the month that Gooden, who began the season 6–1 with a 1.61 ERA, lost consecutive starts before kicking off a streak of 14 wins in his next 14 decisions. During that span, baseball went on a two-day strike; Strawberry missed 43 games due to thumb surgery (and got a five-year contract); Mookie Wilson went down with an injury, allowing Lenny Dykstra to stake his claim on center field; the Mets absorbed the worst defeat in club history, 26–7 at Philadelphia; and they won a surreal 19-inning marathon in Atlanta on July 4. In the 16–13 win, which lasted more than six hours, Hernandez hit for the cycle, Braves pitcher Rick Camp tied the game with a two-out homer in the 18th, and the fireworks display started at 4 a.m. Through it all the Mets dropped from first place to fourth and back to the top again. It was quite a summer. But they could not shake the Cardinals.

The season came down to two head-to-head series in the final three weeks. The Mets took two of three in September at Shea for a slim lead. The game they lost was a double-barreled shutout between St. Louis ace John Tudor and Gooden, who was already the youngest 20-game winner in history. Cesar Cedeno homered off Jesse Orosco for the game's lone run in the 10th, but that was not the most memorable extra-inning, 1–0 game between the clubs that year.

Just under three weeks later, with the Cards in front by three games and six games left to play, the Mets needed to sweep the three-game series at Busch Stadium, or their season was effectively over. Ron Darling threw zeroes for nine innings in the opener. Tudor, by now a 20-game winner, went 10. Finally in the 11th, Strawberry launched a home run off the scoreboard clock to give New York the 1–0 victory. The next night, Gooden put out his fifth outing of nine innings in one month for his final victory of the season. Doc's numbers on the year were from another time: 24–4,

DAVEY JOHNSON

It is one of those great baseball coincidences that the man whose flyball enabled the Mets to become world champions would one day manage the team to its second world championship. Even more coincidental is that Jerry Koosman, the pitcher who retired Davey Johnson to end the 1969 World Series, was eventually traded for Jesse Orosco, the man Johnson had on the mound when the Mets won the 1986 series.

A three-time all-star and Gold Glove second baseman for the great Orioles teams of the 1960s and early 1970s, Davey Johnson became a power hitter in Atlanta, joining Hank Aaron and Darrell Evans in 1973 as the first trio of teammates with 40 home runs in a season. Johnson became the first American to play for the Yomiuri Giants before returning stateside as a solid bench player for the Phillies and Cubs.

Johnson learned the game under legendary Baltimore skipper Earl Weaver. A mathematics major at Trinity College in Texas, Johnson provided computer printouts of the optimum Orioles lineup. "Earl put them in the waste basket," he said.

Johnson's first managing job was in 1979 with the Miami Amigos, winning the lone title in the short history of the Inter-American League. He then went into real estate, but Frank Cashen, who had overseen Johnson's development in the Orioles system, wanted him with the Mets. Johnson managed Class AA Jackson and was a roving instructor before taking over top affiliate Tidewater in 1983. He almost left for the Cardinals after a disagreement, but vice president Lou Gorman convinced him to stay. A year later he was manager for the big league club in New York.

Johnson took over a team that had finished last in five of the previous seven seasons and finished second to last in the other two. *Sports Illustrated* picked the rookie manager's club to finish fifth in 1984, just ahead of the Cubs. As it turned out, New York and Chicago battled all summer for the top spot in the division before the Cubs held off the 90-win Mets. With a talented pitching staff led by Dwight Gooden, New York compiled the best record in baseball over the next seven years. The Mets rolled to a franchise record 108 wins in 1986 and won the pennant and World Series in unforgettable fashion.

Johnson's Mets were a wild bunch, but the manager had a simple rule for handling players: "If they're relaxed and comfortable on the field and in the clubhouse, it's so much easier for them to contribute."

Johnson led the Mets to another division title in 1988 but lost to the underdog Dodgers in the NLCS. With many of his best players traded or let go as free agents, it appeared that the manager would be next following an 87–75 finish in 1989, New York's worst record under Johnson. He was fired after the team started 1990 with a 20–22 record. His 595–417 mark, .588 percentage, and two division titles are tops in club history.

After leaving New York, Johnson took the Cincinnati Reds to the postseason in 1995 and then won a Wild Card berth and a division title with Baltimore in 1996 and 1997; he was named the AL Manager of the Year in the latter season. He left both cities after feuds with ownership and was fired by the Dodgers after a second-place finish in 2000, his last major league managing job. He coached Team USA in the 2008 Olympics and 2009 World Baseball Classic and worked as a consultant with the Washington Nationals. He received his long overdue induction into the Mets Hall of Fame in 2010.

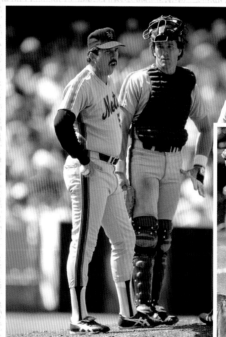

Davey Johnson joined a Mets team on the rise in 1984 and led them to two first-place and four second-place finishes in six full seasons while balancing a mix of savvy veterans, raw youngsters, and at times, all-around mayhem. *Andrew D. Bernstein/Getty Images*

Shown here with his ace closer Jesse Orosco, Johnson celebrated a world championship in 1986, the first for the franchise in 17 years. *Misha Erwitt/NY Daily News Archive/Getty Images*

MVP Books collection

1.53 ERA, 268 Ks, 276⅔ innings. The Mets won in 28 of his 35 starts; twice Sisk blew leads for him, and three times Gooden allowed one run or less and did not get a decision.

Needing to win the third game in St. Louis, the Mets had to go with rookie Rick Aguilera against veteran Danny Cox. The Thursday night game on October 4 was a battle that was not decided until the final at bat—as was the case in most of the previous 17 clashes between the teams. Keith Hernandez went five for five and drove in two runs in the must-win, but he was erased at the plate on a force play in the first inning and stranded in the ninth when Carter popped up to right field. The final was Cardinals 4, Mets 3, giving St. Louis a two-game lead with three games remaining.

A 98-win season, the best in club history next to 1969, was not enough. Over the long, cold winter the gnawing feeling of what might have been turned into what would be in 1986.

"Baseball Like It Oughta Be"

The Mets hit gold across the board in 1986. In the 25th season of Mets baseball, the team got everything right and provided wagons-full of entertainment. Even the annual slogan—"Baseball Like It Oughta Be!"—for once rang true.

After two hard-fought campaigns that ended with the Mets on the outside looking in, the '86 club bashed in the door. The manager felled the first blow in January. "We have a good chance not only of winning our division but of winning it handily," said Davey Johnson. "I want to be on a dominant team, and the Mets can dominate."

General manager Frank Cashen, who had built the team through a rich farm system and shrewd trades, added the final touches to the roster. While the Mets had been fortunate at second base with two of Johnson's players from Tidewater—Wally Backman and Kelvin Chapman—that plan foundered in 1985. The switch-hitting Backman was a force in the second spot in the lineup against right-handed pitching with a .324 average, but he batted more than 200 points lower against lefties; the right-handed Chapman hit a tepid .174 overall before being demoted in July 1985. Clearly, an upgrade was needed, and so New York acquired Minnesota's Tim Teufel for two minor league arms and an outfielder who was picked in the same first round as Darryl Strawberry in 1980: Billy Beane (a so-so hitter who would become an exceptional GM made famous by *Moneyball*). The club's biggest trade, however, was with the Red Sox for 28-year-old southpaw Bobby Ojeda, who had never fit in with Boston's staid clubhouse. The eight-player deal cost the Mets another former first-round draft pick, Calvin Schiraldi, who was then best known for allowing 10 runs during the 26-run shelling the previous June in Philly—but his true place in Mets lore was yet to come.

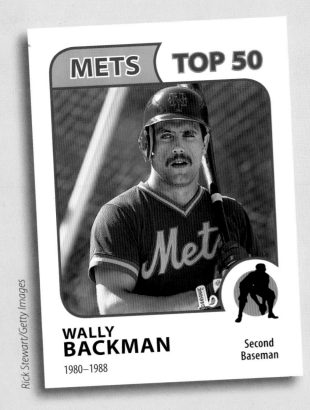

Rick Stewart/Getty Images

METS | TOP 50

WALLY BACKMAN
1980–1988

Second
Baseman

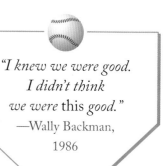

The feisty, fit-inducing combination of Lenny Dykstra and Wally Backman at the top of the Mets order was known as "Backstra." The 5-foot-9 Backman's solid glove caused opponents further consternation in the field.

Switch-hitting second baseman Walter Wayne Backman hit .297 from the left side and .097 from the right in his first full season in 1982 (.294/.165 for his career). He usually sat against lefty starters, but that made him a dangerous asset off the bench late in games, when Backman thrived in doing what it took to win. He did not start Game 3 of the 1986 NLCS, but his drag bunt and circuitous path to first base set the stage for Dykstra's game-winning home run. He didn't start Game 6 of the NLCS, but he entered in the 9th inning and scored the run that proved the difference in the 16th. (He also slid home with the winning run the previous day in the 12th.)

After starting all but one game in the 1988 NLCS loss to the Dodgers, Backman was traded to the Twins, and in 1990 he helped the Pirates win the NL East over his former mates. He retired in 1993. Past legal and financial problems derailed a promising managing career; the Diamondbacks fired him four days after hiring him to manage in Arizona in 2004. He worked his way back through independent baseball, and the Mets hired him to manage the Class-A Brooklyn Cyclones in 2010.

The '86 Mets made their way north after a 13–13 spring training. Amid the constant union–owner rancor, rosters had been reduced from 25 to 24 players. A 10-man pitching staff left six bench players and fewer late-inning options. So in the home opener, the Mets sent in pitcher Rick Aguilera to pinch hit in the 10th inning. The Mets lost in 13, putting them at 2–3. And then, in the blink of an eye, the race was over.

The Mets won all 11 remaining games in April, including a four-game sweep in St. Louis. After losing in Atlanta on May Day, New York reeled off seven more victories to stand at 20–4 with a five-game lead atop the division. The Mets continued to hammer opponents into submission with their bats and, on occasion, their fists.

"People call us one of the cockiest teams in the league, and other people talk about how arrogant we are," Davey Johnson proclaimed. "They're always looking to retaliate. But we enjoy fighting, and if that's what it takes, then we'll fight. We won't be pushed around."

They weren't. After Dodger Tom Niedenfuer allowed a grand slam to George Foster on May 27, he drilled Ray Knight with the next pitch. The ex-boxer charged the mound and punched Niedenfuer's back when the pitcher hoisted him off the ground. Another grand slam provoked another fight on June 30. Gary Carter's two home runs accounted for seven runs in the first two innings against Atlanta's David Palmer, and his curtain call fist pump led Palmer to drill the next batter, Darryl Strawberry. Palmer hit the slugger in the face with his mitt when Straw came running at him.

A fight off the diamond, at a Houston bar called Cooters, led to a night in jail for Darling, Ojeda, Aguilera, and Teufel, who was celebrating the birth of his first child and got slammed against a window by a police officer. In the Astrodome locker room the next day, adhesive tape was hung in stripes over each of the four players' lockers like prison bars. The Mets were 34 games over .500 and 12½ games in front.

The Mets' starting rotation was nearly unstoppable in 1986. Bob Ojeda, Sid Fernandez, Ron Darling, and Dwight Gooden each won at least 15 games and spearheaded a staff that led the NL with a 3.11 team ERA. *Focus on Sport/Getty Images*

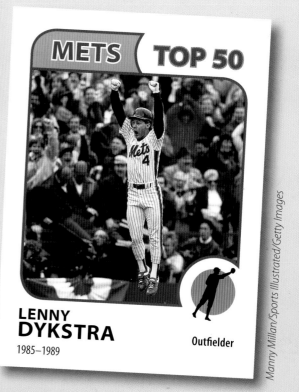

METS TOP 50

LENNY
DYKSTRA
1985–1989

Outfielder

The most memorable night of fisticuffs came three nights later, on July 22, during that same road trip. After trailing the Reds all game, the Mets were down to their last out when Dave Parker's error on a Hernandez flyball allowed two runs to score, tying the game. An inning later Cincinnati's Eric Davis stole second and then third, taking a swipe at Knight with his elbow. Shoving escalated into a full-scale brawl, resulting in the ejection of the two principals, plus Reds hothead Mario Soto and Mets rookie Kevin Mitchell. With Strawberry already thrown out for arguing a call earlier in the game, the Mets were facing a serious player shortage. So Gary Carter moved from catcher to third base, Ed Hearn entered the game behind the plate, Jesse Orosco moved from the mound to right field, and Roger McDowell took over the pitching. But that's not where they stayed.

With a man on second, two outs in the 11th, and lefty-swinging Max Venable coming to the plate, Orosco came in from right field and McDowell took his place in the field. Orosco got the strikeout and stayed on for the 12th; McDowell then reclaimed mound duties in the 13th, sending Orosco back to the outfield. Hearn led off the top of the 14th with a double and Orosco walked to put two men on. Howard Johnson then launched a one-out, three-run home run off Ted Power. For those scoring at home, Cincinnati native McDowell got the win, one of a club-record 14 he garnered in relief in a year when six Mets pitchers won in double figures.

Lenny Dykstra played all-out on every play. A left-handed center fielder with the gap-toothed grin, Dykstra was a hero of the 1986 postseason. His two game-changing ninth-inning hits in the NLCS and leadoff home run in Game 3 of the World Series got the Mets off the mat.

Leonard Kyle Dykstra seemingly grew up in a batting cage in Garden Grove, California. The Mets took him in the 13th round in 1981 and two years later he compiled an astounding 105 steals, 107 walks, 132 runs, and .358 average for a powerhouse Lynchburg club in Class A. He debuted in New York in 1985 and had an immediate impact. He hit .295 the following season and batted .300 in the '86 postseason while making his biggest contributions off the bench in the three October games he didn't start. His walkoff home run in Game 3 against Houston won the first postseason game played at Shea Stadium since 1973.

His subsequent numbers in New York weren't as eye popping, but fans loved the aggressive play of the 5-foot-10 "Nails." His take-chances attitude off the field was not embraced by management, however, and he was sent to the Phillies with Roger McDowell in a regrettable 1989 deal. A three-time all-star in Philadelphia, Dykstra placed second in the MVP voting in 1993, the same year he helped the Phillies win the pennant. Deemed a financial mastermind by experts in the field, he built a fortune and then lost it after his baseball career ended.

It was pandemonium at Shea after the Mets clinched the 1986 NL East division crown with a win over the Cubs on September 17. It was only the beginning of the celebrations for Mets fans that autumn. *Louis Requena/AP Images*

The wins kept coming. With the Mets up by 17 games, the *Daily News* started running a cartoon with the club's magic number for clinching: 41 . . . on August 7. The Mets had a winning percentage of .593 or better in every month of the season. They won 17 of 18 games against the Pirates and grabbed old favorite Lee Mazzilli to boost the bench after Pittsburgh released him. (New York jettisoned George Foster, who called the club's decision racially motivated.) When the *Daily News* caricature of Davey Johnson pulling a rabbit out of a hat reached the magic number two, fans streamed to Philadelphia to see the club clinch the NL East—except the Phillies (the lone club with a winning record against the Mets that year) swept the series. The split of a two-game series in St. Louis still left them a game shy of clinching. Dave Magadan's three-hit major league debut keyed Gooden's

4–2 clincher over the Cubs before fans swarmed the Shea Stadium field on the night of September 17.

The Mets broke the previous year's attendance record with 2,762,417 paid admissions. The '86 Mets were indeed something to see. They dominated at Shea (55–26) and everywhere else (53–28). The 108 wins were the most in the National League since the 1975 Reds and a total unsurpassed in the NL since the 1909 Pirates rang up 110 victories. The Mets had the league's best batting average (.263) and ERA (3.11), finishing 54 games over .500 and 21½ games ahead of the pack. How could they not win it all?

Proving It

Since the NL had little luck containing the Mets, the NFL joined the struggle. A Bears–Oilers game at the Astrodome forced a switch in the NLCS schedule, meaning the Mets no longer had home-field advantage, even though by the practice of the day it was the East division's year to host four of the seven games. So ex-Met Mike Scott got to stand on the mound first, and he was unhittable. Scott fanned 14

A joyous Lenny Dykstra circles the bases after winning Game 3 of the NLCS with a walkoff home run in the ninth. "Nails" led New York with a .304 average in the six-game set.
G. Paul Burnett/AP Images

batters and beat Gooden, 1–0, with the only run coming on a Glenn Davis home run. Ojeda restored order the next night as he went the distance to defeat another former Met, 39-year-old Nolan Ryan.

The last time the Mets had played a postseason game at Shea Stadium was 1973. The winner of that game, the recently retired Jerry Koosman, threw out the first pitch in Game 3 of the 1986 NLCS, but Ron Darling's offerings didn't seem to have too much more on them than Kooz's ceremonial toss. Houston jumped out to a 4–0 lead after two innings, and Bob Knepper held New York scoreless until an error gave the Mets their first run in the sixth. Strawberry crushed the next pitch to tie the game. A Ray Knight error allowed the Astros to take a 5–4 edge, which they carried into the ninth. Backman led off with a drag bunt and veered just shy of the Whitestone Bridge to avoid the tag. He then took second on a passed ball before Danny Heep flied out. Up stepped Lenny Dykstra, who like Backman had not started against the left-handed Knepper. Reliever Dave Smith got ahead 0-and-1, and then Dykstra lined the next pitch over the fence. The Mets mobbed Dykstra, the Astros trudged off the field, and New York led the series, two games to one.

The next night, though, it was back to great Scott and his purported scuffball in Houston's 3–1 win, as the Mets did more complaining than hitting. After a rainout eliminated any more off days in the series, Astros manager Hal Lanier flipped his rotation, bypassing rookie Jim Deshaies for the second straight game in favor of a veteran. Lanier turned to Ryan, who had clinched the 1969 NLCS as a Met at Shea.

For the second straight game, New York was held hitless until the fifth inning. Just after Houston grabbed a 1–0 lead, Strawberry tied the game with a drive that barely cleared the wall in right. Despite nine hits off Gooden in 10 innings, the game remained tied. The Mets still had only two hits when they came to bat in the bottom of the 12th against

Charlie Kerfeld, a certified hater of all things New York. Backman's hard smash off Denny Walling's glove was ruled a single and he took second on Kerfeld's wild pickoff throw. Hernandez was walked to bring up Carter, who was 1 for 21 in the series. Carter's smash up the middle brought Backman home just ahead of the throw to put the Mets one win from the pennant.

The specter of Scott pitching Game 7 loomed throughout the next afternoon at the Astrodome. Houston scored three in the first inning of Game 6 off Ojeda and might have had more if not for a botched suicide squeeze. Knepper had a two-hitter and a three-run lead entering the ninth. Dykstra roped a pinch-hit triple to center field to start an improbable rally, and Knight knocked in the tying run against Dave Smith, who blew his second save—both in Knepper starts with two outs to go. The real drama was just beginning.

Roger McDowell threw five innings of one-hit relief for New York while the Mets hitters were retired in order for four straight innings. That changed in the 14th when Backman singled in the go-ahead run. Orosco came in to try to save it, but Houston's Billy Hatcher answered with a high fly down the line that struck the foul pole. The game marched on.

By now, at the end of the workday in New York, every pitch from Houston was under scrutiny throughout the tri-state area, with people huddled in offices, crammed into bars, or sitting with fingers dug into the easy chair at home. Everyone from the Mets dugout to Madison Avenue knew that losing this game meant almost-certain doom at the hands of Scott.

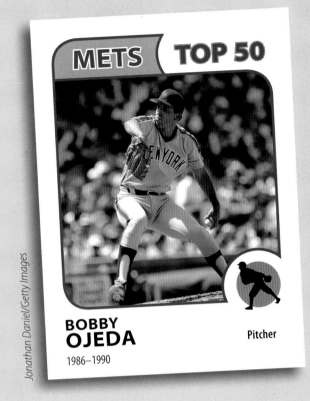

METS | TOP 50

BOBBY OJEDA
1986–1990

Pitcher

Bobby Ojeda was the most consistent Mets starter in 1986. Acquired from the Red Sox in an eight-player deal the previous winter, Ojeda began the season in the bullpen before entering the rotation in late April. He led the National League in winning percentage (.783), was second in ERA (2.57), and paced the 108-win Mets with 18 victories. The southpaw earned New York's first victory in both the NLCS and World Series after losses to open each series. Ojeda started Game 6 in both series, epics eventually won in extra innings.

Robert Michael Ojeda signed with Boston after no team drafted him out of the College of the Sequoias. He was the winning pitcher in the longest game in professional baseball history, tossing the 33rd inning between Triple-A Pawtucket and Rochester in 1981.

Ojeda tossed five shutouts for the Mets in 1988, three by 1–0 scores, and had the NL's best strikeout-to-walk ratio (4.03) when a September accident with electric hedge clippers required microsurgery. He missed the postseason and the Mets lost the NLCS. Sent to Los Angeles after the 1990 season, Ojeda later signed with Cleveland. He was the lone survivor in a March 1993 boating accident that killed Steve Olin and former Dodgers teammate Tim Crews. Ojeda came back from major head lacerations to pitch for the Indians and briefly appeared for the 1994 Yankees. A Mets minor league pitching coach (2001–2003), he later joined SNY as a pre- and post-game analyst.

As it became the longest postseason game in history, suddenly the runs came easily. Strawberry doubled and Knight knocked him in. Two wild pitches plated an insurance run and Dykstra singled home another, giving New York a 7–4 lead. Orosco, beginning his eighth inning of the series—and fifth in just over 24 hours—got the first out in the bottom of the 16th before three consecutive Astros reached base. Hernandez went for the force at second on a groundball, a play that proved crucial when Glenn Davis' subsequent single made it a 7–6 game instead of a tie. The noise was deafening as three Mets conferred on the mound. Hernandez, as he often did, took charge, telling Carter through Orosco in a tone both flippant and serious: "If you throw one more fastball, we're going to fight."

Kevin Bass saw all sliders. The sixth one—on a 3-and-2 pitch—he swung at and missed. The Mets burst out of the dugout to mob Orosco; Dykstra was on top of the pile with an arm raised to the Astrodome roof. With a .304 average, late-game heroics, and as many hits (seven) as anyone in the series, Dykstra was the offensive star for a club that batted .189 in the six-game NLCS yet somehow outscored Houston, 21–17. Orosco's three wins and Game 5 and 6 resolve made him the pitching star for the Mets. The writers in attendance, however, awarded the series MVP to Scott, who never did get that Game 7 start. His Cy Young Award and perhaps that disputed pitch movement helped get him a Wiffle Ball endorsement. The Mets didn't care. Really.

The team's in-flight celebration surpassed the heights—or lows—previously reached by the hard-partying ballclub. In *The Bad Guys Won*, author Jeff Pearlman explained what pushed the Mets from bad to banned by United Airlines was when the plane ran out of beer and little bottles of booze were distributed, along with cake. "I couldn't believe the things I saw going on there," recalled Kevin Mitchell, no shrinking violet himself. When the Mets were presented

Capping a thrilling six-game series against Houston, the Mets pulled off an incredible 16-inning win in Game 6 at the Astrodome to claim the National League pennant. *Ray Stubblebine/AP Images*

with a $7,500 tab, Davey Johnson began reprimanding the team in a closed-door meeting before ripping the bill in half. He paid it himself. The manager may not have been much on discipline, but he knew how to motivate his club.

Johnson also gave the Mets the day off after they dropped the first two games of the World Series to the Red Sox. Boston's Game 3 starter Oil Can Boyd took particular offense. The Mets had been to Fenway Park for an exhibition in September, checking out the ballpark layout and getting to know the locals—the players hitched rides from passing cars after the bus from the airport broke down. Travel arrangements during the World Series worked much better, as did scouting reports. Darrell Johnson, the 1975 pennant-winning Red Sox manager turned New York scout, informed the Mets of Boston's assumption that balls hit off the Green Monster would always be thrown in to the lead base. So with the Mets up 3–0 in Game 4 and a man on first, Mookie Wilson threw to second on a drive off the Monster and nailed Rich Gedman to snuff a rally. Though the Mets tied

the Series that night, the Red Sox won Game 5 and went to New York needing one win for their first title since 1918. Lady luck jumped on the home team's side with a page out of the 1969 Miracle Mets' playbook.

As inevitable as a world championship had seemed a month earlier, it was Amazin' indeed to see "the dream has come true," as announcer Bob Murphy put it moments after Orosco's glove went airborne after the final out. Mookie Wilson, whose place in Mets history was forever etched by that World Series, stood removed from the celebratory champagne spray and summed up the moment for everyone who suffered through the long, lean years at Shea: "When you've been here as long as I have and wondered if you'd ever seen this day, this is good enough."

One for the Ages
THE 1986 WORLD SERIES

Where do you start with the 1986 World Series? You don't start with a frigid opener at Shea Stadium, where the only run scores on an error, and you certainly don't start with a blowout loss the next night that had the T-shirt and hat guys in the parking lot selling their wares for half what they'd been charging on the way in.

You start the '86 series with Lenny Dykstra's leadoff home run in Game 3 at Fenway Park, as the Mets kept putting themselves in comeback mode and rising to the task. They plated four runs in the third game before Bobby Ojeda even stepped on the mound against his former teammates. The next night Gary Carter slugged two homers, Massachusetts-raised Ron Darling pitched seven shutout innings, and the World Series was tied. In Game 5, Bruce Hurst beat the Mets for the second time, and the Red Sox stood one victory from their elusive championship.

As had been the case in Game 6 of the NLCS in Houston, Ojeda took the mound for New York, but this game proved even stranger than the one in the Astrodome. First, a parachutist landed on the infield moments after the game started. The flyboy was ushered off the field, and the Red Sox ushered in a run in each of the first two innings. The Mets tied it in the fifth with a walk, a stolen base, two singles, an outfield error, and an infield groundout. The Red Sox took a one-run lead in the seventh, but Jim Rice was thrown out at the plate by Mookie Wilson—the second assist in the series for the outfielder with a maligned right arm. Coming in to relieve Roger McDowell with two outs and the bases full in the eighth, Jesse Orosco got out of the jam by inducing Bill Buckner to fly out. Orosco was immediately pinch-hit for, but unlike Boston's removal of Roger Clemens for a pinch hitter in the top of the inning, this move paid off. Lee Mazzilli singled and then went to second when former Mets reliever Calvin Schiraldi threw late on a bunt by Dykstra. Backman then bunted Maz over to third, and Mazzilli scored the tying run on Carter's sacrifice fly. The tense game remained tied until Dave Henderson homered in the 10th and Marty Barrett knocked in an insurance run for Boston.

Schiraldi retired the first two Mets in the bottom of the 10th, and the gracious hosts not only wheeled 10 cases of champagne into the Red Sox locker room, but the scoreboard even read—ever so briefly—"Congratulations Red Sox on Your World Series Victory." The message and the bubbly would have to wait.

Carter singled. Kevin Mitchell, who had been in the locker room changing, rushed to the plate and stroked a single. Ray Knight dropped a hit into center field, and the Mets had one run in and men on the corners. Boston manager John McNamara summoned warhorse Bob Stanley from the bullpen to get the last out, but he left his usual defensive replacement at first base, Dave Stapleton, on the bench. Mookie Wilson jackknifed out of the way of a Stanley palmball, and Mitchell crossed the plate with the tying run on the wild pitch. Amazin', but the Mets weren't done. Announcer Bob Murphy called the final pitch: "And a ground ball trickling. It's a fair ball. It gets by Buckner! Rounding third is Knight. The Mets will win the ballgame. They win! They win!"

A rainout the next night allowed the Red Sox to bring back Hurst in the finale to face Darling, both pitchers starting for the third time in the series. Hurst was far sharper, and it took a yeoman's

Bringing an end to a dramatic—almost dreamlike—Game 6, Ray Knight (22) heads home with the winning run in the 10th inning after Mookie Wilson's grounder trickled through the legs of Red Sox first baseman Bill Buckner. *Focus on Sport/Getty Images*

effort by Sid Fernandez out of the bullpen to keep New York in the game after Darling yielded three runs in the second inning. Keith Hernandez stroked a single off Hurst to plate two runs in the sixth and cut Boston's lead to 3–2. Carter drove in the tying run, and Hurst left the game. "Once we got Hurst out of there and they brought in their bullpen," Hernandez said, "we thought we had them where we wanted them." He was right.

With Schiraldi on the mound to start the seventh, Ray Knight lined a home run to left to give the Mets the lead to stay and—with his .391 average—wrap up series MVP honors. New York scored two more in the inning, and the 6–3 lead became 6–5 before Orosco came in and snuffed an eighth-inning Boston rally. Orosco then started a rally of his own with a butcher-boy RBI single in the bottom of the inning to make it 8–5. Orosco's hitting prowess is not what he's remembered for. He's remembered for throwing his mitt to the heavens after striking out Marty Barrett for the game's final out. The Mets didn't have to share their champagne after all.

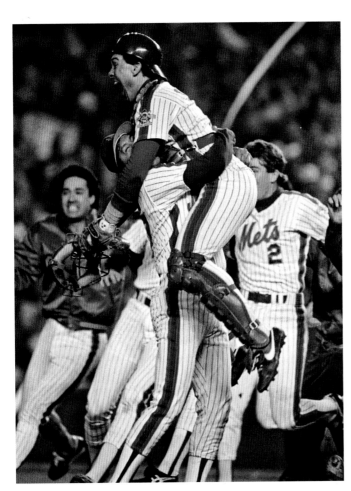

New York Mets are world champions again! *Paul Benoit/AP Images*

ANOTHER MIRACLE IN FLUSHING
(AKA, "The Buckner Game")

New York Mets 6, Boston Red Sox 5
World Series Game 6
Thursday, October 25, 1986
at Shea Stadium, Queens, NY

	1	2	3	4	5	6	7	8	9	10	R	H	E
BOS	1	1	0	0	0	0	1	0	0	2	5	13	3
NYM	0	0	0	0	2	0	0	1	0	3	6	8	2

Boston Red Sox	AB	R	H	RBI
Boggs, 3B	5	2	3	0
Barrett, 2B	4	1	3	2
Buckner, 1B	5	0	0	0
Rice, LF	5	0	0	0
Evans, RF	4	0	1	2
Gedman, C	5	0	1	0
Henderson, CF	5	1	2	1
Owen, SS	4	1	3	0
Clemens, P	3	0	0	0
Greenwell, PH	1	0	0	0
Schiraldi, P	1	0	0	0
Stanley, P	0	0	0	0
Totals	42	5	13	5

2B: Boggs, Evans. **HR:** Henderson. **SH:** Owen. **HBP:** Buckner. **Team LOB:** 14.
E: Buckner, Gedman, Evans.

New York Mets	AB	R	H	RBI
Dykstra, CF	4	0	0	0
Backman, 2B	4	0	1	0
Hernandez, 1B	4	0	1	0
Carter, C	4	1	1	1
Strawberry, RF	2	1	0	0
Aguilera, P	0	0	0	0
Mitchell, PH	1	1	1	0
Knight, 3B	4	2	2	2
Wilson, LF	5	0	1	0
Santana, SS	1	0	0	0
Heep, PH	1	0	0	0
Elster, SS	1	0	0	0
Johnson, PH-SS	1	0	0	0
Ojeda, P	2	0	0	0
McDowell, P	0	0	0	0
Orosco, P	0	0	0	0
Mazzilli, PH-RF	2	1	1	0
Totals	36	6	8	3

SF: Carter. **SH:** Dykstra, Backman. **SB:** Strawberry. **Team LOB:** 8.
E: Elster, Knight.

Pitching Summary

Boston Red Sox	IP	H	R	ER	BB	SO
Clemens	7	4	2	1	2	8
Schiraldi, L (0–2)	2.2	4	4	3	2	1
Stanley	0	0	0	0	0	0
Totals	9.2	8	6	4	4	9

New York Mets	IP	H	R	ER	BB	SO
Ojeda	6	8	2	2	2	3
McDowell	1.2	2	1	0	3	1
Orosco	0.1	0	0	0	0	0
Aguilera, W (1–0)	2	3	2	2	0	3
Totals	10	13	5	4	5	7

WP: Stanley.

Umpires: HP Dale Ford, 1B John Kibler, 2B Jim Evans, 3B Harry Wendelstedt, LF Joe Brinkman, RF Ed Montague.
Time of Game: 4:02
Attendance: 55,078

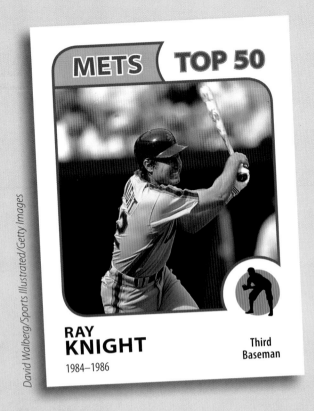

METS TOP 50

RAY KNIGHT
1984–1986

Third Baseman

Ray Knight's career as a Met was relatively brief, but he succeeded when it was needed most. A native of Albany, Georgia, Charles Ray Knight helped the Reds reach the postseason in 1979, his first year replacing Pete Rose at third base. After two and a half seasons in Houston, Knight came to the Mets in August 1984.

Knight batted .218 in his first full season in New York and opened 1986 on the bench. But once he got in the lineup, all he did was hit—and not just the baseball. The former Golden Gloves boxer famously mixed it up with Rose's Reds. Knight batted .298 with 11 homers and 76 RBI in 137 games, all career highs as a Met.

He knocked in the tying run in Game 6 of the NLCS in the ninth inning and seven tense innings later put the Mets ahead for good. In Game 6 of the World Series, his two-out single in the 10th staved off elimination, and then he whooped his way home with the winning run on Bill Buckner's famous error. Knight's tie-breaking home run in Game 7 and .391 series average landed him series MVP honors and a *Sports Illustrated* cover. His trophy still gleaming, the Mets balked at a two-year deal, so he unhappily moved on to Baltimore. Husband of legendary golfer Nancy Lopez, Knight was tabbed in 1996 to replace his former Mets manager, Davey Johnson, as skipper in Cincinnati. Knight lasted a year and a half and returned to broadcasting.

The Hangover

Rousing themselves out of bed with only a couple hours of sleep after their epic celebration the previous night, most of the Mets showed up at the victory parade looking pretty scruffy, but they made it to Manhattan to be toasted by an estimated 2.2 million supporters. But of all the bodies wedged into the "Canyon of Heroes," Dwight Gooden's was not among them.

In November, just before he turned 22, Gooden acknowledged via press release that he had an eight-month-old child and that the wedding with his high school sweetheart was off. It was his comments about his social life that were the most chilling, in hindsight. "Beer is what I drink and not much of that. Wine makes me sick. Drugs? No. I never use them and I never will," he said. Less than a month later he was arrested.

Gooden went wild on police after being pulled over in Tampa with friends, including 18-year-old Gary Sheffield—Gooden's cousin and the Milwaukee Brewers' first-round pick the previous year. Six police offers subdued Gooden during the roadside melee in December. A month after that his ex-fiancée was arrested with a gun in her bag as she went through security to pick up Gooden at LaGuardia Airport. And on April 1 came the announcement that he would miss what turned out to be the first two months of the season to undergo treatment following a positive test for cocaine. The pitcher had insisted on drug testing when he signed a $1.5 million contract during the winter. The idea was to put an end to allegations about his off-field problems and speculation about the reasons for his transformation on the mound from utterly dominant in 1985 to generally outstanding in 1986 (17–6, 2.84 ERA, 200 strikeouts). The Mets were left to pick up the pieces and get on with the business of defending their title without Gooden and with no idea when he'd return.

With his distinctive sidewinder delivery, Terry Leach became a key arm for the Mets in 1987, posting an 11–1 record and 3.22 ERA while doing his share of both starting and relieving for the injury-ravaged staff. *Stephen Dunn/Getty Images*

The world champions went into the season with several changes to the roster. Danny Heep and World Series MVP Ray Knight left as free agents (with acrimony). Kevin McReynolds, a left fielder with superior skills and a laid-back Arkansas manner, arrived from San Diego in an eight-player trade that dispatched Kevin Mitchell. And late in March the Mets sent backup catcher Ed Hearn and two minor leaguers to the Royals for infielder Chris Jelic and a 24-year-old pitcher named David Cone.

Not only did Cone turn out to be one of the great steals in franchise history, the deal was also ideally timed. With Gooden out and Roger McDowell missing a month because of a hernia, the Mets started the season in need of pitching and remained on the lookout for it throughout 1987. The club even tried to bring back Tom Seaver a third time. Acquired by Boston in 1986, Seaver had been in the visiting dugout but unable to play in the World Series. The 42-year-old icon could not physically continue in 1987, a pattern too familiar in Flushing that year. Injuries seemed to leap from one starter to another. Bob Ojeda left after one inning in Atlanta on May

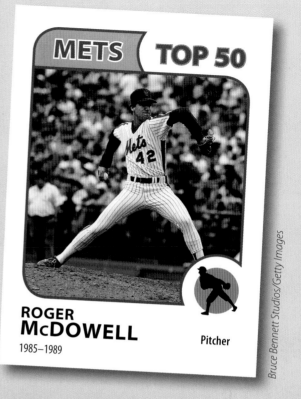

METS TOP 50

ROGER McDOWELL
1985–1989

Pitcher

Prankster Roger McDowell specialized in giving hot foots to teammates and is known for his "second spitter" cameo on *Seinfeld*, but he was also one of the great Mets relief pitchers. Like another reliever who wore number 42, Ron Taylor of the 1969 Mets, McDowell played a key role in winning a championship.

Roger Alan McDowell grew up a Tom Seaver fan . . . in Cincinnati. The Mets drafted him in the third round in 1982 from Bowling Green State and thought enough of his sinker to bring him north in 1985 even though he was coming off elbow surgery. He pitched 62 games as a rookie and a then-club record 75 the next year. McDowell broke Jesse Orosco's club record with 14 relief victories, and they became the first Mets bullpen duo to each save 20 games in the same season. McDowell threw seven shutout inning in the 1986 NLCS, including a career-high five innings in the epic Game 6. Although he gave up two runs and blew the save, McDowell earned the win in Game 7 of the World Series thanks to his team's five late-inning runs and Orosco's save.

In 1989 McDowell and Lenny Dykstra were sent to the Phillies in a horrific deal for Juan Samuel. McDowell spent time with the Dodgers, Rangers, and Orioles before shoulder injuries ended his career. McDowell was voted the top right-handed reliever on the 40th anniversary Mets team in 2002, and he joined the Braves as pitching coach in 2006.

The defending world champions, ten and a half games out in July at the height of their injury bug, had cut St. Louis' lead down to one and a half games on September 11 in the first of a crucial three-game series. (In 1987 the Mets became the second major league team and first New York club to surpass three million fans.) Darling had a 4–1 lead and a no-hitter with one out in the sixth when Vince Coleman tried a drag bunt. Darling, who would later become the first Mets pitcher to win a Gold Glove, landed awkwardly on his thumb. Even with his hand swelling, Darling picked Coleman off second. He was removed the next inning and realized he needed to go to the emergency room. Darling was approaching his car in the players' parking lot when a ball whistled past and dented his Mercedes. It was Terry Pendleton's game-tying home run in the ninth off McDowell. The Cards won the game and eventually the pennant. Darling, who had thumb surgery on September 13, 1987, recounted the climactic Pendleton home run in his book, *The Complete Game*: "He managed to tie the game, erase the lead I'd left behind, and dent my car, all with one swing. It was so almost surreal—so much so that I could never bring myself to fix that dent."

And you thought only Mets *fans* were fatalistic.

Another Title Quest

"The Year of the Home Run," 1987, saw more longballs hit than in any other year in history, and the Mets joined in the fun. Seven players homered in double digits, with Darryl Strawberry and Howard Johnson becoming the first teammate duo in history to hit 30 homers and steal 30 bases in the same season. The Mets set new club records for home runs (192) and batting (.268). They also broke the franchise scoring mark by 60 runs, but the problem was the staff allowed 120 more runs than in 1986. New York still had the bodies to take back the division; they just needed those bodies to be healthy.

9 with elbow pain; he returned in September. Rick Aguilera threw four warmup pitches on May 26 before winding up on the disabled list with a sprained elbow; he returned in August. Cone graduated from decent reliever to eye-opening starter and then broke his right little finger bunting in San Francisco on May 27; he returned in August. Sid Fernandez missed most of August with a knee injury.

The Mets got surprisingly good results from Terry Leach, who had pitched a 10-inning one-hitter for the Mets on the final day of 1982 and then spent most of the next five years buried in the minors. The thoughtful sidewinder filled in as a reliever and then joined the rotation, going 10–0 before losing in August for the only time all year.

The lone healthy starter was Ron Darling, and he was perched on the mound in the biggest game of the season.

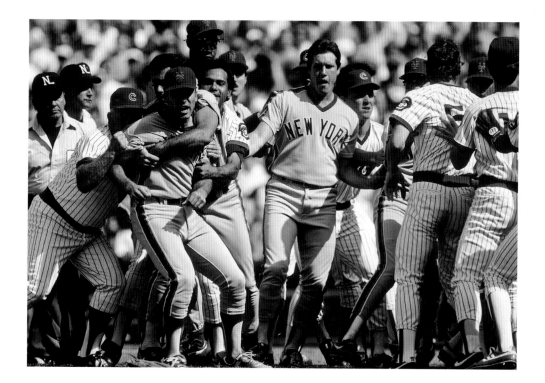

The Mets scraped and scrapped their way to a dominating season in 1988, winning 100 games and leading the league in most categories—including fights. Here they scuffle with the Cubs during a June game at Wrigley Field.
Jonathan Daniel/Allsport/Getty Images

The Mets started the home portion of the 1988 schedule with three straight shutouts and five consecutive wins on their way to an unmatched 56-win season on their home turf. They were almost a full run better per game offensively away from Shea, but the staff allowed 96 fewer runs at home than on the road, fueling a 2.91 ERA overall that was the best in the majors and second best in franchise history. (The 1968 team was the only one to post a better ERA than the 1988 team, but in the "Year of the Pitcher," the 2.72 mark was only good enough for fourth best in the NL.)

The 1988 Mets staff dominated most categories and most batters: fewest hits per game (7.9), fewest home runs allowed (78), lowest opponent batting average (.236), lowest opponent on-base percentage (.293), fewest walks (404), and most strikeouts (1,100). Combine that with the best-fielding team (115 errors), the highest scoring team in the National League (703 runs), and the league leader in home runs (152), and you have a 100-win ballclub that won its division by 15 games.

The Mets dominated the NL West champion Dodgers during the regular season, winning 10 of 11 games, including all six at Dodger Stadium. L.A.'s lone win came on June 1 in a game the Mets nearly pulled out in the bottom of the ninth. New York beat Orel Hershiser, 2–1, the only time they faced him. It was the last game Hershiser lost that season and the second-to-last in which he allowed a run.

Hershiser did not allow a run in any of his six September starts, setting the major league record with 59 consecutive scoreless innings. And though regular season and postseason records do not mix, it's worth noting that he tossed another eight shutout innings in the opener of the 1988 NLCS against the Mets. Then, after 67⅓ consecutive scoreless innings by Hershiser, Darryl Strawberry doubled home Gregg Jefferies. The Mets still trailed in the opener, 2–1, when, with right-handed Kevin McReynolds due up, Tommy Lasorda signaled to the bullpen, removing the shutout machine from the game. He summoned closer Jay Howell, who promptly walked McReynolds and then lost the game on a two-out, two-run double by Gary Carter.

In the ninth inning of Game 4, the Mets were leading by two runs and seemed poised to go up by two games in the series, when Mike Scioscia came to bat with a man on. Scioscia, with all of three home runs during the season, ripped a Dwight Gooden offering into the bullpen to tie the game. Kirk Gibson homered in the top of the 12th against McDowell—only the second blast allowed by the reliever in 90-plus innings all year. With Howell suspended for two games for getting caught with pine tar on his glove, former Mets Tim Leary and Jesse Orosco got the first two outs before Hershiser was summoned from the bullpen, a night after tossing seven innings. He got McReynolds to pop up with the bases loaded. The series was even.

Gregg Jefferies provided a spark for the Mets after getting called up from the minors in late August 1988. Not only did he displace Howard Johnson at third base and bat .321 down the stretch, but he collected a series-high (tied with Strawberry) nine hits in the NLCS against Los Angeles.
Heinz Kluetmeier /Sports Illustrated/ Getty Images

The Dodgers thumped the Mets and Sid Fernandez the next afternoon. "El Sid" had taken the rotation spot of Bobby Ojeda, who had severed the tip of his left middle finger while using electric hedge clippers the week the Mets clinched the division title. With the Mets trying to avoid elimination, David Cone threw a complete game in Los Angeles against Leary. McReynolds went four for four with a homer and knocked in three to keep the Mets alive, for the time being. A crucial error by Jefferies and a terrible outing by Darling doomed New York in Game 7. Hershiser reverted to type with a shutout, and the favored Mets lost an NLCS for the first time in four trips.

The 1988 awards season continued the trend of losses to the now world champion Dodgers. Strawberry led the league with 39 home runs, knocked in 101 runs, and missed another 30–30 season by one stolen base. McReynolds homered 27 times, drove in 99, batted .288, went an unprecedented 21 for 21 in steals, and led NL outfielders with 18 assists. Yet the two Mets split the MVP vote: McReynolds was third, Strawberry second, and Kirk Gibson first despite the Dodgers outfielder's inferior numbers. No one could argue about Hershiser for Cy Young, though Cone had gone 20–3 for a league-best .870 winning percentage. He also placed second in the league in strikeouts (213) and ERA (2.22, which was two points better than Hershiser), but Dodger blue won again.

It was hard to accept that the Mets had been beaten by a team with so little hitting and not much pitching beyond "Bulldog" Hershiser, who appeared in four of the seven NLCS games. Fate had spared the 1986 team. This time, it turned on them. Unlike Buckner in '86, the gimpy-legged, mustachioed veteran of '88—Gibson—held a stake to New York's heart and the battery of Hershiser and Scioscia drove it home.

Jumping the Shark

Five years removed from a National League renaissance in both New York and Chicago, the Cubs made another run at the NL East in 1989 with an almost entirely different cast. Chicago hadn't had a winning record since losing the last three games of the 1984 NLCS in San Diego, but Don Zimmer's club was re-armed with prospects turned into stars:

Shawon Dunston, Mark Grace, and Greg Maddux, plus "Wild Thing" Mitch Williams, who closed out opponents in the Chicago night (the Mets had played the first official night game in Wrigley history on August 9, 1988).

The 1989 Mets were trying to retool on the go, and it was a clunky fit. Over the winter they shipped Wally Backman to Minnesota to make room for Jefferies at second base. Though the deal showed a forward-looking mindset, it angered supporters of "Backstra"—the mythical two-headed beast at the top of the lineup. The other half of the creature was slain on June 18, when the Mets sent Lenny Dykstra and Roger McDowell to Philadelphia for Juan Samuel. A shaky second baseman, Samuel had been moved to center field that year by the Phillies. His arrival displaced Mookie Wilson and led to the banishment of the popular Met to Toronto. Joining Mookie on the Blue Jays was Lee Mazzilli, whom the Mets released the same day they traded Wilson for reliever Jeff Musselman. Maz and Mook ended the year playing in the postseason, which was more than their ex-teammates could say.

The July 31 trading deadline saw New York move five pitchers—including starter-turned-reliever Rick Aguilera, underrated prospect Kevin Tapani, and ballyhooed bust David West—to the Twins for Frank Viola. A Long Island native and St. John's product, Viola had faced Ron Darling in a legendary NCAA tournament game at Yale in 1981. Now the 1987 World Series MVP and 1988 AL Cy Young winner was replacing injured Gooden at the top of the Mets rotation. Seven games behind and in the midst of a seven-game losing streak when the trade was made, the Mets pushed their way north in the standings to stand one and a half games out by the final week of August. The only wins out of the next dozen games came in a three-game sweep in Los Angeles, highlighted by Viola beating Hershiser, 1–0, in the first regular-season meeting of defending Cy Young winners.

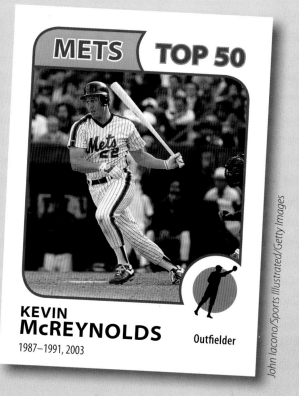

METS TOP 50

KEVIN
McREYNOLDS
1987–1991, 2003

Outfielder

John Iacono/Sports Illustrated/Getty Images

Laconic left fielder Kevin McReynolds never seemed suited for New York, but he made the Mets' lineup more formidable. He finished third in MVP voting in 1988, and his 27 homers, 99 RBI, and .496 slugging percentage all surpassed MVP-winner Kirk Gibson's numbers. Kevin Mac also led NL outfielders in assists (17) and set a major league mark for most steals without getting caught (21). With his team needing a win to force Game 7 in the NLCS, McReynolds had four hits and three RBI in the 5–1 win at Dodger Stadium. Gibson's club, however, got the ultimate prize.

Walter Kevin McReynolds was a star at the University of Arkansas and cover boy on the inaugural issue of *Baseball America* in 1981. He entered the majors as a center fielder and helped San Diego win the 1984 pennant in his first full season, though he missed the World Series because of a broken bone in his hand.

He came and went from the Mets in two December blockbusters. The newly crowned world champs traded future MVP Kevin Mitchell and four minor leaguers for McReynolds and two others in 1986; exactly five years later, the Mets shipped him plus Gregg Jefferies and Keith Miller to Kansas City for Bret Saberhagen and Bill Pecota. McReynolds returned for a final season in 1994 in a deal that rid New York of Vince Coleman. McReynolds, who hit 22 or more home runs in his first four seasons as a Met, retired as fourth on the club's home run ledger (122) and sixth in RBI (456).

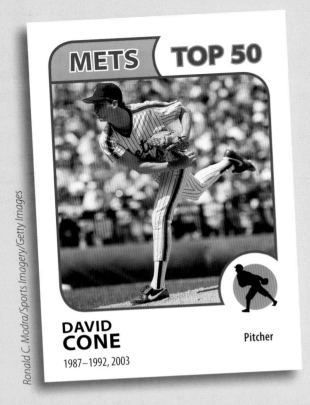

METS · TOP 50

DAVID CONE
1987–1992, 2003

Pitcher

Changing teams five times in less than three seasons, David Cone was a "gunslinger for hire" in the mid-1990s, but the deal that made him a Met in 1987 was one of the great robberies in club history. A native of Kansas City, David Brian Cone debuted for the Royals in 1986 but was dispatched to New York for Ed Hearn, Rick Anderson, and Mauro Gozzo the following March.

A depleted staff forced Cone into the Mets rotation in '87, but a broken finger forced him out. He didn't make his first start in 1988 until May, and he threw a three-hit shutout. He won his first seven decisions and then his last eight to finish 20–3 for the NL East champs. After getting hit hard in his first NLCS start in 1988, he tossed the final inning in the Game 3 victory and then threw a five-hitter in Game 6.

Cone won 14 games in each of his next three seasons as a Met, twice leading the league in strikeouts and racking up 19 K's in the last game of 1991. He led the majors in strikeouts in 1992 but not the NL because he became a Blue Jay in August and won a world championship. He went home to Kansas City and won a Cy Young in 1994, returned to Toronto, and then was shipped back to New York—as a Yankee. He won four more World Series and threw a perfect game in pinstripes before joining Boston in 2001. He briefly came out of retirement with the 2003 Mets before retiring for good.

Even with a loaded rotation and 24 saves from Randy Myers, the Mets failed to win 90 games for the first time since 1983. They split four September games with the Cubs, who had surpassed Montreal atop the division in early August. And a season that began with a fight—Strawberry punched Hernandez during the team photo in spring training because Mex hadn't backed Straw in a contract dispute—ended with a brawl against the Phillies following the final out in the last game of the year at Shea. Again the team was split on support for the instigator. More Mets sided with former teammate McDowell than with Jefferies, who had started the scuffle after McDowell said something to the hot-tempered Met. Phillies manager Nick Leyva observed, "There were thirty guys on our side rooting for Roger and twenty guys on their side rooting for Roger."

That game was also the last Shea Stadium hurrah for co-captains Hernandez and Carter. Two stars imported from division rivals, they had added veteran presence and skill to a young team just learning to win. The Mets of Keith and Kid had mostly moved on by 1989, and now the first two captains in club history—their contracts expiring—would follow.

The Mets captured New York City's only World Series title of the 1980s, but the overwhelming feeling was of promise unfulfilled. The Mets won more games than any major league team from 1984 through the end of the decade, yet the A's, Cardinals, Dodgers, Phillies, and even Royals went to more World Series in the 1980s. Was it the Mets' makeup? Did the party lifestyle curtail the team's ability? Fred Wilpon, closing in on his first decade as team president, had his criteria for what kind of players he thought should represent the Mets.

"I like to see the Mets win within the white lines and be quiet outside the lines," Wilpon said shortly after the 1989 season. "I believe in being responsive, in having that fire in the belly, but as non-dramatic as possible, as conservative as one can be."

1980s METS YEAR-BY-YEAR

YEAR	W–L	PCT.	GB	FINISH	
1980	67–95	.414	24	5th in NL East	Despite new ownership and some early summer magic, the Mets settled in for their fourth straight season of at least 95 losses. Ray Burris led the team with 13 defeats and 170⅓ innings, the first season in Mets history without a pitcher logging at least 200 innings.
1981	41–62	.398	18 ½	5th	The Mets greatly benefited from the split season, washing away a record of 17–34 in the first half; they went 24–28 post-strike to compete for a division title—or half of one. Not bad for a team without a win from top starter Craig Swan or phenom Tim Leary.
1982	65–97	.401	27	6th	The 35-by-26-foot DiamondVision was erected in left field, making Shea once again state of the art (briefly). Close plays were soon barred from being replayed on the color video display board because the men in blue protested being shown up by the facts.
1983	68–94	.420	22	6th	Veteran closer Neil Allen allowed a two-out grand slam to Bo Diaz in a crushing 10–9 loss at Philadelphia on April 13. Emotional stress and control problems resulted in Allen becoming a starter, going back to the pen, and finally on to St. Louis, for Keith Hernandez.
1984	90–72	.556	6 ½	2nd	Along with 1969, 1997, and 2005, this is a watershed season in which the Mets transformed from also-ran to bona-fide contender. Davey Johnson took over as manager, Dwight Gooden, Ron Darling, and Sid Fernandez were rookies, and the club held first place later than any year since 1973.
1985	98–64	.605	3	2nd	The 1985 season is rightly remembered as the Year of Doc, but the Mets bats were alive as well. They tied the 1970 club mark with 695 runs scored and set franchise records for hits (1,425), home runs (134), and RBI (651)—all of which would be broken in 1986.
1986	108–54	.667	–	1st	The best Mets West Coast trip ever (8–1) ended with a bang. Up by a run with one out in the 11th in San Diego on August 27, Lenny Dykstra threw to catcher John Gibbons, who was decked by Garry Templeton. Gibbons got up and threw to third for the final out.
1987	92–70	.568	3	2nd	Despite 457 total days on the disabled list by the pitching staff, the Mets had five double-digit winners: Sid Fernandez (12), Ron Darling (12), Rick Aguilera (11), Terry Leach (11), and Dwight Gooden, who went 15–7 after missing two months to drug rehabilitation.
1988	100–60	.625	–	1st	After reaching 1,000 career RBI in 1987, Gary Carter hit his eighth home run of 1988—career number 299—on May 16. It took 225 at bats before he reached 300, when he went deep at Wrigley against Al Nipper, who had surrendered a Carter homer in the 1986 World Series.
1989	87–75	.537	6	2nd	Sid Fernandez was masterful yet unlucky in Atlanta on July 14, striking out 16—a new record for a Mets lefty—and retiring 16 in a row before Lonnie Smith's game-ending homer. El Sid also threw the first game in NL history without an assist being recorded, on June 25.

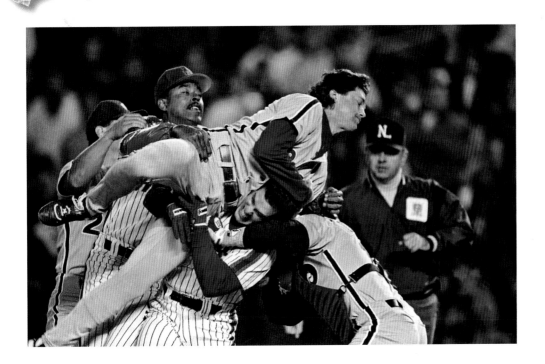

The decade of the 1980s ended with a bang for New York, as an all-out brawl with the Phillies marred the final home game of the 1989 season. It marked the end of a decade filled with both on-field and off-field turmoil from a deeply talented baseball squad.
Susan Ragan/AP Images

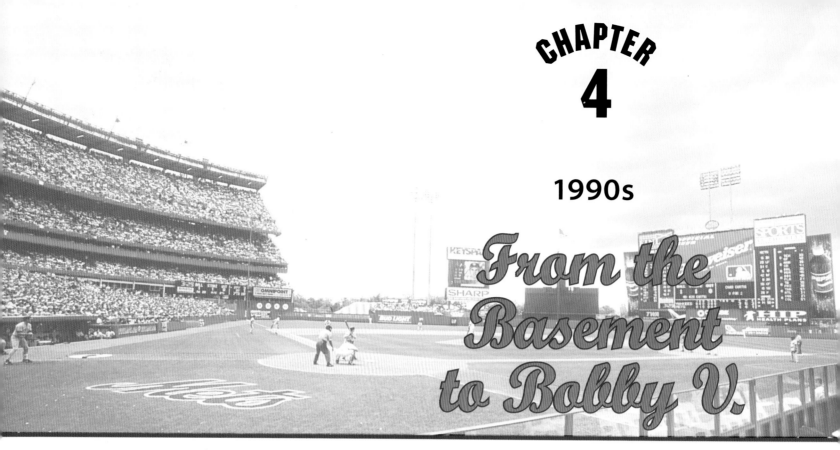

1990s

From the Basement to Bobby V.

David Seelig/Allsport/Getty Images

MVP Books Collection

The Mets entered a new decade with the mindset of the 1980s yet with vastly different personnel. The Opening Day lineup in 1990 had only three starters left from the 1986 championship team. It also opened a week late.

A 32-day lockout kept spring training camps from opening until March 19 and thus delayed the start of the regular season. When the Mets finally hit the field at Shea Stadium on April 9, they were met with a 12–3 drubbing by the Pirates that surpassed the club record for runs allowed on Opening Day, set in the franchise's first game in 1962. The loss also signaled a shift in fortunes in Pittsburgh, which had supplanted New York in the NL East basement in the 1980s. The Mets' glory days ended with them looking up at the first-place Pirates.

Though Frank Viola got off to a 7–0 start, New York had trouble winning when "Sweet Music" wasn't on the mound. Dwight Gooden began the season with a losing record for the first time in his career, Sid Fernandez was 2–4 despite a 3.10 ERA, and David Cone's early season troubles were summed up by his April 30 tantrum in Atlanta.

With two men on and two outs, umpire Charlie Williams ruled Cone missed tagging first base on a seemingly routine infield play. The pitcher argued vehemently with the umpire, his back to the plate as Dale Murphy scored. Gregg Jefferies tried to turn Cone's body to show him lead-footed Ernie Whitt heading for home, but he kept the ball locked in his glove while arguing to no purpose. The first two months of the season were excruciating—especially for Davey Johnson.

Coaches Bill Robinson and Sam Perlozzo had been fired in the wake of the 1989 season, and speculation was that the manager would be next. To the surprise of many, that call did not come during the season. With the Mets in fourth place and staggering around the .500 mark, the month of May became a Johnson death watch, with players-only meetings and GM Frank Cashen traveling with the club. The watch finally ended on May 29, with the Mets at 20–22 and five and a half games behind Pittsburgh.

Johnson had managed and won more games than anyone in Mets history. The club did not want him to meet with the players following his dismissal. Said Johnson, "I wasn't given a reason for my dismissal, and I didn't ask for one."

Ballplayers often say it's unfair for a manager to be fired because of players' mistakes, but Ron Darling summed up the laissez-faire style that had once worked so well for Johnson yet ultimately led to his downfall: "He gave us the room to succeed and we didn't do it." Closer John Franco, acquired from the Reds in a closer-for-closer deal for Randy Myers, was surprised at the attitude of his new club. "We didn't have that fire in our eyes [in 1990]. The Mets had that in 1986. We hated them because they had it."

Organizational soldier Bud Harrelson fulfilled a life's dream by taking over as Mets manager. As is usually the case when a laid-back manager is replaced, Harrelson pledged a no-nonsense attitude and stricter enforcement of the rules. After stumbling through the first week, the Mets won three of four from the Pirates and then found their groove—and first baseman—at Wrigley Field.

Juan Samuel, acquired at such a high price in 1989, had been traded to the Dodgers over the winter for reliever Alejandro Pena and first baseman Mike Marshall, the latter starting most of the first two months of the season while Dave Magadan filled in off the bench. With Marshall slowed by a bad back, Magadan got the start at Wrigley on June 12. He homered in the first inning and went four for four with two walks and six RBI in a 19–8 thrashing of the Cubs. The Mets scored 24 runs the next day, and Magadan had another four hits in a doubleheader sweep in Chicago. Magadan was suddenly among the league leaders in hitting and Marshall was on his way to Boston for three minor leaguers.

The Mets, nine and a half games out on June 7, were tied for first on June 29. Despite decimating injuries, New York took sole possession of first for a few days each in July, August, and September. Kevin Elster's injury hurt the team the most. A steady shortstop with pop, Elster underwent shoulder surgery that forced Howard Johnson to shift to short, while Jefferies moved from second to third, and new acquisition Tommie Herr took over at second base. Herr, a thorn in New York's side as a Cardinal, was one of three late-season

The Last Straw

Darryl Strawberry was treated for alcoholism and battled marital problems as well as the Mets front office over his contract in 1990. He vowed not to sign with the team after Davey Johnson was fired, and he called the club's subsequent offer of $9.1 million for three years "insulting." In the end, Strawberry signed with his hometown Dodgers for five years and $20.3 million—and wishing he'd stayed with the Mets.

Joe McIlvaine also left New York for the West Coast after a decade with the organization. While running the scouting department, McIlvaine had signed Strawberry, along with many of the names that helped turn the Mets into champions. The heir apparent to Frank Cashen, McIlvaine bristled at the slow timetable for the transfer of power and the criticism laid his way over the Johnson firing and the dubious trades of the late 1980s.

Coming back to the Mets from California was Hubie Brooks. Now a right fielder, Brooks took Strawberry's place following another questionable deal—this one sending Bob Ojeda and Greg Hansell to L.A. Brooks matched his 1984 Mets high of 16 homers in 1991, but he missed the last six weeks of the season. His .238 average was his lowest since coming to the majors in 1980, and 50 RBI was not what was expected of Strawberry's replacement in the cleanup spot. Brooks was out of the four-hole by Memorial Day.

By then Bud Harrelson had gotten angry with reporters over questions of his handling of his fielders and had quit his own WFAN pregame show because he thought the show's host—lifetime Mets fan Howie Rose—was too negative. Gregg Jefferies made news of his own by sending a fax to WFAN begging for fan sympathy; he was mocked in all corners as a whiner. Yet with all this—plus Gooden getting hit like never before—the Mets began July by winning 10 straight games, including the first 7–0 road trip in club history. Less than a month after that streak concluded, the

additions to try to bolster the injury-riddled club. Charlie O'Brien took over the catching duties, and Pat Tabler helped off the bench and filled in at the corner outfield spots as the Mets limped to the finish. Their chances diminished greatly following the fateful decision to start Julio Valera over Ron Darling in a crucial series the first week of September. The Mets were coming off a 6–0 homestand and had won seven straight heading into a three-game, two-day series at Three Rivers Stadium. They scored only once in a doubleheader sweep by the Pirates, and then Valera didn't make it out of the third inning in the third game. Valera never won another game for the Mets. The Mets never again were in first place in 1990.

Though New York was eliminated from postseason contention before the season-ending series in Pittsburgh, Magadan was contending for a batting title (he finished third at .328) and two pitchers had a shot at 20 wins. Gooden, who had bounced back from a slow start to win 16 of 17 decisions, failed in his bid for number 20 in the penultimate game. Viola, loser of three straight close games, topped the disinterested Pirates in the season finale for his 20th. What the Mets would give for such hollow victories in 1991.

Despite incredible promise and expectations, Darryl Strawberry never quite reached the Hall of Fame potential many expected of him. By 1990, his home life was starting to generate more headlines than his home runs. In his eighth and final season as a Met, Straw belted 37 homers and drove in 108 runs before moving on to his hometown Dodgers in 1991. *Jonathan Daniel/Getty Images*

Mets endured the first 0–10 road trip in franchise history. The Jekyll and Hyde club was summed up best by Kevin McReynolds, "We show signs of being good and signs of being Little Leaguers."

The Dodgers staged a 1986 reunion tour at Shea with Darryl Strawberry and Gary Carter launching home runs off David Cone in the first inning. A few starts earlier, Cone had gotten into a heated argument with Harrelson in the dugout over an ignored pitchout. Harrelson admitted sending pitching coach Mel Stottlemyre out to remove a pitcher so he wouldn't have to endure the boos at Shea. And there was the argument between coach Mike Cubbage and Vince Coleman, who'd signed a four-year, $12 million contract. The result was that the Mets, 15 games over .500 and two and a half games out the weekend after the All-Star break, were six games under and eighteen and a half games back when Harrelson was fired the last week of the season.

Still, there were scattered rainbows in the first losing season in eight years. Howard Johnson became the first Met to lead the league in both home runs (38) and RBI (117), and he picked up his third 30–30 season while playing at least 25 games at three different positions. Cone, the NL strikeout leader (241), fanned a record-tying 19 Phillies in the final game of the year, as retiring GM Frank Cashen called the game with Ralph Kiner in the broadcast booth. A very odd season to say the least, but the oddest was yet to come.

The Worst Team Money Could Buy

The first order of business for new GM Al Harazin was to open the checkbook to try to make the lingering ugliness from 1991 disappear. He threw $27.5 million over five years at free agent Bobby Bonilla, making him the richest athlete in history. Harazin pulled the trigger on a blockbuster deal that sent Jefferies, McReynolds, and Keith Miller to the Royals for two-time Cy Young winner Bret Saberhagen and infielder

After taking over a struggling team from Davey Johnson early in 1990, longtime Mets infielder Bud Harrelson got the club back on track and a second-place finish by winning 71 of 120 games under his leadership. The success didn't last, however, as tension in the clubhouse and losing on the field led to his dismissal in the final week of the 1991 season. *Andrew D. Bernstein/Getty Images*

Stephen Dunn/Getty Images

METS **TOP 50**

HOWARD JOHNSON
1985–1993

Third Baseman

A beloved Met with ties to the team over three decades, Howard Johnson remains an all-time fan favorite. He was a key component to the 1980s Mets, a three-time 30–30 man, an MVP candidate in the 1990s, and returned in the 2000s as a coach in the minors—plus one season managing Class-A Brooklyn—before becoming the Mets hitting coach in 2007.

Howard Michael Johnson was especially valuable as a power hitter and for his flexibility. Though primarily a third baseman, HoJo was the shortstop in Davey Johnson's "power lineup." He was the shortstop in extra innings in Game 6 of the 1986 World Series and played five games at short in the 1988 NLCS. Jeff Torborg made him a center fielder in 1992.

Johnson had a World Series ring before he even got to New York (in a steal of a deal for pitcher Walt Terrell). A 1979 first-round pick by Detroit out of Clearwater, Florida, HoJo hit 12 homers for the 1984 world champion Tigers, though he batted just once in the World Series. During the 1987 season, his bat was confiscated and X-rayed under suspicion of being corked—but it wasn't the bat, it was HoJo getting to play every day. He was part of the first 30-homer, 30-steal tandem with Darryl Strawberry in 1987, and in 1991 his 38 homers and 117 RBI led the league, making him the first Met and the first switch hitter to lead the NL in RBI. He left the Mets after the '93 season ranked second on their all-time list in home runs, RBI, and extra-base hits.

Bill Pecota. He brought in slugger Eddie Murray and former Yankees all-star Willie Randolph to man the right side of the infield. Ron Darling had been traded the previous summer, Frank Viola left as a free agent, and ailing Hubie Brooks was traded once more, bringing in outfield reserve Dave Gallagher. Leading this newly molded club was the 1990 AL Manager of the Year, Jeff Torborg, lured from the White Sox.

The club's exorbitant $44.5 million payroll kept the Mets as the big story while Yankees owner George Steinbrenner was suspended and his team endured its fourth straight losing season. But the news about the 1992 Mets was rarely good. The top story occurred in spring training when the Port St. Lucie police reported that three players were being investigated for rape: Darryl Boston, Vince Coleman, and Dwight Gooden, at whose house the incident was alleged to have taken place in 1991. While the district attorney later declined to prosecute (as had happened in a separate case alleging Cone threatened three women with lewd behavior during a game at Shea), the disquieting scene shattered the serenity that the front office had labored so hard to create. A media boycott by the players lasted a week, ending following a plea from Randolph prior to an exhibition game at Baltimore's new ballpark, Camden Yards.

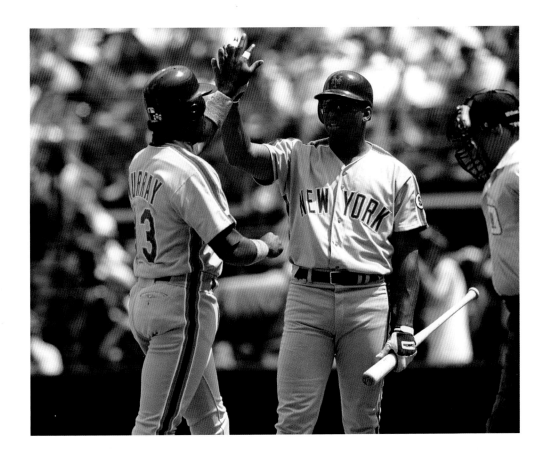

Eddie Murray (left) and Bobby Bonilla (right) were signed within five days of each other during the offseason, and the duo epitomized the team's lack of frugality in trying to rebuild. Although they were the top two producers of home runs and RBI in 1992 (16 and 93 for Murray, 19 and 70 for Bonilla), it didn't quite make up for their combined salary of $10.2 million. *Bernstein Associates/Getty Images*

Despite no words from the Mets, the club had the appearance of a paper tiger coming out of spring training. As beat writers Bob Klapisch and John Harper would write in their book on the season, *The Worst Team Money Could Buy*, "On paper the players looked wonderful. Under the hot Florida sun, they looked like a fifth-place team. They were slow and heavy-legged, in the field as well as on the bases, and the ball never seemed to jump off their bats."

All seemed right on Opening Night in St. Louis. Down by a run in the 9th inning, catcher Mackey Sasser tied the game on a fielder's choice. Coleman singled to lead off the 10th and scored on Bonilla's long home run. Comparisons were made to Gary Carter's Mets debut in 1985, when his homer beat the Cardinals. But this was not 1985.

New York split the four-game series in St. Louis and was swept by the Expos in the first series at home. Yet the Mets won five of their next six series and stood at 16–10 and two games out of first on May 4. The deficit was the same exactly a month later when the Mets and Bobby Bo rolled into Pittsburgh for his first trip back to his former home. The fans were unkind and the Pirates more so, taking three of the four games. The Mets sought revenge the following weekend at Shea, but they dropped three straight one-run games to fall seven back.

The club's miseries compounded on and off the field. Ownership, burned by so many long-term deals to so many brittle players, was uneasy about giving Cone the five-year contract he wanted, so Harazin took the first decent offer he got for the stud pitcher, sending him to Toronto. How weak was the pitching? Bill Pecota became the first Mets position player in history to take the mound, during a 19–2 shellacking at Three Rivers Stadium on September 26 in which the Pirates clinched their third straight division title.

In New York, without Barry Bonds to protect him in the lineup, Bobby Bonilla wasn't nearly as imposing—though he was an easy target. Bonilla wore earplugs because of the fan booing at Shea and then was pilloried in the media—and yelled at by his manager—for calling the press box after a seven-run first inning to complain about being charged with an error after butchering a ball hit at him by the opposing pitcher. Anthony Young lost that game, just a tiny sample of the atrocious luck that followed the hurler from the rotation to the bullpen to the closer role after John Franco was injured. Young won his first two outings in 1992 and then lost his next 14 decisions of the year. Watching the losses pile up would continue for both Young and his team.

The Worst Team Money Could Buy: The Sequel

In 1993, expansion returned to the National League for the first time since 1969 with the addition of two new teams. One was in Florida, in the NL East, and the other hailed from Colorado. The NL West's Rockies entered the world of the major leagues through the portal of Shea Stadium, and the Mets shut out the newbies on Opening Day.

Even after winning the first two games against Colorado, the Mets were under .500 before the first homestand was over, dropping three straight to the Astros. But then they won twice at Denver's Mile High Stadium and twice in Cincinnati to stand at 6–4. It took nearly another month for the Mets to win another six games. It was ugly on and off the field. In a locker-room battle of the Bobs, Bonilla threatened to fight Klapisch following the publication of *The Worst Team Money Could Buy*. The players seemed determined to prove the press and everyone else wrong, but all they did was prove that the 1992 book's title was a year premature.

Torborg, whom many players had taken an immediate dislike to thanks to his no-drinking policy on flights, was the first to go. With the 13–25 club sinking fast, the manager was fired just before Memorial Day and replaced by disciplinarian Dallas Green. Green had won a World Series with the 1980 Phillies, broken the Cubs' postseason drought as Chicago's GM in 1984, and had New York experience managing the 1989 Yankees. Al Harazin resigned and left the rudderless ship to Joe McIlvaine, who had departed San Diego when ownership insisted on a fire sale of the players he'd brought in. Yet neither the losing nor the unfathomable behavior at Shea stopped. The Mets lost 103 games and finished with baseball's worst record for the first time since 1967. They also managed to finish behind an expansion team and get no-hit by Houston's Darryl Kile. And there was so much more.

Tony Fernandez, called by the *New York Times* "the best all-around shortstop to play in New York since Pee Wee Reese," played like he couldn't wait to leave. A four-time Gold Glove winner in Toronto and an all-star a year earlier with San Diego, he sleepwalked through 48 games in New York, batting .225 and committing six errors. Traded back to the Blue Jays, Fernandez batted .306 in 94 games and had the second-best fielding percentage in the American League. Darrin Jackson, whom the Mets got from Toronto, missed six weeks with hyperthyroidism and batted .209. Jackson signed with the White Sox almost immediately after declaring free agency.

One of the few, if short-lived, bright spots in the 59–103 nightmare of 1993 was rookie Tim Bogar. The hardworking infielder had the game of his life in August, collecting four hits and two homers against the front-running Phils to help Bobby Jones win his major league debut. Bogar's second home run of the game, an inside-the-park job, was his last act as a Met in '93. He tore a ligament in his hand diving across the plate and missed the last seven weeks of the season.

Future Hall of Famer Eddie Murray led the club with 100 RBI, including a walk-off double that finally ended Anthony Young's major league record 27-game losing streak in July. Murray was long known for his loathing of the press, and a team official—part of a growing army of anonymous sources speaking out to the media—said the 38-year-old Murray "can't be part of the kind of club we want to go with." (Young didn't stick around, either, for more obvious reasons.)

Vince Coleman, who had clipped Dwight Gooden while swinging a golf club in the clubhouse in April, tossed a firecracker in a Dodger Stadium parking lot in July and injured three people, including an infant. Coleman was with teammate Bobby Bonilla and Dodger Eric Davis when he lit the fuse and tossed it over a fence. He later said in court, "They were thirty feet away and we were just having fun. We do it all the time." Fred Wilpon declared Coleman would never play for the team again. He didn't.

Saberhagen, who was basically untradable thanks to a three-year, $15.4 million contract extension signed before the season, took out his hostilities on the press in two separate incidents: first throwing a firecracker at reporters and later spraying them with bleach. The night the club dropped to 50–100, catcher Todd Hundley told the press, "If you'd told me at the beginning of the year we'd lose one hundred games, I'd have spit in your face." Saliva was about the only thing Mets players didn't hurl at reporters in 1993.

LOSING IT: ANTHONY YOUNG'S 27-GAME LOSING STREAK

Anthony Young's record streak of futility began following a win in relief on April 19, 1992, at Montreal. It ended 15 months later with a win in relief against Florida on July 28, 1993.

Date	Opponent	Score	Start/Rel.	ERA
1992 (14 straight losses)				
May 6	@CIN	5–3	Start	3.96
May 11	SD	4–2	Start	4.25
May 17	LA	7–6	Start	4.69
June 8	@MON	6–0	Start	4.66
June 15	MON	4–1	Start	4.46
June 20	STL	6–1	Start	4.42
June 25	CHI	9–2	Start	4.65
June 30	@CHI	3–1	Rel.	4.65
July 4 (2)	HOU	3–1	Rel.	4.70
Sept. 3	@CIN	4–3	Rel.	3.72
Sept. 5	@CIN	6–5	Rel.	3.86
Sept. 13	@MON	7–5	Rel.	4.07
Sept. 17	STL	3–2	Rel.	4.08
Sept. 29	PHI	5–3	Rel.	4.17
1993 (13 straight losses)				
April 9	HOU	7–3	Rel.	18.00
April 25	SD	9–8	Rel.	3.72
April 30	@SD	7–6	Rel.	3.86
May 16	@MON	4–3	Rel.	3.24
May 28	CIN	5–2	Rel.	4.09
June 8	CHI	5–1	Rel.	3.44
June 13	PHI	5–3	Start	3.60
June 18	@PIT	5–2	Start	4.02
June 22	MON	6–3	Start	4.08
June 27	STL	5–3	Start	4.35
July 2	SF	3–1	Start	4.43
July 7	SD	2–0	Start	4.19
July 24	@LA	5–4	Rel.	4.24

precipitous downturn), while the Braves landed in the East (just as they established a dynasty), along with the Expos, Phillies, and Marlins. There was also now a fallback position in the postseason: the Wild Card. Had this alignment been in place from 1984 to 1990, the Mets would have been in the postseason every year, instead of five on-the-outside-looking-in finishes intermingled with two division titles. But the Mets were putting the past behind them, even as they celebrated the silver anniversary of the 1969 championship. No miracles in 1994, just a better brand of baseball—albeit truncated.

A strike appeared as inevitable as rain from blackening skies, yet the game almost danced along for much of that summer. As the New York Yankees and Cleveland Indians emerged from long slumbers, and the hockey hotbed of Montreal housed the team with the best record in baseball, the Mets too were improving on the field and were doing their best to cover up the odor from the 1993 squad. In conjunction with Nickelodeon, rides and games were set up beyond center field at Shea Stadium. With the improvements came an old friend: a reborn Mr. Met. Other than depictions in various yearbooks, the Met with the giant ball for a head had been in hiding for the better part of a quarter century. Mr. Met—all 6 feet 10 inches of him—roamed the stands for the first time since Mets employee Dan Reilly had worn the bulky papier-mâché head in 1967. It was fun to be a Mets fan again.

Things got off to a good start in 1994, as New York pulled off a 12–8 Opening Day victory at Wrigley Field, keying a sweep of the Cubs. After 113 games, the Mets nearly put together as many wins as they had in 162 games a year earlier. The revitalized cast was led by Bret Saberhagen, who looked like his old Kansas City self. He transformed into the ultimate control freak, allowing just 13 walks in 24 starts en route to a 14–4 record. In his first full season (sort of), Bobby Jones went 12–7 with a 3.15 ERA. John Franco saved

Was it any wonder that the media started flocking to the improving Yankees after nearly a decade of making the Mets the top baseball story in town? John Franco spoke the obvious truth behind the desertion by media and fans alike: "On and off the field, we've been terrible for two years."

Cutoff Men

The Mets were determined to turn a new leaf in 1994. Fan annoyance at the reacquisition of stoic Kevin McReynolds vanished when it was revealed that the cost was Vince Coleman, still under contract to the Mets. Anthony Young's 1–16 season—following a 2–14 campaign in 1992—made it necessary to get him a fresh start. GM Joe McIlvaine not only worked out a deal, but he got a starting shortstop from the Cubs in Jose Vizcaino. While fans were sad to see Howard Johnson and Sid Fernandez leave as free agents after long and meritorious service, they were at the end of the line, and the team needed new blood.

New blood also arrived in the Mets' division. After the 1993 season, Major League Baseball realigned each league into three divisions. Along with the Cubs and Cardinals, the Pirates departed the NL East (just as they began a

Jeff Kent proved to be a good return from the David Cone trade, as the infielder hit .279 and averaged 18 homers and 71 RBI in his three full seasons in New York (1993–1995). *Mitchell Layton/Getty Images*

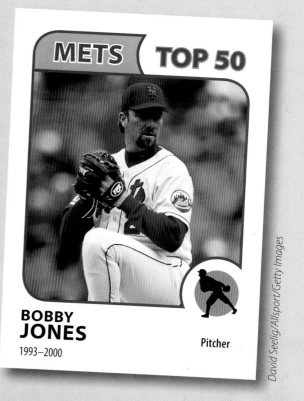

METS TOP 50

BOBBY JONES
1993–2000

Pitcher

30 games to lead a much improved bullpen. Offensively, Jeff Kent—acquired with Ryan Thompson in the David Cone deal in 1992—showed unexpected production at second base, homering seven times in the first 11 games and leading the team in RBI. First baseman Rico Brogna, acquired in a minor deal with Detroit just before the season, was promoted to New York in late June and pounded out a .351 average. But the positive events of 1994 were quickly undone, not just by the strike, which everyone saw coming, but by Dwight Gooden's failed drug test. That was a complete shock.

Gooden was suspended at the end of June for failing a drug test and received a 60-day suspension from Major League Baseball. Contract negotiations, which had been in the $6 million per year range, were put on hold. Permanently. A positive drug test for the now injury-prone Doc ended his 1994 season six weeks before the MLB Players Association shut down the game for all. Gooden—second to Tom Seaver in franchise history in wins and strikeouts—never threw another pitch as a Met. His suspension was subsequently extended for all of 1995 when he failed numerous drug tests after going through treatment. Manager Dallas Green said it was "time for Doc to go elsewhere."

Bobby Jones was not flashy. He took the ball 190 times as a Met, won 74 games, threw 1,215⅔ innings, and fanned 714, placing him among the top 10 in Mets history in those categories. And one day in 2000, he threw eight perfect innings to clinch a postseason series, although those eight innings were split in half: 12 straight batters retired to start the game, and after allowing a hit and two walks in the fifth, 12 more consecutive outs to clinch Game 4 of the NLDS against San Francisco. He had gone to the minors that spring at the club's request and returned a new man, or more fittingly, the old Bobby Jones.

The flashiest things about him was where he came from and how he became a Met. Robert Joseph Jones was born in Tom Seaver's hometown of Fresno, California, and he was selected with the 1991 first-round pick that the Mets received as compensation when Darryl Strawberry signed with the Dodgers. Jones was no Seaver or Strawberry, but he did reach the majors two years after signing. He posted double-digit wins every year from 1994 to 1997, including a career-best 15 in 1997, when he also pitched a scoreless inning in the All-Star Game.

Jones did not lead the league in any notable category until he joined the Padres as a free agent in the wake of his breakthrough one-hit playoff gem: He allowed the most home runs in the National League and lost 19 times in 2001.

The Replacements

Eight months after baseball abruptly ceased, it resumed when future Supreme Court Justice Sonia Sotomayor issued a New York District Court ruling that prevented baseball owners from implementing a new collective bargaining agreement and using replacement players. It ended the strike as well as the dreams of many fringe players who had gotten a paid fantasy camp experience in March 1995. While the idea of "scabs" taking the place of major leaguers set the stage for future tension when some of these men later reached the big leagues on merit, the spring of the replacement players at least gave sportswriters and their readers a respite from covering the strike and labor negotiations. There were plenty of interesting stories, whether it was former Met Doug Sisk giving the game one last shot, or unknowns like Alex Coghen, a 37-year-old pitcher 16 years removed from his last minor league game, who went from Bronx truck driver to number five in Port St. Lucie. That number had previously belonged to Jeromy Burnitz, the young, power-hitting right fielder who Dallas Green had urged to play winter ball. Burnitz declined and was soon the property of the Cleveland Indians, traded for pitchers Paul Byrd, Jerry DiPoto, and Dave Mlicki, a trio who had chances to show their mettle as Mets, once the 1995 season finally got started.

With 18 fewer games on the schedule, the Mets finished 21 games out, but there were silver linings, given how the decade had gone so far. Opening Day came later than any in club history—April 26—with a lid lifter from hell that

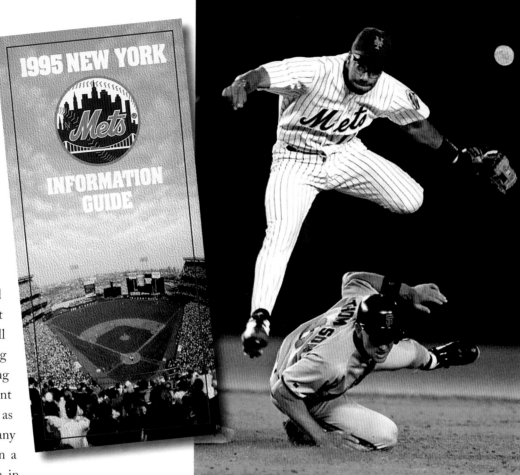

Jose Vizcaino, acquired in exchange for Anthony Young in 1994, not only provided slick fielding at shortstop, but he chipped in with his bat as well in 1995. The young infielder was eventually traded to Cleveland, with Jeff Kent, in an ill-advised transaction the following year. *Mark Phillips/AFP/Getty Images*

future visiting clubs to Denver's new ballpark would simply deem a "Coors Field game." The Mets were unable to hold leads in the 9th, 13th, and 14th innings, and the next day could not maintain a 7–2 sixth-inning lead as the Rockies again won in their last at bat. Not much went right for the Mets in the first two months of the season; they stood 19 games under .500 and 19 games out at the All-Star break. During a late July slump, New York dumped the bloated contracts (and clubhouse headaches) of Bobby Bonilla and Bret Saberhagen on anxious contenders. The Mets accepted that they just weren't going anywhere in 1995. And then suddenly they started going somewhere.

Following a six-game winning streak in early August, the Mets lightened the load further by shedding aging speedster Brett Butler on the Dodgers—and then they swept the same

Dodgers at Shea. The Mets continued to jettison players, trading or releasing Mike Remlinger, Josias Manzanillo, David Segui, Mike Birkbeck, Jason Jacome, and Eric Gunderson through the summer. While the return on these deals was minimal—the only players who ever appeared in a Mets uniform were obscurities Damon Buford, Reid Cornelius, and Juan Acevedo, plus overrated Alex Ochoa— Joe McIlvaine's moves afforded the Mets the freedom to play their younger players. Carl Everett showed an explosive bat—and moderately controlled temper—with 12 homers in 79 games; shortstop Jose Vizcaino hit .287 and knocked in 56 runs; Tim Bogar batted .290 in 78 games and started at every infield position; journeyman Chris Jones hit .400 as a pinch hitter in 32 appearances; one-time scrawny catching prospect Todd Hundley showed power and patience behind the plate with 15 home runs and a .280 average; and Rico Brogna and Jeff Kent each launched 20 home runs. Infielder Edgardo Alfonzo, just 21, showed as much promise as anyone, batting .278 while ably handling both second and third base.

The Mets finished the year with a 27–15 flourish, culminated by a season-ending six-game home winning streak against Davey Johnson's Reds and Bobby Cox's Braves (who would go on to meet each other in the NLCS, with Atlanta ultimately winning the World Series). A walk-off walk by Bogar in the season finale left New York tied with Philadelphia for second place in the division. Joe Orsulak, the only regular over 30 at year's end, left as a free agent. The Mets were continuing the youth movement.

Generation K Goes Down Looking

The Mets had reason for optimism. Topps, *USA Today*, and *Baseball America* all chose the Mets as Organization of the Year. Two of their top pitching prospects had been promoted during the year and showed early promise. Bill Pulsipher came up in June 1995 and displayed a lively left arm and an even livelier personality. The southpaw went 5–7, pitching into the seventh inning in 14 of his 17 starts until he was shut down in mid-September with a sprained ligament in his elbow following almost 220 innings in the majors and minors. Jason "Izzy" Isringhausen, who debuted in July, threw a similar number of innings and won 20 games all told at three different levels, including a stellar 9–2 mark and 2.81 ERA in 93 innings for New York. Excitement was building. Pulsipher, a 1991 second-round pick, was listed as *Baseball America*'s 12th-ranked prospect; Izzy, a 44th-round pick that same year, ranked 37th.

But these two were deemed mere tremors before the big one: Paul Wilson, the first overall pick in 1994 and ranked second by *Baseball America* coming into the season. This confluence of projected greatness and hype boiled together to create an entity known as Generation K.

The phenomenon of phenoms intensified over the long winter. By spring the Mets were down to two. Pulsipher's elbow sprain became a tear, and he was done for the year.

With a contract on the line, Bernard Gilkey earned a big payday with a career year in 1996. His 153 games, 181 hits, 108 runs, 44 doubles, 30 homers, 117 RBI, 73 walks, .317 average, .393 OBP, and .562 slugging all qualified as high-water marks for the left fielder. *Ron Frehm/AP Images*

Lance "One Dog" Johnson set all sorts of team records with his speed and his hits in 1996. Here he beats the tag from Hall of Fame shortstop Cal Ripken to snag a stolen base during that season's All-Star Game. *Al Bello/Getty Images*

Wilson debuted in the third game of the season and should have gotten the win, but the bullpen coughed up a five-run lead in the eighth before the offense scraped together two unearned runs in the bottom of the ninth for a 10–9 win. It was the last day the Mets were in first place.

Despite expectations to the contrary, the 1996 Mets had a high-caliber offense but an atrocious pitching staff. The team's two uncharacteristic traits were apparent from the first day, when they fell behind the Cardinals, 6–0, and still came back to win. The club's 4.22 ERA on the year was the highest since the Mets moved into Shea Stadium in 1964. The 779 runs, 1,517 hits, and 159 home runs allowed were the most by the team since 1962. On the other side, Mets bats produced a club-record .270 batting average. The franchise hits record (1,515) and the triples explosion that tied the 1977 high (47) were made possible largely by the work of one man—or One Dog—Lance Johnson.

Johnson crashed into the Mets record books with 227 hits, 21 triples, and 117 runs (since broken) in 1996. The speedy Johnson's accumulation of triples wasn't a surprise;

Todd Hundley was another Mets player who took it up in notch on the field in 1996 in the pursuit of a new contract. He set a new franchise (and career) record with 41 homers while playing 150 games behind the plate. *Al Bello/Getty Images*

One Dog was a four-time American League leader in that category with the White Sox. His dominance in New York, however, was staggering. Johnson established career highs in steals (50), average (.333), doubles (31), RBI (69), and slugging (.479). He played in his lone All-Star Game and got the start due to an injury to Tony Gwynn. Johnson went three for four with a steal to lead the NL to victory (its last until 2010).

But among great 1996 performances that were never duplicated, Bernard Gilkey belongs near the top of the list. Unlike Johnson, who signed as a free agent for $5 million per year before the season, Gilkey was acquired in a trade from St. Louis in his contract year. He sang for his supper quite convincingly, knocking out a club-record 44 doubles and tying Howard Johnson's 1991 mark of 117 RBI (broken by Mike Piazza's 124 and Robin Ventura's 120 in 1999). It landed him a four-year, $20.4 million contract.

Todd Hundley got an even bigger payday, thanks to 41 home runs that set the franchise record and surpassed the all-time record for home runs in a season by a catcher, established by Brooklyn's Roy Campanella in 1953 (one of Campy's homers that year came as a pinch hitter). The switch-hitting Hundley subsequently received a four-year, $21 million contract that was unique in that it granted him permission to use a team logo for local endorsements.

The Mets had so much offense in 1996 that they even gave some of it away. Jose Vizcaino was benched in favor of Cuban defector Rey Ordonez, who swung hard at any and every pitch, drawing just 10 unintentional walks in 530 plate appearances. Though he made 27 errors as a rookie, Ordonez routinely conjured up the spectacular with his glove. Stationed to his right was Jeff Kent, moved to third base by the club and manning the position as if he were being held hostage. Kent hit .290 but committed 21 errors in 89 games before the Mets sent him to Cleveland, along with Vizcaino, for all-star second baseman Carlos Baerga and reserve Alvaro Espinoza. Kent never played third base after 1996, but he did become the best slugging second baseman since Rogers Hornsby. Baerga, coming off four straight .300 seasons with the Indians, hit .193 as a Met the rest of the year while nursing injuries.

But 1996 was supposed to be about the pitching. Reliever John Franco earned his 300th career save and was subsequently tossed from a game during a brawl with the Cubs on John Franco Day. Speaking of the Cubs, they had a hand in squashing early dreams of Mets pitching greatness. Paul Wilson, with two down in the ninth on a gray May Friday at Wrigley Field, was ordered to walk Mark Grace intentionally to face Sammy Sosa. The ensuing blast onto Waveland Avenue turned a 2–1 win into a 4–2 loss in what

METS TOP 50

JOHN FRANCO
1990–2004

Pitcher

The Mets celebrated John Franco Day at Shea Stadium on May 11, 1996, to honor the pitcher for reaching 300 career saves. Franco celebrated by joining in a brawl with the Cubs, resulting in his ejection, along with eight other players. *Louis Requena/AP Images*

John Franco stands first among Mets in saves and appearances, second in years of service, as the third captain in club history, four-time all-star, and the all-time leader in saves by a lefty. A 5-foot-10 changeup pitcher with the guts of a burglar, Franco came back after Tommy John surgery in 2002 and pitched until age 44.

The son of a Brooklyn sanitation worker, John Anthony Franco starred at Lafayette High School, the same school as Sandy Koufax and Mets owner Fred Wilpon. Originally drafted out of St. John's by the Dodgers in 1981, Franco was traded to Cincinnati two years later. He was a three-time all-star in his six years with the Reds and 1988 Rolaids Fireman of the Year. He won the award again in 1990; that year, Randy Myers, the reliever he was traded for, led the Reds to a championship.

The local kid and lifelong Mets fan was not always embraced at Shea Stadium, as the public seemed to focus on Franco's 64 blown saves more than his 276 saves as a Met. (Franco was 424 of 525 in save attempts for his career.) After injuring his middle finger in 1999, Franco became the setup man for closer Armando Benitez. That year he also appeared in his first postseason, picking up the win in the clinching game of the NLDS. Franco also fanned Barry Bonds to save Game 2 of the 2000 NLDS, and a few weeks later he beat the Yankees for the first Mets win in a World Series game since 1986. Only Ed Kranepool spent more years in a Met uniform than Franco.

proved to be Wilson's only complete game as a Met. Jerry DiPoto got in on the heartbreak when Sammy slammed his final pitch for another walk-off win that Sunday. The Mets scored 14 runs two weekends later in a drubbing at Candlestick Park and then scored just twice the next day during a Giants' doubleheader sweep. The road was cruel in 1996, as the Mets won just 29 times away from Shea while allowing more than five runs per game. And it was on the road in Mexico—the first regular-season series ever played in that country—that Dallas Green began his last stand as a manager.

The Mets lost to the Padres, 15–10, in that first game in Monterrey, won the next night, and then dropped the rubber game, 8–0, as a woozy Ken Caminiti used an IV, a Snickers bar, and perhaps some other elixir to crawl off the bathroom floor and slam two home runs against Wilson. A 12–11 loss in San Francisco sent the Mets on an eight-game losing streak during which Green, age 62 and the oldest manager in the National League, uttered a fateful assessment of Isringhausen and Wilson to reporters: "These guys don't belong in the big leagues. That might sound harsh and negative, but what have they done to get here?" They stayed. Green left. But the young pitchers, who combined for an 11–26 mark and a 5.05 ERA in '96, would spend far more time in doctors' offices and tuning up in the minor leagues in the seasons to come than on a major league mound.

Valentine's Day

Bobby Valentine became the 16th Mets manager and the club's fifth skipper in the seven years since Davey Johnson was let go. In that time the club's only winning record came during the season in which Johnson was replaced. The Mets of the early 1990s stocked up on free agents and veterans as the team became unwatchable. They then tried to gear up through the farm system and found the growing pains intolerable. "The main thing I'm looking for from Bobby is a new approach, a new touch," GM Joe McIlvaine told the press at the August 27 announcement. "Maybe it will feel a little different."

It felt pretty much the same as the Mets were swept in their first series under Valentine and stumbled to a 12–19 finish; 1997 didn't start off any better. Opening the season with a nine-game West Coast swing, the Mets were pounded in the opener in San Diego, 12–5, and returned home with a 3–6 record, including losses in three games that lasted 12 innings or more. Rain postponed Opening Day at Shea, creating an Easter Sunday doubleheader that the Mets dropped to the Giants in front of just 21,981 fans, the smallest home-opener crowd since 1981. When San Francisco completed the series sweep the next night (Jeff Kent went 7 for 16 with two homers and six RBI in his first five games against his former team), the Mets stood at 3–9 and already in last place. Following six seasons without a winning record, New York appeared to be on the road to number seven.

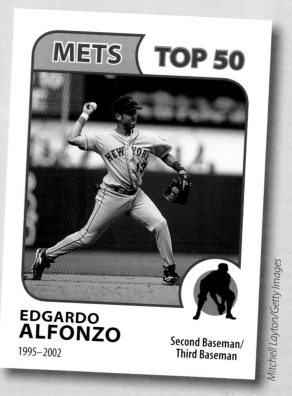

METS TOP 50

EDGARDO ALFONZO
1995–2002

Second Baseman/ Third Baseman

Edgardo Alfonzo never won a Gold Glove Award and went to just one All-Star Game, but he was as vital as any Met during his career in Flushing. Batting in front of John Olerud and Mike Piazza in 1999, Alfonzo set a club record with 123 runs (later surpassed by Carlos Beltran) and led the club with 315 total bases, 191 hits, and 41 doubles. He also went six for six (the first in Mets history), scored six runs, knocked in five, and hit three homers in a game at the cavernous Houston Astrodome. His .324 average and .967 OPS helped the Mets claim another Wild Card in 2000.

Brought from Venezuela to Class A at age 18, Edgardo Antonio Alfonzo hit .331 his first year in the minors and .350 his second. He landed in New York at 21 and held his own before breaking out with a .315 average in 1997. Fonzie homered two batters into the 1999 one-game playoff in Cincinnati; the next night his grand slam broke a ninth-inning tie in the NLDS opener in Arizona. He homered three times in that series, batted .444 in the 2000 NLCS, and knocked in 16 runs in 19 postseason games as a Met.

A superb fielder who switched positions to accommodate the club (524 games at second base, 515 at third), the Mets let him leave for the Giants after 2002. He signed with Triple-A Norfolk in 2006, a stop he hadn't made during his meteoric rise a decade earlier. Fonzie did not get a call to New York, but he retired in the top five in RBI, runs, total bases, hits, doubles, extra-base hits, and multi-hit games.

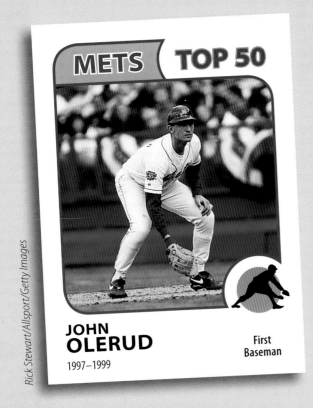

METS TOP 50

JOHN OLERUD
1997–1999

First Baseman

Toronto took pitcher Robert Person and paid the Mets $5 million, the highest amount in a transaction at the time, to take the first baseman who would transform their lineup. A .363 hitter in 1993, the Blue Jays tried to make Olerud a pull hitter. New York let the sweet-swinging lefty be, and he responded in his three seasons with the club, starting off with a team-best 102 RBI in 1997.

Olerud's .354 average in 1998 topped Cleon Jones' .340 club mark from 1969. Olerud also surpassed Keith Hernandez as the all-time leader in average (.315) and took out Dave Magadan as the all-time leader in on-base percentage (.425). His OBP in '98 (.447) and '99 (.427) rank as the two highest by a Met, helped by his record 125 walks the latter season. He became the first Met besides Darryl Strawberry to slug higher than .500 with the team. He did all this while acting as the glue for the "best infield ever." His two-run single in Game 4 of the 1999 NLCS overcame a 2–1 deficit in the eighth inning. His two-run homer the next day was his team's only scoring until the Mets dramatically won in 15 in what would be Olerud's last game at Shea.

John Garrett Olerud had suffered a brain aneurysm at Washington State and wore a batting helmet in the field as protection and to keep his mother from worrying. He made his family happy—but Mets fans despondent—by returning to his native Washington as a Mariner in 2000.

On April 15, 1997, the Mets served as hosts for the 50th anniversary celebration of Jackie Robinson's major league debut. Because the historic moment had taken place at Ebbets Field in Brooklyn, Shea Stadium was the closest alternative. The Mets–Dodgers national event—featuring President Bill Clinton, commissioner Bud Selig, and Rachel Robinson (Jackie's widow)—worked better on the East Coast, where a fifth-inning ceremony would take place in the middle of prime time instead of the middle of the night (for eastern viewership). The weather was harder to manipulate. Still, the frigid night produced the only 50,000-plus crowd of the year, even though most of them left as soon as the ceremony ended. Many kind and fitting words were spoken about Jackie Robinson, his legacy, and his foundation, but the most lasting moment came from Bud Selig, who announced that number 42 would hereafter be retired "in perpetuity." The Mets' number 42, Butch Huskey (who, like everyone who wore 42 at the time, was allowed to keep wearing the number until his career ended) had one of the team's 10 hits that night. Lance Johnson knocked in four runs, and Armando Reynoso and Toby Borland combined to blank Los Angeles for a 5–0 win.

From that night onward, the Mets produced the second-best record in the National League (85–65), despite lacking a lineup or a rotation that caused anyone to quake in fear. Todd Hundley's health problems—and a propensity for feuding with his manager—left Todd Pratt, who had been managing a Domino's pizza establishment a year earlier, to get a fair share of the playing time behind the plate in the second half. Bernard Gilkey reverted to his pre-1996 form but still contributed 18 homers and 78 RBI. Despite a .216 average, Rey Ordonez committed just nine errors in the field and won the first of three straight Gold Glove Awards. Carlos Baerga bounced back to hit .281, and Edgardo Alfonzo had a breakthrough season with a .315 average and

The ticket stub and inside program cover from the first Mets–Yankees interleague series, held at Yankee Stadium. The Mets took the opener, 6–0, on June 16, 1997, but lost the next two. *Author's collection*

was stellar at third base. The anchor of the infield—and the team—was John Olerud, who had won a batting title and two world championships in Toronto, but the Blue Jays tired of him. Not only did they pay the Mets $5 million to take Olerud off their hands, Jays manager Cito Gaston predicted he'd crumble under the pressure in New York. The Mets gladly took the money and his team-leading .400 on-base percentage, 85 walks, 34 doubles, 90 runs, and 102 RBI. Olerud embraced his new home, riding the subway to work unrecognized without the helmet that he wore in the field because of a brain aneurysm a decade earlier.

The rotation was led by low-key all-star Bobby Jones (15–9) and loaded with even lesser known talents like Reynoso, Brian Bohanon, and former replacement player Rick Reed. Dave Mlicki was just 8–12 with a 4.00 ERA, but his lone complete game was a shutout at Yankee Stadium in the first interleague game between the Mets and Yankees—a triumph that forever placed the otherwise-average right-hander in the gallery of Mets of fleeting greatness. The Mets lost the other two games of that midweek series to the Yankees, but getting the first shot in against the world champions on their home turf was a triumph for Mets fans everywhere.

FIRST METS–YANKEES INTERLEAGUE GAME
Now It Counts

New York Mets 6, New York Yankees 5
Monday, June 16, 1997
at Yankee Stadium, Bronx, NY

	1	2	3	4	5	6	7	8	9	R	H	E
NYM	3	0	0	0	0	0	2	0	1	6	9	2
NYY	0	0	0	0	0	0	0	0	0	0	9	1

New York Mets	AB	R	H	RBI
Johnson, CF	5	0	0	0
Gilkey, LF	3	1	2	1
Olerud, 1B	5	1	2	3
Hundley, C	2	1	0	0
Huskey, DH	4	0	2	1
Everett, RF	4	0	0	0
Baerga, 2B	4	0	0	0
M Franco, 3B	4	2	2	0
Lopez, SS	2	1	1	0
Totals	**33**	**6**	**9**	**5**

2B: Olerud, Gilkey. **SF:** Gilkey. **SH:** Lopez. **HBP:** Lopez. **SB:** Hundley, Huskey.
Team LOB: 6.
E: Baerga, Johnson.

New York Yankees	AB	R	H	RBI
Jeter, SS	5	0	1	0
Kelly, 2B	4	0	1	0
O'Neill, RF	3	0	1	0
Fielder, DH	4	0	1	0
Martinez, 1B	4	0	0	0
Hayes, 3B	3	0	1	0
Whiten, LF	4	0	1	0
Curtis, CF	4	0	0	0
Girardi, C	4	0	3	0
Totals	**35**	**0**	**9**	**0**

2B: Girardi, Fielder. **Team LOB:** 10.
E: Lloyd.

Pitching Summary

New York Mets	IP	H	R	ER	BB	SO
Mlicki, W (3–5)	9	9	0	0	2	8

New York Yankees	IP	H	R	ER	BB	SO
Pettitte, L (8–4)	7	8	5	5	3	4
Lloyd	2	1	1	0	0	0
Totals	**9**	**9**	**6**	**5**	**3**	**4**

Umpires: HP Tim Tschida, 1B Don Denkinger, 2B John Shulock, 3B Mike Everitt.
Time of Game: 2:44
Attendance: 56,111

At the start of the 1990s, fans at Shea Stadium didn't have a whole lot to cheer for, even going so far as to wear bags over their heads and—worse yet—don Yankee jerseys. By the end of the decade, however, there was plenty of hope and reason to believe as winning ways returned to Queens.

1 *Bill Hickey/Getty Images*

2 *Steve Moore/Allsport/Getty Images*

3 *Howard Earl Simmons/NY Daily News Archive/Getty Images*

4 Howard Johnson's versatility in the field and at the plate made him an invaluable contributor in New York for many years. After spending most of his career playing the left side of the infield, he spent the entirety of 1992 roaming the outfield. *Bernstein Associates/Getty Images*

5 First baseman John Olerud (5) and manager Bobby Valentine were at the center of the team's resurgence in the 1990s. Here Olerud gets congratulations from his skipper and his teammates after hitting a two-run walkoff homer against Colorado in May 1997. *Gerald Herbert/NY Daily News Archive/Getty Images*

Renaissance Manager
BOBBY VALENTINE

Bobby Valentine was the Mets' renaissance manager—a dancer, a ballplayer, a restaurateur, a crafty third-base coach, a tell-it-like-it-is TV analyst, an international hero, a humanitarian. In New York, he came along at a time when the Yankees were donning their dynastic robes and the Mets were an afterthought, but he brought plenty of personality to the job. Valentine also went on to accumulate the second-highest win total (536) of any manager in Mets history.

The fifth overall pick in baseball's 1968 amateur draft as a player, Valentine was selected by the Dodgers ahead of Steve Garvey, Ron Cey, and Bill Buckner. He became a utility player after suffering a gruesome leg injury while with the Angels in 1973. In 1977 he was traded from the Padres to the Mets for Dave Kingman as part of the "Midnight Massacre." Valentine served as a Mets coach (1983–1985) before Texas hired him to manage. He was the most successful manager in Rangers history and winner of the 1986 American League Manager of the Year Award, but Valentine was fired in 1992 by the Rangers' managing general partner, George W. Bush. Valentine then became the first American to manage in the Japanese professional leagues before he returned to the United States as skipper of the Mets' Triple-A farm club in Norfolk in 1994. He was ready when Dallas Green was fired in New York in 1996.

Many fans hold the 1997 season dear because there were so few expectations heading in, yet the club won 88 games and battled for the Wild Card spot up until the final week. A late-season swoon in 1998 was followed by a sluggish start in 1999, leading to the dismantling of Valentine's coaching staff in early June. A few days later, in perhaps the most infamous Bobby V. episode, he was ejected from a game against Toronto, only to return to the dugout in a moustache-and-sunglasses disguise. Valentine was suspended for the incident, and that, plus a

Matthew Stockman/Getty Images

seven-game skid in late September, seemingly put his job in jeopardy; a controversial *Sports Illustrated* article on the manager added fuel to the fire. But the Mets reversed course in the final days of the season to secure the Wild Card, and Valentine led them to victory over the 100-win Diamondbacks in the Division Series and then to rally from a three-games-to-none deficit before losing a heartbreaking NLCS to Atlanta.

The Mets won a second straight Wild Card in 2000 and marched as underdogs all the way to a long-awaited return to the World Series—and a match-up with their formidable cross-town mates, the Yankees. Though the Mets had Mike Piazza surrounded in the lineup by Edgardo Alfonzo and Robin Ventura, the rest of Valentine's pennant club was pedestrian. The manager's specialty in New York seemed to be showing faith in unheralded but hardworking ballplayers, such as minor leaguers Melvin Mora, Matt Franco, and Benny Agbayani, as well as former replacement player Rick Reed.

Off the diamond, Valentine worked tirelessly to help coordinate relief efforts at Shea Stadium following the terrorist attacks of September 11, 2001. He earned the Joan Payson, Branch Rickey, and Bart Giamatti Awards, among many other honors, for his humanitarian work.

After a late-season rally for the division title fell short in 2001, the Mets crumbled in 2002, and Valentine was fired. He returned to Japan to manage the Chiba Lotte Marines, immersing himself in the language and culture and becoming one of the most popular—and merchandized—sports figures in the country. He topped it off by taking the downtrodden club to the Nippon Series title. Cost-cutting by the Marines sent Valentine back to the United States, where he worked as an analyst on ESPN's *Baseball Tonight* while waiting for the next major league club to take a chance on Bobby V.

The Mets drew more than 49,000 fans to Shea Stadium for the home opener against the Phillies on March 31, 1998, and they would reach that total only one more time through nearly three full months to start the season. That changed dramatically with the acquisition of Mike Piazza. *Ezra Shaw/Getty Images*

Joe McIlvaine, who had assembled the roster, did not get to see them contend into the final week of September. He was replaced in July by underling Steve Phillips, a smooth-talking former minor leaguer whose handiness with a cell phone (McIlvaine didn't like having one glued to his ear) seemed as much a reason as any for the change. The new general manager's first trade created more stir than substance: center fielder Lance Johnson, utility infielder Manny Alexander, and starter Mark Clark (22–18 with a 3.76 ERA since coming from Cleveland in 1996) to the Cubs for center fielder Brian McRae and relievers Turk Wendell and Mel Rojas. With a bullpen of John Franco, veteran sidearmer Greg McMichael, swingman Joe Crawford, rookie Cory Lidle, and Takashi Kashiwada (the first Japanese player in Mets history), the bullpen was a project that Phillips would continually tinker with during his six years on the job.

Pizzaz Needed; Piazza Delivered

The turnaround year of 1997 had defied the experts and was achieved without any big-name stars. The Mets' 1,766,174 attendance was their highest in four years, yet it still put them in the bottom third in the National League and about 800,000 behind the Yankees. The popularity disparity was most apparent when the Yankees were forced to play a game at Shea Stadium because of a beam collapse at Yankee Stadium early in the 1998 season. It created the first time in more than a century that four teams played in one stadium in one day, and the strange twin bill on April 15 demonstrated the imbalance in the sizes of the two teams' fan bases. (GM Steve Phillips referred to being a Mets fan as "an acquired taste.") The Yankees hosted the Angels in the impromptu

afternoon game and drew 40,743 to Shea; the Mets–Cubs game that night was seen by just 16,012. Both New York teams picked up victories.

Competing with the 114-win Yankees of 1998 was tough enough—the Mets were fortunate to sneak a win at Shea in the lone interleague series between these new on-field rivals—but they also had trouble holding their own against their National League foes. By May 21 the Mets were nine games behind Atlanta in the NL East and two and a half games behind the Cubs in the Wild Card race.

With early-season injuries to Alfonzo and Gilkey, and Hundley not due to return from elbow surgery until the second half, Bobby Valentine's creativity was put to the test to come up with a lineup that could generate offense. In Hundley's spot behind the plate, he tried a quintet of nobodies, with Tim Spehr, Jim Tatum, Todd Pratt, Rich Wilkins, and Alberto Castillo all getting starts at catcher through the first 35 games. Only Pratt, who began the year in the minors, remained a Met after the season, and the lone notable offensive contribution by a catcher in 1998 was Castillo's 14th-inning, game-winning single that ended the majors' longest Opening Day game since 1919. The Mets could wait for the return of Hundley, coming off successive 30-homer years, but there might not be much of a race for him to come back to. There was a catcher available on the market, *the* catcher on the market: Mike Piazza.

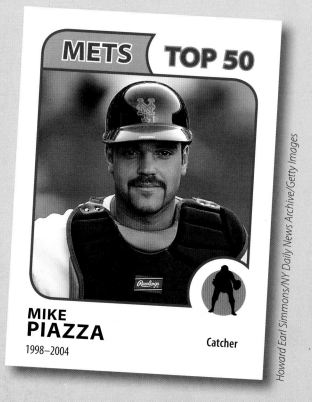

METS TOP 50

MIKE PIAZZA
1998–2004

Catcher

You don't find many catchers who can hit like Mike Piazza. The ball exploded off his bat, especially to the opposite field. And he did it while playing most of his career at two of the most difficult stadiums to hit in: Dodger Stadium and Shea Stadium.

Growing up in Phoenixville, Pennsylvania, Michael Joseph Piazza served as Dodgers batboy when the team visited Philadelphia. His selection in the 1988 draft seemed almost as ceremonial. Los Angeles took Piazza in the 62nd round because manager Tommy Lasorda was a close friend of Mike's father, Vince. Converted to catcher in the minors, he began 1992 batting .377 in Class AA, moved up a level and hit .341. Piazza started for the Dodgers the first day rosters expanded and went three for three with a walk. The Dodgers let longtime catcher Mike Scioscia leave as a free agent. Piazza earned the first of a dozen all-star nods, was named Rookie of the Year, and placed ninth in MVP balloting, the first of nine straight seasons he was voted in the top 15 (though he never won). His .318 average as a rookie would be his lowest in five full seasons in Los Angeles.

He peaked for L.A. in 1997, when he hit 40 home runs, drove in 124 runs, and had a staggering line of .362 average, .431 OBP, and .638 slugging. Problems with Dodgers management and turning down an $80 million offer resulted in a seven-player deal that sent Piazza and Todd Zeile to Florida in May 1998. The Marlins, who'd made the trade to shed their own big contracts, dealt Piazza eight days later to New York.

MIKE PIAZZA

Born: September 4, 1968, in Norristown, PA
Acquired by New York Mets via trade, 1998
Mets Debut: May 23, 1998
Bats: Right. **Throws:** Right

New York Mets Batting Record

YEAR	AB	H	HR	RBI	BA
1998	394	137	23	76	.348
1999	534	162	40	124	.303
2000	482	156	38	113	.324
2001	503	151	36	94	.300
2002	478	134	33	98	.280
2003	234	67	11	34	.286
2004	455	121	20	54	.266
2005	398	100	19	62	.251
Mets Totals	3478	1028	220	655	.296
MLB Totals	6911	2127	427	1335	.308

The New York experience and a $91 million outlay kept Piazza in town through 2005. The club reached the postseason twice and the World Series once, but this period of renewed fan interest revolved around Piazza. When Roger Clemens, a pitcher he'd hammered, beaned Piazza at Yankee Stadium in July 2000 and then threw a broken bat barrel at him in the World Series, fans acted as if a family member had been threatened. His game-winning home run the night baseball returned to New York in the wake of the 2001 attacks made him that much more beloved.

Piazza's offensive numbers are among the best ever at the position, including 396 homers as a catcher (he hit 427 overall and 220 as a Met). He batted .308 for his career (.296 as a Met), drove in 1,335 runs (655 as a Met), and scored 1,048 runs (532 as a Met). Though throwing out runners on the basepaths was not a strength (just 23 percent over his career), Piazza took great pride in catching and endured constant abuse to his 6-foot-3 frame.

The ovation Piazza received during his last game as a Met in 2005 and his first time back as a Padre in 2006 were among the loudest and longest ever at Shea Stadium. Mets ownership showed its opinion of Piazza by having him catch the final ceremonial pitch at Shea from Tom Seaver on September 28, 2008—and the first pitch at Citi Field the following April. Although he played for three West Coast teams during his career, New York considers Piazza theirs. For all time.

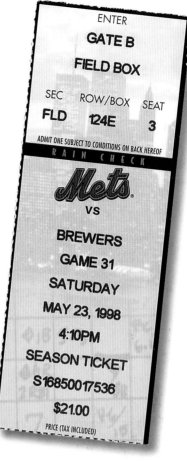

A .331 hitter with a .571 career slugging percentage and an average of 36 homers per year through his first five-plus seasons, Piazza had been traded from the Dodgers to the Marlins on May 14 after a contract dispute. The Marlins, who had gone from world champions to clearinghouse in one year, were unloading veteran after veteran for prospects—the Mets had grabbed Dennis Cook and Al Leiter in two deals for five prospects (including A. J. Burnett) during the winter sale-a-thon. Yet when Steve Phillips was asked on WFAN on May 19 about trading with the Marlins for Piazza, he said the Mets had other priorities. New York's viewpoint on Piazza quickly changed, however, because other teams looking to trade with the Mets wanted major leaguers in return. Suddenly, trading a few more prospects seemed a more palatable solution, and Florida GM Dave Dumbrowksi did have quite an appetite for Mets minor leaguers.

Phillips sat with director of personnel Carmen Fusco, advisor Dave Wallace (who became Mets pitching coach in 1999), and two assistants who would eventually succeed Phillips as Mets GM—Jim Duquette and Omar Minaya—to discuss options. A Piazza deal was no longer out of the question, though it was not without risk. The catcher had already turned down $80 million from the Dodgers and would be a free agent after the season. Preston Wilson, Mookie's stepson, was a key to the deal. The recently promoted outfielder and 1992 first-round pick displayed both power and speed, but ownership concurred that the Mets should step up the Piazza pursuit.

The Cubs, meanwhile, made a run at Piazza. On Thursday, May 21, as the Mets completed three dates with the Reds while drawing barely 40,000—total—for the series, it seemed like New York would come up short in the Piazza chase. Of the eight other interested teams, the Cubs were the clear frontrunners—Piazza's agent even told the catcher that Chicago would be the destination—but the Mets' final offer won the day. They sent Wilson and two highly ranked lefty prospects, Ed Yarnall and Geoff Goetz, to Florida in exchange for the all-star catcher. That day, May 22, was heralded as "Great Friday" by the *Daily News*, and it was one hell of a way to kick off Memorial Day weekend.

Piazza arrived at Shea Stadium a day later and started behind the plate against a Milwaukee club making its first trip to Shea as a National League franchise after a lifetime in the American League. Fans roared Piazza's every move, held up pizza (Piazza) boxes, and were generally in disbelief that the team had pulled off the trade. Piazza doubled and caught Leiter's shutout in his Mets debut. New York took off, winning nine straight. The Piazza era began with a bang indeed.

The suddenly larger crowds brought in a fair share of boo birds, but Piazza didn't seem to notice. When Hundley came back in July, it was as a left fielder, and by the end of the season he was used mostly as a backup to Piazza and a pinch hitter. Although Piazza struggled in his first full month with the team (four homers, .318/.365/.511), his numbers went up every month thereafter. His final line of .348/.417/.607 with 33 doubles, 23 homers, and 76 RBI in 109 games as a Met was Shea Stadium's answer to the "home run chase" between Mark McGwire and Sammy Sosa. The Mets were also chasing their first postseason berth in a decade. Almost got it, too.

The Cubs tried to hand the Wild Card to New York, but the Expos ruined that. The Mets dropped their last two home games to Montreal to finish 4–8 against the last-place

Roger Cedeno slides home with the winning run during New York's 5–4 comeback victory over the Phillies on May 23, 1999. Cedeno was one of the bright newcomers that year, as the 24-year-old outfielder contributed a .313 average and a team-high 66 stolen bases. *Lou Requena/AP Images*

Turk Wendell was a workhorse for the Mets in the late nineties, appearing in 146 games during 1998 and 1999 while posting a record of 10–5 with a 2.99 ERA over those two seasons. *Ezra O. Shaw/Allsport/Getty Images*

Expos. The division-champion Braves then swept the Mets in Atlanta to end the season. All Mets fans could do was sigh and pray that the team could re-sign Piazza. The Mets broke the bank, throwing $91 million and seven years at him before any other team could try to woo him. After drawing 2,287,942 fans in 1998, the highest attendance since Darryl Strawberry's departure, it was a prudent investment. Once past those few early mind-boggling boos, Piazza was forever after worshipped at Shea Stadium. "You know where you stand with these people," he said when the deal was signed. Piazza was *the man*—as evidenced by the army of number 31 jerseys in every corner of Shea—and the catcher would soon get another chance to help end the postseason drought.

A Little of Everything

The 1998 Mets had more going for them than just their new all-star catcher. John Olerud set a club record with a .354 average, three Mets hit 20 homers—including Brian McRae, who also led the team with 20 steals—Al Leiter went 17–6, Rick Reed was 16–11, and John Franco saved 38 games. But after two oh-so-close 88-win seasons, the Mets needed to

crack 90 wins to get to the promised land of October. The Mets spent the winter upgrading: out with Butch Huskey, in with Roger Cedeno; Carlos Baerga dumped for Robin Ventura (with Edgardo Alfonzo moving to second base); ineffective Hideo Nomo replaced with old Mets nemesis Orel Hershiser; and ageless speedster Rickey Henderson taking over in left field. In a lightning-fast trick, the Mets sent minor leaguer Arnold Gooch and extraneous catcher Todd Hundley to the Dodgers for Cedeno and Charles Johnson and then immediately swapped Johnson to the Orioles for reliever Armando Benitez.

Though Benitez would bring years of late-season angst to Mets fans, his arrival transformed the bullpen in 1999, providing a power arm to go with the left–right tandem of Dennis Cook and Turk Wendell, who had pitched 73 and 66 games, respectively, in 1998. (Wendell had set a club record with appearances in nine straight games that year.) New York still had Franco, the all-time leader in saves by a lefty, and in April he became the second reliever in history to collect 400 career saves. Despite an Opening Day loss in Florida, the Mets reeled off seven wins in their next eight games. Piazza's two-out, two-run homer off San Diego's Trevor Hoffman turned an excruciating one-run loss into a thrilling one-run win and launched a six-game winning streak that carried the Mets into May. Later that month, Olerud's two-run single in the ninth against Curt Schilling rallied New York from a four-run ninth-inning deficit to a 5–4 win over the Phillies. The Mets followed that by taking two of three in Pittsburgh to improve to 27–20 before coming back home for Memorial Day weekend. That's where the team started improvising on the script—and the dialogue got a bit choppy.

The Mets were swept out of Shea in back-to-back series by the Diamondbacks and Reds. When the Mets went to the Bronx and dropped the first two games to the Yankees, things got hot for Bobby V. The eight straight losses cost the manager his top lieutenants: pitching coach Bob Apodaca, hitting coach Tom Robson, and bullpen coach Randy Niemann. With the season looking precarious, Leiter stopped the bleeding (and Roger Clemens' 20-game winning streak) with a 7–2 win over the Yanks.

The Mets then took the first two games of an interleague series with Toronto at Shea and rallied in the ninth inning of the finale for three runs to steal a win from avowed Valentine basher David Wells. As the game went into extra innings, Bobby V. was ejected for arguing. He changed his uniform, put on a Mets T-shirt and sunglasses, and then, the pièce de résistance, used eyeblack tape to create a mustache that turned the ensuing dugout scene into something out of Groucho Marx. The Mets beat the Blue Jays in 14 innings, and Valentine was suspended for two games and hit with a $5,000 fine, but his team was finally rolling.

In the meantime, Phillips brought in reinforcements. Veteran southpaw Kenny Rogers came from Oakland on July 23 (for Terrence Long and Leo Vazquez) to boost the wearied starting staff. Another trade with the A's a week later, however, proved costly. Because of a finger injury to

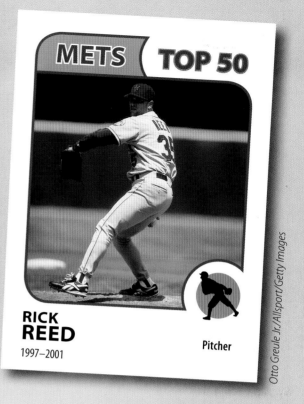

METS TOP 50

RICK REED
1997–2001

Pitcher

Otto Greule Jr./Allsport/Getty Images

Several unheralded minor leaguers thrived when given a chance by manager Bobby Valentine, but no Met made more of his opportunity than Rick Reed. Branded a replacement player for crossing the picket line to support his family in 1995, he spent 1996 at Triple-A Norfolk with Valentine and pitching coach Bob Apodaca, who were elevated to New York in August. Reed joined them the following spring at age 32.

Richard Allen Reed's first win as a Met was a complete game. He won six straight decisions during the summer, and his 13 victories nearly doubled his previous career total with four major league clubs. He won 16 games in 1998 and twice took no-hitters into the seventh inning. He made the all-star team, but as was the case in 2000, he did not pitch. He endured many slights due to his actions during the strike, but he did win 59 games as a Met, forged a tie for the Wild Card with a shutout in the penultimate game of 1999, beat the Diamondbacks in the NLDS, and in 2000 started the only World Series game won by the Mets.

Months after signing a three-year deal, Reed was dealt to Minnesota in July 2001 for Matt Lawton. The West Virginian loved pitching in New York, later saying that "baseball kind of died" for him and his wife with that trade. He went 25–25 as a Twin and pitched in three postseason series with Minnesota. He became pitching coach at his alma mater, Marshall University, but left to be with his family.

THE BEST INFIELD EVER!

The cover of the September 6, 1999, issue of *Sports Illustrated* posed the question "The Best Infield Ever?" and featured an image of four smiling Mets. It sounded like a bold claim, but writer Tom Verducci went through the other candidates who rated high with the glove: the 1906 Cubs, 1950 Dodgers, 1961 Yankees, 1969 Orioles, 1969 Cubs, 1980 Phillies, 1982 Cardinals, and 1998 Orioles. They all had their strengths, but the 1999 Mets were smoother than smooth.

The infield of John Olerud at first base, Edgardo Alfonzo at second, Rey Ordonez at short, and Robin Ventura at third committed just 27 errors all season in 1999. Even with six additional fielding gaffes by reserves, New York still broke the record of fewest infield errors, set a year earlier by Baltimore (45). Ordonez (four errors), Alfonzo (five, all on throws), Olerud (nine), and Ventura (nine) had a composite fielding percentage of .992.

The left side of the infield got Gold Gloves—Ordonez his third and Ventura his sixth—but the hardware was withheld from the right side. That was a shame, because Alfonzo's switch from third base to second so Ventura would sign as a free agent changed the whole infield dynamic.

"They exemplify the saying that strength up the middle wins championships," said Giants first baseman J. T. Snow, who won the Gold Glove over Olerud. (Pokey Reese got the award at second over Alfonzo.) "It's hard to get four guys like that on one infield, and that's why they're going to make the playoffs." *Sports Illustrated* cover jinx and Snow's prediction aside, the Mets managed to reach the postseason after a one-game playoff with Reese's Reds.

The Mets committed a major league low 68 errors and allowed just 20 unearned runs all season, both shattering marks held by the 1998 Orioles. Al Leiter was the only Mets starter to allow more than one unearned run in 1999.

The infielders' bats did their part, too. Alfonzo set a Mets record (since broken) with 123 runs scored while smashing 27 home runs and 104 RBI for a line of .304/.385/.502. Olerud scored 107 times, collected 125 walks, hit 19 homers, drove in 96 runs, and posted a line of .298/.427/.463. Ventura had 32 HRs, 120 RBI, three grand slams (plus another in the NLCS that didn't count), and a line of .301/.379/.529. And Ordonez . . . did we mention how good a fielder Rey-Rey was?

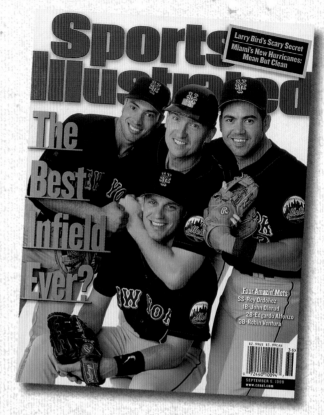

The Mets had an all-around solid infield in the late 1990s, but shortstop Rey Ordonez brought home the most hardware. Seen here making a bare-handed catch and throw to nail Chicago's Brian McRae at first base in July 1997, Ordonez won three straight Gold Glove Awards from 1997 to 1999. Third baseman Robin Ventura also won the award in 1999. *John Dunn/AP Images*

Somewhere in the middle of that pile is Melvin Mora, who has just scored the winning run on a wild pitch against Pittsburgh in the final inning of game number 162. The win allowed New York to finish in a tie with Cincinnati for the NL Wild Card spot, forcing a one-game playoff. *Jon Naso/ NY Daily News Archive/Getty Images*

Mets fans were hoping for another miracle on the 30th anniversary of the original Miracle Mets. *Jon Naso/NY Daily News Archive/Getty Images*

John Franco, the Mets saw the need for veteran bullpen help. Jason Isringhausen, nursed to health through repeated injuries and setbacks, and Greg McMichael—deemed so valuable in 1998 that he was traded to the Dodgers for one starter (Hideo Nomo) only to be reacquired a month later for another starter (Brian Bohanon)—were sent to the A's for Billy Taylor. Isringhausen became a top closer with Oakland, while Taylor, who had notched 26 saves with the A's in 1999, compiled an 8.10 ERA as a Met and was buried in the bullpen, just as Mel Rojas had been before being swapped in the spring for Bobby Bonilla in a headache-for-headache deal. While Rojas was traded once and released twice by Independence Day, Bonilla was a weight on the Mets bench all year, petulantly complaining about Valentine and a lack of playing time. A .160 hitter with a $5.9 million salary, Bonilla came to bat just 15 times in the second half. And the fans didn't like him much more than they had in his first sojourn with the Mets.

The Mets won 25 of their next 30 series (with one split) following the coach firing. They spent seven days in first place in August and another week tied with Atlanta atop the NL

Rickey Henderson (24) congratulates Edgardo Alfonzo after Fonzie's two-run homer gave the Mets a first-inning lead in the one-game playoff with Cincinnati, which New York won 5–0.
Mark Lyons/Allsport/Getty Images

East. The Braves had been the lone team to beat the Mets in more than one series during New York's dominant summer. As fall arrived on the calendar, the Mets headed to Turner Field trailing by one game. Given Atlanta's five straight series wins over New York, it was a tall order to come away with the division lead, but at least they had the Wild Card pretty well in hand. And then suddenly they didn't.

Chipper Jones wrapped up his MVP candidacy with four homers and seven RBI as the Braves swept the Mets. Then the Mets went to Philadelphia and were swept there. New York ended the seven-game skid with a club-record nine hits in one inning against Greg Maddux and the Braves at Shea, but they still lost the series. A four-game Wild Card lead over Cincinnati with a dozen games to play had become a two-game deficit with just three games left on the schedule.

The Reds, still alive for the NL Central crown, had reeled off six straight wins while the Mets had gone 1–8. All Cincinnati had to do was win once and New York lose once and it was over. Starting a three-game series on the road against fifth-place Milwaukee, the Reds blew a 3–0 lead in the eighth before losing in 10 innings. The Mets, meanwhile, pushed their winning run across the plate against Pittsburgh on Robin Ventura's hit, as reliever Pat Mahomes ran his record to 8–0. On Saturday afternoon the Brewers scored seven times in the third and beat the Reds; the Mets scored seven late runs Saturday night while Rick Reed blanked the Bucs. The Mets and Reds were now tied in the standings. If they both won—or lost—on Sunday, they would play each other on Monday.

Two years' worth of disappointment built on top of a decade of frustration at packed Shea Stadium—and wouldn't you know it, the Pirates scored first against Orel Hershiser. It seemed like an eternity until a line drive by Darryl Hamilton, a trade-deadline acquisition from Colorado, tied the game in the bottom of the fourth against rookie Kris Benson. Pittsburgh thwarted several chances by New York to take the lead, until the bottom of the ninth. Unknown sub Melvin Mora thrust himself into the consciousness of a hypersensitive Mets fan base by delivering a one-out single. Reliable Edgardo Alfonzo then singled to right, sending Mora to third. The Pirates walked John Olerud to set up a force at any base and bring up Mike Piazza, who had hit his 40th home run the night before but also owned the club record by grounding into 27 double plays in 1999. Brad Clontz, a side-arming groundball pitcher, came in to face Piazza. His first pitch went to the backstop. Mora crossed home plate on the wild pitch, and the Mets had come through on the last day of the season to live for another day.

Given what had happened the previous year, it was a moment of intense satisfaction and relief. After waiting all afternoon and most of the night for a weather front to move out of Wisconsin, the Reds finally escaped County Stadium with a win. The Mets and Reds had each seen a sure thing go out the window, and now came the chance to see which of them could salvage what was left on the sill.

Mister Mojo Risin'

After playing 162 games to get to this one-game playoff, the Mets took control quickly. Forty-year-old Rickey Henderson, the leading hitter (.315) on a team with five regulars batting over .300, led off with a single. Alfonzo promptly drilled a home run off rookie Steve Parris for two runs two batters into the game in Cincinnati. That was all Al Leiter needed. The southpaw, off and on all season with a 12–12 record and 4.41 ERA entering his do-or-die start, tossed his best game as a Met. He allowed a single in the second inning, a double in the ninth, and scattered four walks in a 135-pitch, 5–0 masterpiece. The wait for the sweet champagne had been long, but the Mets were quickly on to their next stop for a date in Phoenix with the Diamondbacks, the second-year expansion team with 100 wins.

Fonzie again played the hero. His ninth-inning grand slam provided the winning margin in the Division Series opener. Arizona evened the series the next night, but even more important was a thumb injury aggravated by Mike Piazza. He could not catch or swing a bat. As the NLDS shifted to New York, many fans were not even aware until game time that Piazza couldn't play. Todd Pratt, who had caught one inning and batted twice over the last two hectic weeks of the season, was in the lineup. He called a good game and Rick Reed pitched a superb one as the Mets blew out the Diamondbacks, 9–2.

Pratt caught Game 4 and the Mets held a 2–1 lead in the eighth with Leiter again working on a two-hitter. A walk and a mishandled grounder that went for a hit brought in Armando Benitez. Since John Franco's injury in July, the hard-throwing right-hander had taken over as closer; Franco shifted to setup role when he returned in September. Benitez had earned the promotion, allowing just one run in 17 appearances dating back to August, and he had picked up the win against Pittsburgh that forced the one-game playoff with Cincinnati.

Benitez entered in the eighth inning against Arizona and promptly served up a two-run double to give the Diamondbacks the lead, making a fifth game in Phoenix against Randy Johnson a frightening possibility. The top of the eighth ended with Melvin Mora throwing to Pratt to nail Jay Bell at the plate and keep it a 3–2 game. That proved key, because Tony Womack, moved from shortstop to right field, dropped a flyball that enabled the Mets to tie the score in the bottom of the inning. Diamondbacks closer Matt Mantei escaped further trouble by getting Pratt to ground out.

When Pratt came up again to face Mantei in the 10th inning, it seemed like maybe the Mets were running low on mojo—luck, attitude, or simply the refrain from The Doors' "L.A. Woman" that Robin Ventura played when the Mets won. Pratt took a mighty cut and sent a line drive to deep center. Gold Glove center fielder Steve Finley jumped at the base of the wall and seemed to have it. As everyone watched Finley, the outfielder slapped his glove and put his hands on his hips. Pratt jumped and Shea erupted. With only the fourth postseason series-ending homer to that point in history, the ultimate Mets understudy had become an unlikely hero. Mister Mojo risin' indeed.

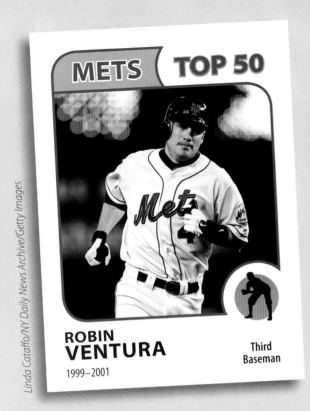

METS **TOP 50**

ROBIN VENTURA
1999–2001

Third Baseman

Robin Ventura hit 18 grand slams in his career, which at one point tied him with Willie McCovey for third most all-time. Ventura slammed three his first year as a Met in 1999—and became the first player to hit grand slams in each game of a doubleheader—but with the bases loaded in the 15th inning of Game 5 of the NLCS, all he needed was a flyball to bring in the winning run against Atlanta. He cleared the wall on a rainy night at Shea, but he only reached first when Todd Pratt hugged Ventura, passing the runner and negating the home run trot but not the win. The "Grand Slam Single" remains a singular postseason moment.

Robin Mark Ventura hit safely in 57 consecutive games at Oklahoma State and was taken in the first round by the White Sox in 1988. Signed as a free agent, Ventura came to the Mets and, while pushing Edgardo Alfonzo from third base to second, created what *Sports Illustrated* called the "best infield ever." Ventura kept the team loose by playing the "Mojo Risin'" refrain from the Doors song after wins in '99, and he kept the club in the Wild Card race with a walkoff single on the last Friday of the season. Though he and Mike Piazza became the franchise's first 120-RBI Mets that year, Ventura never again approached that level. Traded to the Yankees after 2001, the California native retired a Dodger. His last two homers were grand slams.

Catcher Mike Piazza congratulates Armando Benitez after the reliever pitched a perfect ninth inning against the Braves to earn the save in Game 4 of the 1999 NLCS. Benitez wasn't always perfect in his years with the Mets, but he does hold the franchise single-season record for saves (43, set in 2001). *Matt Campbell/AFP/Getty Images*

In the League Championship Series, the Braves were all business as they continued their dominance of the Mets. Even with Piazza back in the lineup, the Braves won the first two games at Turner Field in Atlanta. Greg Maddux won the opener and John Smoltz made his first career relief appearance to save Game 2. Two New York errors led to the Braves sneaking across the only run of Game 3 as Tom Glavine outdueled Al Leiter. John Olerud's single following a Mets double steal brought in the tying and go-ahead runs in Game 4 to avoid the sweep. Olerud homered to account for two more runs the next day in the first inning off Maddux, but runs would be hard to come by in a game with no shortage of drama.

Orel Hershiser relieved an ineffective Masato Yoshii in the fourth and was brilliant for three and one-third innings, even tagging out Ryan Klesko at the plate in a rundown to end a sixth-inning threat. When the Braves threatened in the seventh, Bobby Valentine brought in Turk Wendell. With Otis Nixon having stolen second and Brian Jordan ahead in the count 2–0, Valentine summoned Dennis Cook, running on fumes after pitching 71 times during the season. Cook intentionally walked Jordan, and with a southpaw on the mound, Atlanta skipper Bobby Cox sent up Brian Hunter to bat for Klesko. Valentine got the matchup he wanted and called in Pat Mahomes, who retired Hunter. The chess match lasted almost six hours in a steady rain that gave the proceedings a surreal quality. When the game reached inning 13, it became *The Twilight Zone*.

With rookie Octavio Dotel replacing Kenny Rogers on the mound, the Mets appeared about ready to crack. Keith Lockhart tried to score on a Chipper Jones double, but Melvin Mora threw to Piazza to end the inning. Lockhart got his revenge with a triple that plated the go-ahead run in the 15th. That's when things turned epic.

Shawon Dunston, who had been acquired at the trade deadline seemingly for just this purpose, fought Braves rookie Kevin McGlinchy through a 12-pitch at bat before singling to open the home 15th. Valentine somehow had two bench players left, and he sent up top pinch hitter Matt Franco, who had set a record with 20 walks off the bench during the season. Franco walked and Alfonzo bunted the runners over. Olerud was passed intentionally to load the bases, and Pratt, who had taken over for Piazza an inning earlier, walked to send in the tying run. With the infield and outfield playing in, Ventura crushed a 2–1 pitch. The ball somehow made it

GRAND-SLAM SINGLE
New York Mets 4, Atlanta Braves 3
NLCS Game 5
Sunday, October 17, 1999
at Shea Stadium, Queens, NY

	1	2	3	4	5	6	7	8	9	10	11	12	13	14	15	R	H	E
ATL	0	0	0	2	0	0	0	0	0	0	0	0	0	0	1	3	13	2
NYM	2	0	0	0	0	0	0	0	0	0	0	0	0	0	2	4	11	1

Atlanta Braves	AB	R	H	RBI
Williams, LF	7	0	1	0
Boone, 2B	3	1	1	0
Nixon, PR	0	0	0	0
Lockhart, 2B	4	0	2	1
C Jones, 3B	6	1	3	1
Jordan, RF	7	0	2	1
Klesko, 1B	2	0	0	0
Hunter, PH-1B	3	0	0	0
A Jones, CF	5	0	0	0
Perez, C	4	0	2	0
Battle, PR	0	0	0	0
Myers, C	1	0	0	0
Weiss, SS	6	1	2	0
Maddux, P	3	0	0	0
Hernandez, PH	1	0	0	0
Mulholland, P	0	0	0	0
Guillen, PH	1	0	0	0
Remlinger, P	0	0	0	0
Springer, P	0	0	0	0
Fabregas, PH	1	0	0	0
Rocker, P	0	0	0	0
McGlinchy, P	1	0	0	0
Totals	55	3	13	3

2B: Boone, Williams, Weiss, C Jones 2, Perez. **3B:** Lockhart. **SH:** A Jones.
HBP: Boone. **SB:** Weiss, Battle, Nixon. **Team LOB:** 19.
E: Klesko 2.

New York Mets	AB	R	H	RBI
Henderson, LF	5	1	1	0
Rogers, P	0	0	0	0
Bonilla, PH	1	0	0	0
Dotel, P	0	0	0	0
M Franco, PH	0	0	0	0
Cedeno, PR	0	1	0	0
Alfonzo, 2B	6	0	1	0
Olerud, 1B	6	1	2	2
Piazza, C	6	0	1	0
Pratt, C	0	0	0	1
Ventura, 3B	7	0	2	1
Mora, RF-CF-RF	6	0	1	0
Hamilton, CF	3	0	2	0
Agbayani, PH-RF-LF	1	0	0	0
Ordonez, SS	6	0	0	0
Yoshii, P	1	0	0	0
Hershiser, P	1	0	0	0
Wendell, P	0	0	0	0
Cook, P	0	0	0	0
Mahomes, P	1	0	0	0
J Franco, P	0	0	0	0
Benitez, P	0	0	0	0
Dunston, PH-CF	3	1	1	0
Totals	53	4	11	4

2B: Hamilton. **HR:** Olerud. **SH:** Alfonzo. **SB:** Dunston, Agbayani. **Team LOB:** 12.
E: Olerud.

Pitching Summary

Atlanta Braves	IP	H	R	ER	BB	SO
Maddux	7	7	2	2	0	5
Mulholland	2	1	0	0	0	2
Remlinger	2	1	0	0	0	2
Springer	1	0	0	0	1	1
Rocker	1.1	0	0	0	0	2
McGlinchy, L (0–1)	1	2	2	2	4	1
Totals	14.1	11	4	4	5	13

New York Mets	IP	H	R	ER	BB	SO
Yoshii	3	4	2	2	1	3
Hershiser	3.1	1	0	0	3	5
Wendell	0.1	0	0	0	1	1
Cook	0	0	0	0	0	0
Mahomes	1	1	0	0	2	1
J Franco	1.1	1	0	0	0	2
Benitez	1	1	0	0	0	1
Rogers	2	1	0	0	1	1
Dotel, W (1–0)	3	4	1	1	2	5
Totals	15	13	3	3	10	19

Umpires: HP Jerry Layne, 1B Jerry Crawford, 2B Ed Montague, 3B Jeff Kellogg, LF Charlie Reliford, RF Ed Rapuano.
Time of Game: 5:46
Attendance: 55,723

through the rain and fog into the bullpen. The game was over—but not the spectacle. Pratt turned and gave Ventura a bear hug, thereby passing the batter and discounting three runs. No game-winning homer, but the "grand-slam single" was an instant part of the lexicon, and the Mets lived on.

It was a precarious life, though, one that began in a 5–0 hole when Al Leiter, so tough in his last four starts, could not retire a single batter in Game 6. The Mets relievers allowed just two runs in seven innings, while the offense gradually dug the team out of the hole. New York tied the game in the seventh on Piazza's three-run homer off Smoltz in relief and then took the lead an inning later on Mora's RBI single

off Mike Remlinger. That's when John Franco, charged with only one run in 17 games since coming back from his finger injury, surrendered the lead. Pratt came through once more by driving in the go-ahead run in top of the 10th against celebrated New York hater John Rocker, but Atlanta pinch hitter Ozzie Guillen singled in the tying run in the bottom of the inning against Benitez.

The whole series—the whole month—was like a dream now. Kenny Rogers pitching in the 11th . . . missing to Andruw Jones with the bases loaded . . . Braves celebrating at home plate . . . the end of a storied run, the end of a decade, a century, a millennium.

1990s METS YEAR-BY-YEAR

YEAR	W–L	PCT.	GB	FINISH	
1990	91–71	.562	4	2nd in 6-team NL East	David Cone's 233 strikeouts were the most in baseball, Sid Fernandez led the NL with 6.5 hits per nine innings, Frank Viola's 249⅔ innings topped the league, and John Franco led the NL with 33 saves in his first year as a Met.
1991	77–84	.478	20 ½	5th	Because part of Olympic Stadium collapsed, a rescheduled Expos doubleheader on September 17 drew just 4,335 fans. It was the smallest crowd at Shea Stadium since another doubleheader with Montreal drew just 2,251 in September 1982. Nine years apart, the Mets split both twinbills with the Expos.
1992	72–90	.444	24	5th	The over-the-hill and overpaid club went 18–39 in games on artificial turf in 1992, making for a long season when four division opponents played on the stuff. The Mets had more DL stints (18) than triples (17), at the time setting a franchise mark for the most of the former and the fewest of the latter.
1993	59–103	.364	38	7th in 7-team NL East	For the worst Mets team in a quarter century, this squad put up some big offensive numbers. Three Mets surpassed 20 homers and 80 RBI—Bobby Bonilla (34, 87), Eddie Murray (27, 100), and Jeff Kent (21, 80)—yet the team was second-to last in the league in runs and dead last in on-base percentage.
1994	55–58	.487	18 ½	3rd in 5-team NL East	Mets batters led the majors with 52 hit by pitches. Three Mets were hit in double digits: Fernando Vina (12), Jeff Kent (10), and Ryan Thompson (10). Yet 5-foot-8 John Cangelosi, who was hit by pitches only twice, made the cover of *Sports Illustrated* getting punched by ex-Met Charlie O'Brien in a brawl at Shea.
1995	69–75	.479	21	2nd	The Mets went 34–18 after August 5, including wins in their last 11 home games to tie a franchise mark. They won nearly as many games in the final two months as they had in the first three. The Mets walked the fewest batters in baseball, and their 3.88 ERA was third in the NL.
1996	71–91	.438	25	4th	On Friday the 13th against first-place Atlanta in September, rookie Derek Wallace came on for the save. He fanned Terry Pendleton, who took first on a passed ball. After striking out Chipper Jones, Wallace allowed a double but then struck out the last two batters to become the first Met to fan four in one inning.
1997	88–74	.543	13	3rd	The Mets won 17 more games than in 1996 and led the majors with 47 come-from-behind wins, including on September 13 against Montreal. Down 6–0 with two outs in the ninth, Roberto Petagine singled in two runs and Carl Everett launched a grand slam to tie the game. Bernard Gilkey's three-run homer won it in 11.
1998	88–74	.543	18	2nd	Nine rainouts in 1998 were the most of the decade. The result was a 4–1–3 mark in doubleheaders, but the last twin bill was on the original schedule at the Astrodome in September. The Mets split the doubleheader and took the other two must-win games in Houston in extra innings.
1999	97–66	.595	6 ½	2nd*	Benny Agbayani gave the Mets a nice Hawaiian punch in his first full season in the majors, slamming 10 home runs in his first 73 at bats after being called up and batting .286 on the season. A ballroom dancer—like manager Bobby Valentine—B-B-B-enny and the Mets were a graceful pair.

* Won one-game playoff for Wild Card.

Before he can even reach second base after hitting the ball over the fence, Ventura is hoisted up by Todd Pratt, preventing Ventura from completing his circuit around the bases. Although he was credited officially with a single, it was enough to send in the winning run. *Bill Kostroun/AFP/Getty Images*

The 2000s

So Close and Yet. . .

G Fiume/Getty Images

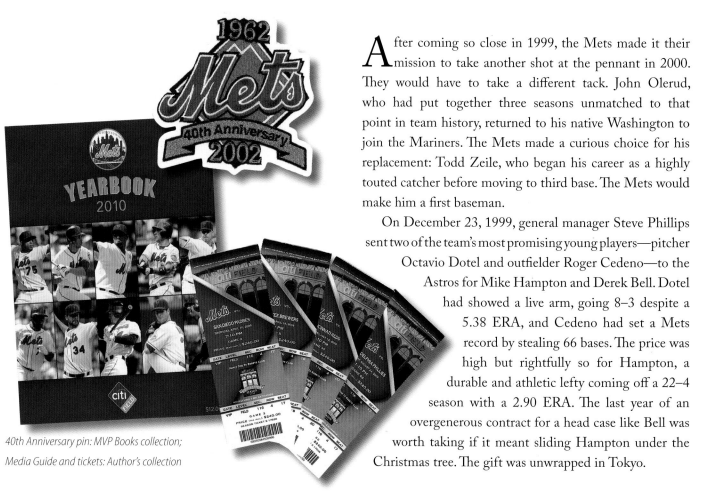

YEARBOOK
2010

*40th Anniversary pin: MVP Books collection;
Media Guide and tickets: Author's collection*

After coming so close in 1999, the Mets made it their mission to take another shot at the pennant in 2000. They would have to take a different tack. John Olerud, who had put together three seasons unmatched to that point in team history, returned to his native Washington to join the Mariners. The Mets made a curious choice for his replacement: Todd Zeile, who began his career as a highly touted catcher before moving to third base. The Mets would make him a first baseman.

On December 23, 1999, general manager Steve Phillips sent two of the team's most promising young players—pitcher Octavio Dotel and outfielder Roger Cedeno—to the Astros for Mike Hampton and Derek Bell. Dotel had showed a live arm, going 8–3 despite a 5.38 ERA, and Cedeno had set a Mets record by stealing 66 bases. The price was high but rightfully so for Hampton, a durable and athletic lefty coming off a 22–4 season with a 2.90 ERA. The last year of an overgenerous contract for a head case like Bell was worth taking if it meant sliding Hampton under the Christmas tree. The gift was unwrapped in Tokyo.

For years Major League Baseball had played exhibitions in Japan, but it had to take the next step and stage games that fans in the United States genuinely cared about to truly expand the MLB brand to the most baseball-obsessed country outside the western hemisphere. Logistically, playing overseas required the season to start five days before everyone else. Stylistically, the draw was Chicago's Slammin' Sammy Sosa against New York's Mike Piazza. The hype would have been far greater if either team employed a Japanese player (the Mets had traded Masato Yoshii to Colorado in January), but New York did have a manager with Japanese experience. Bobby Valentine had managed the Chiba Lotte Marines to a second-place finish in 1995, and he relished every minute of the March 2000 trip.

Benny Agbayani was on the Opening Day roster only because the Mets didn't need all their starting pitchers for the two-game series in Japan. Agbayani made the trek knowing he would likely be farmed out upon returning stateside since he had minor league options remaining. The Mets lost the first game—Hampton looked groggy and fans watching on TV felt even more so with the 5 a.m. New York start time—but the second game went late, or until almost 9 a.m. eastern time. Agbayani's grand slam in the 11th at the Tokyo Dome led the Mets to their first win of 2000. He received a traditional shogun helmet as the star of the game. He did not have to lug the souvenir back to the minors.

Newcomer Derek Bell hit the tiebreaking homer in the Shea Stadium opener, but the Mets dropped six of eight. They were streaky all season. A nine-game April winning streak was followed by a 5–8 road trip. They won nine of ten in late June, punctuated by a 10-run eighth inning on fireworks night to stun the first-place Braves, 11–8. The Mets then dropped six of eight heading into the All-Star break, including a sweep in the first two-stadium, two-league doubleheader in New York history.

A rainout at Yankee Stadium a month earlier forced the Mets and Yankees to hop on buses (forget that it was called the *Subway* Series) and go from Shea by day to Yankee Stadium at night. The afternoon game featured Dwight Gooden pitching against the Mets for the first time in his career. After the Mets cut him loose in 1994 for his continued drug problems, Gooden had signed with the Yankees—and pitched a no-hitter—in 1996 and then bounced around for a few years before returning to the Bronx in the summer of 2000. His first start was at Shea against his former team. Gooden pitched five innings and the bullpen stymied the Mets. It was a strange scene, but it got downright scary that night at Yankee Stadium. Roger Clemens, lit up by Mike Piazza for a grand slam one month earlier, drilled Piazza in the head in the rematch. Piazza was helped off the field, and he missed the next game as well as the All-Star Game. And it could have been far worse. Mets starter Glendon Rusch plunked the first Yankee in the bottom of the inning, but it wasn't enough for Valentine. "I hope someday he'll pitch in a National League park when we're playing against him," the Mets skipper said of Clemens.

Piazza was back behind the plate when the Mets returned from the All-Star break, but one error altered the club's thinking. Melvin Mora had taken over at shortstop after Rey Ordonez broke his arm on May 29 in Los Angeles. The resulting lineup was far more dynamic, with Mora batting leadoff and left fielder Agbayani in the eight hole. (Increasingly cantankerous Rickey Henderson had been released in May after watching his "sure" home run go for a

It was a scary scene for Mets fans everywhere when Mike Piazza dropped to the ground after getting beaned by Roger Clemens in the first inning of the second game of the Mets–Yankees cross-town doubleheader on July 8, 2000. *Mark Lennihan/AP Images*

ridiculously long single). Mora couldn't approach Ordonez's glove, but his offensive production far outpaced Rey-Rey's. In the first game after the break, Mora's error on a potential game-ending double play at Fenway Park led to a game-ending double by Brian Daubach. Though Mora homered and knocked in three runs the next night—and Piazza showed he was all right with a go-ahead home run in the eighth—the wheels were in motion for another regrettable midseason deal.

Phillips tried to get shortstop Barry Larkin in a trade that would have cost New York nobody who wound up spending much time in the majors, yet Larkin said "no" to coming to the Mets. *New York Times* speculation about Baltimore's Mike Bordick was spot on: "Bordick appears to be the only available shortstop the Mets value more than their own Melvin Mora." The Mets acquired Bordick for Mora and three others. Phillips then prudently traded two former first-round draft choices, Paul Wilson and Jason Tyner, to Tampa Bay for outfielder Bubba Trammell and reliever Rick White. The trio paid immediate dividends: Bordick and Trammell each homered their first times up and White won his first appearance. After that rare show of

power, however, Bordick hit meekly and proved both injury prone and homesick. He returned to Baltimore as a free agent, joining future all-star Mora.

But the Mets were going for it in 2000. They even got their annual September swoon out of the way early. The 8–1 homestand during which those trades were made propelled the Mets to a 20–9 August and catapulted them from five and a half games behind Atlanta to a half-game ahead on August 31. Hearts sank with three straight walk-off losses in St. Louis, two less dramatic but equally disheartening defeats in a three-game set in Cincinnati, and two consecutive losses to the Phillies at Shea. Yet that was as bad as things got in the regular season. The Mets won 13 of their last 20, closing the season with five straight victories while becoming the first NL team to win the Wild Card twice.

Matterhorn High, Grand Canyon Low

The Mets and Giants had ravaged each other in 2000. The Giants welcomed the Mets into the new Pac Bell Park by sweeping them four straight in May, and the Mets took the first three of four from San Francisco at Shea in August. The Division Series began in Pac Bell with New York losing both

the opening game and right fielder Derek Bell to a leg injury. Though the Mets would not win a regular season game at San Francisco's jewel of a ballpark until 2003, they won when they had to in the Division Series.

Al Leiter was brilliant in Game 2, and Bell's understudy, Timo Perez, knocked in the game's first two runs. Perez also scored in the 9th on an Edgardo Alfonzo home run that gave New York a seemingly safe 4–1 lead, but J. T. Snow's pinch-hit blast off Armando Benitez with two men on and tied the game. Darryl Hamilton doubled with two outs in the 10th and chugged home on Jay Payton's single. After Benitez allowed a single to open the bottom of the inning, John Franco, all-time Mets saves leader turned setup man, notched the save by freezing Barry Bonds with strike three.

The late-inning drama continued at Shea Stadium. After Alfonzo's two-out double tied Game 3 in the 8th inning, both clubs tried not to squander their most valuable extra-inning assets: reliable arms. Rick White allowed two hits in the top of the 13th, but he got Bonds to pop up to end it. In the bottom of the inning, Agbayani hammered an Aaron Fultz pitch through the stiff wind and put the Mets one game from winning the series. That's where an even better redemption story came in.

"Fresno" Bobby Jones, one of two Mets pitchers by that name on the club in 2000, had been sent to the minors. He returned from two weeks in Norfolk and went 10–3 the rest of the way, looking like the man who was among his team's most consistent starters until an arm injury derailed his 1999 season. Having missed the previous year's October run, Jones got his first career postseason start for Game 4. He tossed a one-hit shutout, allowing base runners in only the fifth inning and escaping that jam when three-time manager of the year Dusty Baker let pitcher Mark Gardner bat—and pop up—with the bases loaded. Jones retired the final 13 batters. As

announcer Bob Murphy called it, "The Mets have never had a better game pitched in their 39-year history than this game pitched by Bobby Jones." And Murph would know.

The Mets owed a sincere thanks to the Cardinals for sweeping the Braves, the first time America's perennial postseason team had not advanced to at least the second round since the Division Series debuted in 1995. The Cards were favored over the Mets in the NLCS, just as the Giants had been in the NLDS. Bobby Valentine's club dispatched both Dusty Baker and Tony LaRussa with complete-game shutout clinchers at Shea. This time Mike Hampton was the center of the celebration. He threw seven shutout innings in the opener and—with Payton again getting the tiebreaking hit in Game 2 and Glendon Rusch coming to the rescue out of the pen to hold off St. Louis in Game 4—Hampton blanked the Cards on three hits in Game 5. Todd Zeile's bases-clearing double in the fourth inning gave the Mets

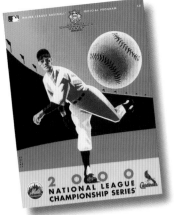

a six-run lead, and the countdown commenced for the first Mets pennant since 1986. Edgardo Alfonzo hit .444, Mike Piazza batted .412, Timo Perez scored eight runs, and Zeile knocked in eight, but the NLCS MVP was Hampton. He held St. Louis to a measly .158 average in 16 shutout innings of work (the Cards batted .317 against the rest of the Mets staff).

Without Olerud and Ordonez, this was not the "Best Infield Ever," and the outfield of Agbayani-Payton-Perez did not remind anyone of Cleon-Agee-Swoboda or Mookie-Dykstra-Darryl, but just like those clubs, these Mets were a World Series team. And this series would be a local affair.

The Yankees clinched their division title with 87 wins, seven fewer than the Mets and the lowest win total by any Yankees postseason team over a full season. The Yankees stayed right on the heels of the Mets during this march through October: clinching the Division Series the same day and taking the pennant one day and one game later than the Mets. Their swagger restored after defeating Oakland and Seattle, the Yankees now looked just like the team that swept through the 1998 and 1999 World Series. In the end, the Yankees won in five, with two games decided in the final inning; the difference in every game was one or two runs. In a city like New York, there are no parades for second place, and all that history would note was that the one time the Mets and Yankees played with everything on the line, the Yankees had won. The Bronx is up . . .

It seemed that nothing could hurt Mets fans more than what happened in 2000, but a year later a national tragedy in the city offered the ultimate perspective. Baseball is just a game, a distraction, an activity far down the list of what truly matters. And then, lump still in throat, baseball provided the opportunity to show that life does go on, even after the unimaginable.

Mike Hampton was the Mets pitching hero and series MVP against St. Louis in the NLCS. The righty struck out eight while yielding just three hits and one walk in a complete-game win to clinch the pennant for New York. *Jeff Zelevansky/AFP/Getty Images*

Mets fans and Yankee fans exchange words on the number 4 train to Yankee Stadium for the first World Series meeting between the two clubs. *Spencer Platt/Newsmakers/Getty Images*

The Return of the Subway Series
THE 2000 WORLD SERIES

For Mets fans who long wished for a chance to take on the crosstown Yankees on the World Series stage, October of 2000 was a classic case of be careful what you wish for. The Subway Series dominated the media in New York for the 10 days it was a reality, but it caused barely a ripple nationally amid low TV ratings. Even in New York, it was not a novel concept, as the Bronx Bombers had faced off with the New York Giants or the Brooklyn Dodgers a total of 13 times between 1921 and 1956, winning 10 of those contests.

The Mets and Yankees players tried to downplay the rivalry that had been ignited with the introduction of interleague play in 1997, after years of facing each other only in spring training and Mayor's Trophy exhibition games. Now with a championship on the line, the hype was at full bore. And Roger Clemens' hurling a shattered bat at Mike Piazza in Game 2 turned the 2000 World Series into a circus—a circus the Yankees controlled like a seasoned pro on the high wire.

During the long winter that followed, recurring images flickered in darkened bedrooms late at night. A moment's hesitation by Timo Perez cost him on the base paths in the 6th inning of the opener, negating a run the Mets desperately needed, especially after Armando Benitez frittered away the lead in the 9th. When an RBI single by ex-Met Jose Vizcaino won it for the Yanks in the 12th inning, years of condescension and cracks

Game 2 of the 2000 World Series took a bizarre turn when Yankee pitcher Roger Clemens tossed a piece of Mike Piazza's broken bat toward Piazza as he ran to first. Piazza didn't take kindly to the action, and both dugouts cleared, but order was restored without further incident. *Doug Kanter/AFP/Getty Images*

from peers weighed heavy on the almost always outnumbered Mets fan. This series had offered a lasting chance at retribution; after one game, it was slipping away.

A Game 2 comeback fell short, and the Mets returned to the relative safety of Shea Stadium, where Benny Agbayani broke a tie in the eighth inning. John Franco earned the Game 3 win, ending the Yankees' 14-game World Series winning streak and providing a morsel of dignity for his people. Derek Jeter led off Game 4 with a home run and former Met David Cone retired the only batter he faced in the series—Mike Piazza, with the bases loaded. Al Leiter gave everything he had the next night, but when his 142nd pitch was dribbled through the middle by Luis Sojo to snap a tie in the ninth inning, the worst of all possible worlds came to be for Mets fans: the Yankees celebrating a world championship on the Shea Stadium field.

"Nobody wins a Subway Series. Or maybe everybody does," contemplated Robert Lipsyte in the *New York Times*. Maybe that's how it felt in the press box, but on the subway ride home after Game 5, Mets fans felt a mixture of numbness, regret, and an unexpected kinship with teams that long ago traded riding in trains for cruising on California freeways.

Yankee catcher Jorge Posada waits to make the tag on Timo Perez as the Mets right fielder attempts to score from first on a Todd Zeile double. A slight hesitation on the base paths ensured that Perez was a dead duck, spoiling a chance for the Mets to get on the board first in Game 1. *V. J. Lovero/Sports Illustrated/Getty Images*

The first baseball game played in New York after 9/11 was an emotional moment for all in attendance at Shea Stadium on September 21, 2001. Mike Piazza's game-winning home run in the bottom of the eighth brought a moment of joy for Mets fans. *Matt Campbell/AFP/Getty Images*

Carry On

The first four and a half months of the 2001 season were interminable. The Mets won on Opening Day and took two series from Atlanta in the first 10 days of the season, but by June the club was 10 games under .500 and 13 games out. The Mets finally had a winning month in July, but by the end of the month, trailing Atlanta by 11½ and even further out in the Wild Card race, New York decided to be sellers at the trade deadline. A few days after trading Todd Pratt to the Phillies, the Mets' overworked bullpen tandem of Turk Wendell and Dennis Cook went to Philadelphia as well. A seven-game losing streak in mid-August put the Mets a season-worst 14 games under .500 and 14 behind Atlanta in the loss column. Then suddenly they couldn't be stopped.

The Mets embarked on a 16–5 run that included several late-game comebacks: Alfonzo singling in the tying run and Agbayani driving in the go-ahead run to end the slump in Los Angeles; beating San Francisco on a walk-off hit by Rey Ordonez in 11 innings as the Mets took three of four from the Giants; scoring five runs in the ninth to commence a sweep of the Phillies; and down to their last out in Florida, and with reserve Mark Johnson walked intentionally to face him, Matt Lawton (acquired from the Twins for Rick Reed) doubled in the tying and go-ahead runs. Just eights games back and the closest they had been since May 16, baseball was fun again, and the Mets still had six games remaining with first-place Atlanta. The date was September 9, 2001.

The World Trade Center attacks were so utterly beyond words that explaining what happened, what it meant, and what people felt was compartmentalized into two numbers: 9/11. Shea Stadium remained intensely busy, as the parking lot was used as a police command center and a location for collecting food and clothing for rescue efforts. The Mets, who had been in Pittsburgh the morning of September 11, took a nine-hour bus ride back to New York. After six days, baseball games resumed with the Mets back in Pittsburgh after swapping the location of a later series. When the Mets took the field, they wore hats honoring New York's emergency personnel. The Mets swept the Pirates to go over .500 for the first time since the third game of the season. The Mets were five games out, and the Braves were coming to New York.

It felt strange to be home. Several players, like many other people throughout the world, suffered from depression, but the Mets returned to work realizing the value in the entertainment and distraction they provided. "There will be some people who take a break from the local news and CNN, take a deep breath and enjoy what they did before," said Bobby Valentine, who had flown to Pittsburgh a day later than his team because he was helping to coordinate the relief efforts at Shea Stadium. The place was ready for baseball on Friday, September 21.

Flags waved, people sang, and for the first time in a long time, nary a head was covered for the playing of the national anthem, sung by Marc Anthony. Also singing were Diana Ross and Liza Minnelli, high stepping with a line of New York firefighters in a lively rendition of "New York, New York." Bruce Chen, acquired from Philadelphia a month earlier, threw the game's first pitch, and with it baseball returned to New York.

Mike Piazza at Shea Stadium, September 21, 2001. *Howard Earl Simmons/ NY Daily News Archive/Getty Images*

The Braves took a 2–1 lead in the top of the eighth, but Edgardo Alfonzo worked out a walk in the bottom of the inning. Mike Piazza, who had battled to keep his emotions in check on the field earlier in the game, crushed Long Islander Steve Karsay's 0–1 pitch to center as the stadium erupted in cheers.

An even greater test—especially for Mets followers—was how to react when the team did something maddening. After the Mets won for the 21st time in 27 games the next night to pull within three and a half games of Atlanta, Armando Benitez coughed up a three-run lead with two outs in the ninth on Sunday. The Mets lost in 11 innings. New York swept Montreal to pull within three games of first, but then lost the opener in Atlanta. The next day Al Leiter allowed just one run in eight innings for the second straight start, only to see the bullpen implode, this time to the tune of seven runs in the ninth. Even after all that had happened in the too-real world, it was OK to be angry at the Mets. It just wasn't the end of the world anymore.

NEW YORK'S FIRST POST-9/11 BASEBALL GAME

New York Mets 3, Atlanta Braves 2
Friday, September 21, 2001
at Shea Stadium, Queens, NY

	1	2	3	4	5	6	7	8	9	R	H	E
ATL	0	0	0	1	0	0	0	1	0	2	9	0
NYM	0	0	0	1	0	0	0	2	x	3	8	1

Atlanta Braves	AB	R	H	RBI
Giles, 2B	3	0	0	0
Franco, 1B	3	0	0	0
Aldridge, PR	0	1	0	0
Karsay, P	0	0	0	0
C Jones, LF	4	1	2	0
Jordan, RF	4	0	1	1
Caminiti, 3B	3	0	2	0
Garcia, PR	0	0	0	0
Helms, 3B	0	0	0	0
Martinez, PH-1B	0	0	0	0
A Jones, CF	4	0	0	0
Lopez, C	4	0	3	0
DeRosa, PR	0	0	0	0
Sanchez, SS	3	0	1	0
Surhoff, PH	1	0	0	0
Marquis, P	2	0	0	0
Reed, P	0	0	0	0
Remlinger, P	0	0	0	0
Gilkey, PH	1	0	0	0
Lockhart, 3B	1	0	0	0
Totals	**33**	**2**	**9**	**1**

2B: Jordan, Caminiti. **SB:** Sanchez, Garcia. **Team LOB:** 7.

New York Mets	AB	R	H	RBI
Lawton, RF	4	0	1	0
Alfonzo, 2B	3	0	1	0
Relaford, PR-2B	0	1	0	0
Piazza, C	4	2	3	2
Ventura, 3B	4	0	1	0
Shinjo, LF	3	0	1	1
Zeile, 1B	3	0	1	0
Payton, CF	3	0	0	0
Ordonez, SS	3	0	0	0
Chen, P	2	0	0	0
Johnson, PH	0	0	0	0
McEwing, PH	1	0	0	0
Franco, P	0	0	0	0
Benitez, P	0	0	0	0
Totals	**30**	**3**	**8**	**3**

2B: Zeile, Piazza. **HR:** Piazza. **SF:** Shinjo. **Team LOB:** 5.
E: Piazza.

Pitching Summary

Atlanta Braves	IP	H	R	ER	BB	SO
Marquis	6	7	1	1	0	4
Reed	0.2	0	0	0	0	0
Remlinger	0.1	0	0	0	0	0
Karsay, L (3–5)	1	1	2	2	1	1
Totals	**8**	**8**	**3**	**3**	**1**	**5**

New York Mets	IP	H	R	ER	BB	SO
Chen	7	6	1	0	1	5
Franco	0.2	1	1	1	1	1
Benitez, W (6–3)	1.1	2	0	0	1	1
Totals	**9**	**9**	**2**	**1**	**3**	**7**

Umpires: HP Wally Bell, 1B Marty Foster, 2B Mark Hirschbeck, 3B Ron Kulpa.
Time of Game: 3:07
Attendance: 41,235

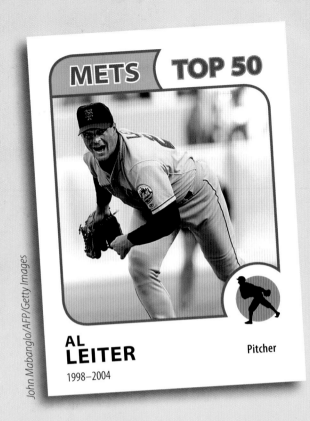

METS · TOP 50

AL LEITER
1998–2004

Pitcher

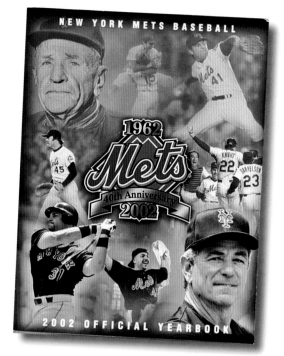

While celebrating the 40th anniversary of the franchise, the 2002 incarnation of the Mets seemed to have more in common with Casey Stengel's 1962 squad than with the championship clubs featured on the yearbook cover. *Author's collection*

Al Leiter was a Mets fan who grew up to be a Mets ace. The Leiter household in Toms River, New Jersey, produced two big league pitchers. Older brother Mark spent 11 years in the majors, but younger brother Al, a southpaw, was drafted higher, debuted earlier, lasted longer, and pitched in three World Series.

Alois Terry Leiter was drafted by the Yankees, but his career hit a roadblock with a series of arm injuries traceable to a 163-pitch effort under manager Dallas Green in 1989. Traded shortly thereafter to Toronto, he was hurt for much of his time as a Blue Jay. He earned the win in the opener of the 1993 World Series, but he failed to notch a victory in his next 14 postseason appearances. He left with leads in three Mets postseason games only to see each one blown by Armando Benitez.

Leiter became a Met four months after starting Game 7 of the 1997 World Series for the Florida Marlins. In 1998, he had a 2.47 ERA, and his 17 wins were the most by a Met since 1990. His two-hit shutout in a one-game playoff in Cincinnati in 1999 put the Mets in the postseason for the first time in 11 years. He took the loss in both the All-Star Game and the deciding game of the World Series in 2000, though he deserved a better fate in each. A pitcher who wore his emotions on his sleeve, Leiter is among the leaders in many Mets all-time categories.

Up in Smoke

Change continued to be the constant under Steve Phillips in 2002. A year earlier the GM had understandably let mega-priced Mike Hampton leave and did not pursue Alex Rodriguez. Reserves Desi Relaford and Tyoshi Shinjo, picked up at marginal cost in 2001, performed ably enough to net southpaw Shawn Estes in a trade with San Francisco. Despite the club making up 10 games in the standings in a 29-game span while dealing with circumstances far beyond anyone's control in 2001, Phillips picked apart the core of the team. Robin Ventura was traded to the Yankees for David Justice, who was sent to Oakland for two relievers. Todd Zeile was shipped to Colorado with Benny Agbayani, while Lenny Harris, who had become baseball's all-time pinch-hit king the final weekend of 2001, went to Milwaukee with Glendon Rusch; the return was ex-Met Jeromy Burnitz and Jeff D'Amico.

The big trade was with Cleveland: Roberto Alomar and a couple of minor leaguers for Matt Lawton and four Mets prospects, notably Alex Escobar, who had not yet been traded despite three years ranked high by *Baseball America*. Phillips also lavished a four-year, $18 million contract on Roger Cedeno. They kept bringing in the same type of

player: veterans past their prime, in peak earning years, and not so sturdy anymore. For the fifth straight year, the Mets got older. Two days after Christmas, a mistake-for-mistake trade turned out to be, not surprisingly, crippling.

Kevin Appier, handed a $40 million, four-year contract after Hampton left, was traded for a former all-star who had just missed an entire season: Mo Vaughn. A Norwalk, Connecticut, native beloved in his hometown for his charitable endeavors and good-guy persona, the former Seton Hall star had left the Red Sox after the 1998 season and put together two solid seasons for the Angels before missing all of 2001 with a biceps tendon injury. Phillips and Valentine agreed to go forward with the deal after watching Vaughn hit in an indoor batting cage. Vaughn's bloated contract (three years, $42 million) and body (270 pounds, minimum) came to symbolize what was wrong with the Mets.

Vaughn committed a league-high 18 errors in 139 games in 2002. Even for a player who'd led the league in this dubious category six times, this was a career worst. His 18 doubles, 26 homers, 72 RBI, .259 average, and .456 slugging were his lowest marks in a decade. But it wasn't just Vaughn. Alomar, coming off a superb year in Cleveland, fell off a cliff in New York. His 12 consecutive all-star appearances ended

and his .266 average was his lowest since he was a rookie in 1988. Worst of all, Alomar went from Gold Glove to barely adequate at second base; his range and speed were reduced, not to mention his aversion to contact around the bag. Two 34-year-old veterans the Mets had hoped would anchor the infield sank it instead.

A club-record 16 wins in April kept the Mets going early, and they managed to hold the NL East lead for much of May. A month later the deficit was double digits. Even winning a series from the Yankees and finally getting Roger Clemens in the batter's box was marred when Shawn Estes missed drilling The Rocket; Estes—and Piazza, fittingly— both homered off Clemens, however, in a Mets rout. Estes would be traded a few weeks later.

The July 31 trading deadline had routinely filled other teams' rosters with young talent while mostly adding to the roll of veteran Mets middle relievers. As if David Weathers, Scott Strickland, Mark Guthrie, Satoru Komiyama, and Armando Benitez did not constitute a veteran enough bullpen, Phillips traded minor leaguer Jason Bay (stolen from Montreal's Omar Minaya) to San Diego with two others for 37-year-old sidearmer Steve Reed and dead-end prospect Jason Middlebrook. Phillips then acquired cranky

Colorado starter John Thomson and outfielder Mark Little (who would play three games as a Met) in exchange for 2000 postseason hero Jay Payton and Mark Corey. Corey had suffered a seizure after smoking marijuana shortly after a game at Shea Stadium. That same subject came up later when a photo of reliever Grant Roberts using a bong was made public. Bobby Valentine's parody of a batter trying to hit while high was frowned upon by management, but what really brought down his regime was how the $95 million Mets tanked.

After sitting in second place with a 55–51 record the day the two trades were made, the Mets went 20–35 the rest of the way. Four straight home losses to the Diamondbacks ended both Mark Guthrie's record-tying 33-appearance scoreless streak as well as any realistic shot at contention. The Mets briefly gathered themselves to nudge back over .500 and then promptly dropped 12 in a row. An August strike would have spared the club the indignity of a record home losing streak, but the work stoppage was averted and the Mets concluded their winless month at Shea (0–15). If Bobby V., the second-winningest manager in club history was going to get the axe, it seemed a fait accompli that Steve Phillips, the man who assembled the dysfunctional roster, would also be shown the door. Valentine left alone.

Howe Low Can You Go?

Phillips not only got to stay, he got to hire the new manager. The Mets wanted someone with experience to handle this veteran-heavy club. They talked to the Mariners about Lou Piniella, but Seattle adamantly refused to let him out of the last year of his contract without compensation—and they wanted teenage shortstop Jose Reyes. Phillips balked. (Tampa Bay forked over outfielder Randy Winn to get Piniella, who lost 91 or more games in each of his three years in his hometown.) A generation of Mets fans can thank Phillips for holding on to Reyes, but fans of the 2003–2004 club may not be so forgiving about the manager he brought in: Art Howe.

Oakland, which began an AL-record 20-game winning streak the same time the Mets were losing 12 straight, still had Howe under contract. Yet GM Billy Beane was only too happy to let the Mets have his three-time AL West champion manager. The Mets interviewed Terry Francona, Willie Randolph, and Buck Showalter, among others, but chose to hire Howe rather than risk losing him if they waited for Dusty Baker, pennant-winning manager of the Giants, whose contract was up after the World Series. So the decision was made to give a four-year, $9.4 million contract to Howe, the club's admitted second—or maybe third—choice.

A rare bright spot for the 2003 Mets, Steve Trachsel is shown here delivering a pitch during his one-hit, complete-game victory over Colorado in August. Other than an injury-shortened 2005, Trachsel posted double-digit wins in each of five full seasons with a Mets club that managed only one postseason appearance. *Andrew Savulich/NY Daily News Archive/Getty Images*

The offseason acquisitions seemed less concentrated and more a mishmash than the previous year's. New York brought in lefties who'd excelled for their enemies—Tom Glavine (Braves), Mike Stanton (Yankees), and Graeme Lloyd (Yankees by way of Toronto, Montreal, and Florida)—traded one shortstop named Rey (Ordonez) and tabbed another Rey (Sanchez) to take his place; tried and failed to sign Japanese third baseman Norihiro Nakamura and seemed more upset about losing him than star homegrown third baseman Edgardo Alfonzo; signed Tony Clark one day and watched Brady Clark go on waivers the next; brought in outfielder Cliff Floyd and brought back Tyoshi Shinjo; and the starting rotation was depleted enough for David Cone to come out of retirement and make the club.

While Glavine's debut turned into an Opening Day record 15–2 rout, Cone's return on a windy, frigid night was ideal for a 40-year-old making a comeback, as the Expos

METS TOP 50

JOSE REYES
2003–

Shortstop

Mike Ehrmann/WireImage/Getty Images

There are many ways to measure a player's worth to his team, but with Jose Reyes it's pretty simple: when he's playing, the Mets are a superior team. From June 2003 through 2009, New York was a .531 team (420–371) with him on the field and a .416 club (117–164) without him. He missed significant time with injuries in 2003, 2004, 2009, and 2010.

Jose Bernabe Reyes debuted the day before he turned 20. By age 25 he already held the franchise records for steals and triples. By then Reyes had switched to second base to make room for Kaz Matsui and then switched back to shortstop, led the National League in triples and steals three times (setting the single-season Mets mark in the latter category with 78 in '08), scored 100 runs three times, and led the league with 204 hits in 2008. Though he hasn't won a Gold Glove through his first eight seasons, in 2007 *Baseball America* picked him as the NL's best defensive shortstop, along with best infield arm, best base runner, and most exciting player.

Reyes has his detractors, especially those who deride his dugout celebrations, and he batted just .210 during the 52 games that constituted the club's disastrous Septembers in 2007 and 2008. But Reyes did come through in the 2006 NLCS, when he hit .281, led off the must-win Game 6 with a home run, and nearly won Game 7 with two on in the ninth inning, had Jim Edmonds not nabbed his shot to center field. Reyes' Mets legacy rides on getting another October chance.

In 2004, Kaz Matsui (left) had to learn a new language and culture, and Jose Reyes had to learn a new position, but the double-play duo found a way to communicate with each other—even if the Mets committed the second-most errors in the league that year. *Al Bello/Getty Images*

shivered and barely hit. In sultry Puerto Rico, the new home away from home for the vagabond Expos (owned by Major League Baseball), it was a different story. The "home" club pounded Cone in a 10–0 rout that led to a four-game sweep. Howe's club returned from its first road trip already in last place and rarely budged from there in 2003.

Mo Vaughn went on the disabled list in May batting .190 and never played again for the Mets due to an arthritic left knee. An insurance policy made it financially palatable, but the decision to bring him to New York in the first place was completely laughable. The 96-loss Mets were like an unfunny comedy with a cheesy laugh track.

★ Rey Sanchez was caught getting a mid-game haircut in the clubhouse while the Mets were getting slammed in St. Louis. (Armando Benitez was the purported barber.)

★ Art Howe spoke in a television interview about Mike Piazza playing first base before talking with his all-star catcher about it, creating a chasm between them. Howe then lost his best player to a groin injury for three months.

★ Steve Trachsel and Al Leiter won 16 and 15 games, respectively, for a team that managed just 35 wins without them on the hill.

★ An August blackout throughout the Northeast spared the Mets having to face Barry Bonds a third night, giving New York a two-game sweep of the 100-win NL champs. If only the lights could have gone out during either series

with the Yankees. The Mets lost all six games, the first sweep in seven seasons of interleague play.

★ Tom Glavine's brother Mike, 30, a former Indians and Braves farmhand who had been playing independent ball, was signed by the Mets and promoted to New York in September for his only major league action. Tom out-hit his first baseman kid brother, .151 to .143.

★ Amid Fred Wilpon's promise for "meaningful games in September" in 2004, the only September game of meaning in 2003 was the home finale, a Thursday night affair against the perennial doormat Pirates. It was Bob Murphy Night, to honor the announcer who was retiring after 41 years in the booth. One of Murph's final calls was Piazza's first play as a first baseman.

★ The Mets did play games that were meaningful to others, and boy were those clubs glad. The Mets were 1–20 against teams contending for postseason berths (not counting runaway winner Atlanta). The eventual world champion Marlins clinched the Wild Card against the Mets during the final weekend.

The only Mets in the news were from 1962. The Tigers lost 119 games in 2003 and threatened New York's modern day record of 120 losses before winning their last two games. A mythical confrontation in the *New York Times* pitted the '62 Mets against the '03 version, and Casey Stengel's club beat Art Howe's in seven games with Timo Perez thrown out at the plate to end it. If only there'd been that much excitement.

"No Light at the End of the Tunnel"

Steve Phillips' reprieve from the gallows was revoked midway through the 2003 season. He was replaced by Jim Duquette, whose main order of business was to rid the Mets of his predecessor's onerous contracts. No players of note came back, but the Mets were just happy to be rid of Alomar, Benitez,

Burnitz, Lloyd, and Sanchez. It took until the next year to unload Roger Cedeno's contract, while eating part of it, which was only fitting since Cedeno's weight topped the list of his numerous problems. Duke's hands were tied by the team's refusal to go beyond three years for a contract—essentially ending any chance to get Mets killer Vladimir Guerrero in a down market—so the GM signed an outfield of Mark Cameron, Shane Spencer, and Karim Garcia (plus reserves Eric Valent, Gerald Williams, and recidivist Met Todd Zeile). It was in the infield where Duquette had problems. He let infielder Marco Scutaro go on waivers, which was a mistake because Scutaro turned out to be a better shortstop than the club's ballyhooed 2003 signing, Kaz Matsui.

Matsui homered in his first at bat in each of his three seasons as a Met, but he was remarkably ordinary the rest of the time. His arm was weak and erratic, and the Mets had moved shortstop prodigy Jose Reyes to second base to accommodate him. Reyes endured an unnerving series of hamstring problems, and the Mets shuttled in double play partners all season. His target at first base also changed often. Mike Piazza was behind the plate until he broke Carlton Fisk's record of 351 home runs by a catcher. Then Piazza moved to first base as everyone always said he would. He just wasn't very good there. Fans still thought of Piazza as a catcher, voting him to start the All-Star Game in Houston, where he caught hometown hero—and Queens public enemy number one—Roger Clemens, who was lit up for six runs.

The 2004 season had started like a carbon copy of 2003. The Mets were stuck at 9–15 a month into the season. Looking back, it is hard to believe how one winning month could change the whole perception of the franchise. Their 15–12 May was the same record they'd produced the previous August, which barely caused a sniff. The rest of the division was snoozing early on, watching groggily as the Mets went to Philadelphia's new Citizens Bank Park for the first time

and swept the Phillies. Duquette sent David Weathers to Houston for Richard Hidalgo, who had the last good month of his mercurial career with a 10-homer July.

The Mets were frisky in interleague play, dropping five straight in the club's first trips to Minnesota and Kansas City and winning five of six as Cleveland and Detroit came to Shea for the first time since the place housed the Yankees in the mid-1970s. It was against those Yankees that the Mets had 2004's signature moment. A sweep of the Yanks on July Fourth weekend at Shea was a first against their rival (the Mets had lost two of three in the Bronx the previous weekend). Yet the overestimation of the Mets' chances turned out to be the team's biggest gaffe.

Duquette's unloading of veterans for prospects had girded Mets fans to wait for a gleaming future raised on the farm. When 20-year-old third baseman David Wright debuted on July 21, that future was getting closer. Despite dropping below .500 and falling from two to six games back in a week, that old nemesis—the July 31 deadline—teased the Mets into thinking they could trade their way back into contention.

Trading the cream of their farm system in two separate deals for Kris Benson and Victor Zambrano made fans as angry as Jack's mother when he sold the family cow for a handful of beans. Pitching coach Rick Peterson could not, as newspapers claimed he said, "fix Zambrano in ten minutes." Three players traded—Ty Wigginton, Jose Bautista, and Scott Kazmir—later became all-stars. The dreams of contention in

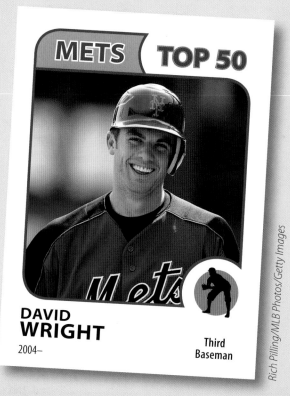

METS TOP 50

DAVID WRIGHT

2004–

Third Baseman

Rich Pilling/MLB Photos/Getty Images

When Mike Hampton signed with the Colorado Rockies in December 2000, Mets fans were infuriated that the pitcher who had helped the Mets reach that year's World Series would spurn New York for the Rockies, who was offered him an eight-year, $123 million deal. While that contract became an albatross for the Rockies and subsequent clubs, the compensation pick the Mets got for losing the pitcher became one of the greatest choices in this franchise's history.

David Allen Wright was the Gatorade Player of the Year in Virginia as a senior at Chesapeake's Hickory High School. The Mets took Wright with the 38th pick in the 2001 amateur draft after choosing Aaron Heilman earlier in the first round with the 18th pick (also courtesy of the Rockies). Wright landed in the majors at age 20 on July 21, 2004, and by year's end he was the team's number three hitter. He hit 14 homers in 69 games and knocked in 40 runs while batting .293, tied for highest among rookies, although that average would be Wright's lowest over his first seven seasons.

In his first full season with the big league club, Wright posted his first of four straight years in which he had at least 25 home runs, 100 RBI, 96 runs, and a .300 average. With Wright at third and Jose Reyes at short, the Mets had a reliable and durable left side of the infield. They became the first pair at their positions under age 22 to play 150 games in the same year (Wright played 160 games and Reyes, who was actually

DAVID WRIGHT

Born: December 20, 1982, in Norfolk, VA
Drafted by New York Mets, 2001
Mets Debut: July 21, 2004
Bats: Right. Throws: Right

New York Mets Batting Record

YEAR	AB	H	HR	RBI	BA
2004	263	77	14	40	.293
2005	575	176	27	102	.306
2006	582	181	26	116	.311
2007	604	196	30	107	.325
2008	626	189	33	124	.302
2009	535	164	10	72	.307
2010	587	166	29	103	.283
Mets/MLB Totals	4335	1149	169	664	.305

21, played 161). When Mike Piazza left the Mets that offseason, Wright became the heartthrob successor for New York's National League affection. His face appeared on magazines, in advertisements, and in pitchers' nightmares.

Wright made the all-star team every year from 2006 through 2010, won Silver Slugger Awards in 2007 and 2008, and (despite defense in which the spectacular play sometimes seemed to come easier than the routine throw) earned Gold Gloves at third base in those same two years. In 2007 the speedy Wright stole 34 bases, hit 30 homers, and had career highs (so far) with a .325 batting average, .416 on-base percentage, and .546 slugging percentage. He also tied Todd Helton for the league lead by reaching base 296 times. The performance was good enough to net Wright fourth place in the NL MVP voting in 2007.

Wright upped his power numbers in 2008 (33 homers, 124 RBI), but in the inaugural season of Citi Field, his increasing strikeout total and diminishing home run output were cause for alarm (10 HRs, 140 K's). So was a frightening beaning by San Francisco's Matt Cain in August. But Wright showed a renewed power stroke in 2010 and even extended his All-Star Game hitting streak to five games.

In year seven of his major league career, Wright broke Ed Kranepool's club record of 225 doubles, and he is in striking distance of many Mets career batting records.

Stephen Dunn/Getty Images

2004 evaporated quickly, a 13–28 freefall sucking the life out of Shea. "Things aren't looking bright," said ever-honest outfielder Cliff Floyd as New York lost 19 times in 21 games. "There's no light at the end of the tunnel."

Both Howe and Duquette were relieved of their posts in September. Duke stayed with the organization and Howe remained as lame-duck manager the last three weeks of the season; the team actually "battled" (Howe's favorite term) against a contender after playing dead for two Septembers. Call-up Victor Diaz blasted a three-run homer against the Cubs to tie the game with two outs in the 9th, and Craig Brazell launched his only career homer in the 11th for the win. Al Leiter won the next day and Chicago lost its Wild Card lead to Houston in the final week of the season.

The final game of 2004 saw Montreal bid adieu to baseball. Owned—and squeezed—by MLB, the Expos were the first team to relocate since 1971, when Washington played its final game before moving to Texas. Now Montreal was on its way to Washington. Amid a carnival in the parking lot, the Expos folded up their tent at Shea, where they had come into existence 35 years earlier against Tom Seaver and won. This time they faced Tom Glavine and lost, Montreal's spritely Endy Chavez hitting the grounder that bounced the Expos out of existence. Even before the Expos' gear was packed away for good, the Mets already had Montreal's general manager.

Meet the New Mets

Fred Wilpon, who had bought out Nelson Doubleday as sole owner of the Mets in 2002, liked Omar Minaya as assistant GM of the Mets, a job he'd shared with Duquette in the 1990s. Wilpon had tried to get Minaya back in 2004 and share the general manager's job with Duquette. Minaya, the first Latino GM, saw that as a demotion and remained in Montreal. Less than a year later, Fred and Jeff Wilpon—the son handling the club's day-to-day operations—flew to Montreal and offered Minaya the job outright. With the Expos' management future in doubt, Minaya returned to Queens, where he'd grown up a Mets fan after his family moved there from the Dominican Republic.

Given more authority—and cash—than his predecessor, Minaya quickly went to work transforming the Mets. Yankees great and one-time Met Willie Randolph, passed over after interviewing for a dozen managerial jobs, finally got the call in Queens. A month into the job he knew he'd have Pedro Martinez as his Opening Day starter. Next up was the hottest star on the free agent market, Carlos Beltran, who had gone from Kansas City to Houston in midseason and exploded in his first postseason, hitting eight home runs and scoring 21 runs in 12 October games. He not only signed for seven years and $119 million with the Mets—though he offered to jump into the Yankees' lap at the last moment if they'd wanted him—he also dubbed the team "the New Mets" at his press conference. (In truth, agent Scott Boras did both the negotiating and the brand naming.)

The New Mets opened with a magnificent effort by Martinez, who fanned 12 Reds in six innings, but reliever Braden Looper undid it in three batters in the ninth, allowing two home runs. When Martinez's next start came around, the team was 0–5 and on the verge of being swept for the second time when Beltran homered off John Smoltz in the eighth. Randolph took no chances in his first win, keeping in Pedro, who retired the last 16 Braves. The Mets went in the other direction and won six straight, including the home opener by roughing up John Franco, now an Astro. Shea was even more

Author's collection

hopping for Pedro's Queens debut. Pitching against Al Leiter, who had left in a dispute with Minaya and went to the Marlins and was booed as much as Franco, Martinez was again in line for the win—and again Looper blew it. (Looper's troubles in 2005 could in part be attributed to a shoulder injury that he didn't reveal until year's end.) This time the Mets won on a walk-off hit by Ramon Castro, one of the several unnoticed additions who helped transform the ballclub.

Jose Reyes led the league with 17 triples and 60 steals and paced the Mets to a major league high 153, but the most important number was that he led the NL with 161 starts at shortstop (despite a league-high 18 errors). With Reyes healthy again, the lineup had a rhythm and an urgency. David Wright cranked out 27 homers, 102 RBI, and a .306/.388/.523 line in his first full season. He slotted in behind Cliff Floyd, finally healthy, who hit 34 home runs and knocked in 98 runs. Floyd's signature moment was a two-run homer in extra innings with the Mets a run down to beat the Angels; Marlon Anderson had tied the game in the ninth with the team's first inside-the-park home run in five years and the first ever by a Mets pinch hitter.

In contrast to his predecessors, Minaya was reluctant to part with his top prospects at the trading deadline. He watched July 31 pass with the Mets three games behind Wild Card leader Washington and did not indulge in pricey veterans. One thing that did happen was another September swoon. The Mets stood half a game out of the Wild Card on August 30 after Castro hit a dramatic three-run homer off Phillies closer Ugueth Urbina, but three weeks later the Mets were out of the race, in last place, and seemingly resigned to their fourth straight losing season. The Mets reeled off an 11–3 string, ruining divisional foes' postseason hopes left and right, clinching a winning record, at least a tie for third place, and leaving only one order of business for the last day: Mike Piazza's farewell.

Unlike the previous year, when Leiter had thought one thing and Minaya another, the tacit understanding was that this was the end of the line in New York for the 37-year-old star. Piazza's seven and a half years hadn't been long enough to set career marks except for slugging (.542), but few argued that he was the best hitter in club history, certainly the best who batted right-handed. Or caught. Piazza was cheered wildly every time he stepped to the plate—even while Victor Zambrano was booed off the field by a jammed house. When Randolph removed Piazza in the seventh inning, when he still might have gotten another at bat, the waves of cheers poured down for eight minutes as the other Mets and Rockies stood on the dugout steps looking around in awe.

"I'm humbled," Piazza said afterward. "Genuinely humbled. I just feel like part of the family." Some would call him the head of the family.

"Get Your New York Sports Here"

The 2006 season opened with a new station on the dial: SportsNet New York. In a move similar to when the club's radio home, WFAN, became an all-sports station and then moved to clear channel 660 in the late 1980s, getting a television network of its own changed the way fans followed

the game. The YES Network had been the first to break up Cablevision's monopoly on New York sports channels, becoming the 24-hour Yankees station in 2002. YES also gave a blueprint on what to avoid, especially the channel's relentless self-love that might make other fans queasy. SNY—owned by the Mets, Time Warner, and Comcast—adopted a more citywide approach, with a repeating highlight show covering all of New York, yet the station's focus remained the Mets. They took care to assemble a trio of broadcasters that fit Mets fans' taste better than any combo since Nelson, Murphy, and Kiner. Gary Cohen moved from radio to television, Ron Darling was brought in from Washington, and Keith Hernandez stayed in the TV booth, with Ralph Kiner, now in his 80s, making occasional appearances. The trio was embraced as insightful, funny, and your no-homer home for New York sports. Gary, Keith, and Ron even became a brand, lending their name to charities and other community works. But what most helped launch the trio, the programming, and SNY was a team that fans couldn't wait to watch.

Omar Minaya's remaking of the bullpen was a major part of his second-year Mets makeover. Pedro Martinez would have won 20 games in 2005 had the bullpen not blown five of his leads. After blowing 21 saves in 2005, New York finished with the fewest blown saves in the league (15) in 2006 and boasted the NL's best bullpen record (32–15) and highest save percentage (74 percent). Chad Bradford and Pedro Feliciano handled the middle innings; 35-year-old Darren Oliver, who hadn't pitched at all in the majors in 2005, was the long man; Aaron Heilman, who wanted to be a starter, had been one of the game's top setup men a year earlier; and unhittable Duaner Sanchez, acquired from the Dodgers for Jae Seo, locked down the eighth. For a closer, the team signed former Philadelphia gunslinger Billy Wagner, who racked up 40 saves—including his career 300th—for the 2006 Mets.

All the attention on the bullpen was good, because the starting rotation was held together with bailing wire. The club's first division title since 1988 was won with 13 different Mets making at least three starts. John Maine, the unknown pitcher the Mets got in the Jorge Julio for Kris Benson deal with Baltimore, started 15 games. Maine's 26 consecutive scoreless innings broke Dwight Gooden's 1984 club mark for rookies. Other starters briefly plugged in, including Mike Pelfrey and Brian Bannister (anticipated debuts), David Williams and Alay Soler (never won after 2006), plus Jose Lima and Geremi Gonzalez (since deceased). The four

Paul Lo Duca's double tag of two Dodgers at the plate helped John Maine out of a jam in the second inning of the 2006 NLDS opener. He is about to notch the second out of the play with a tag of J. D. Drew, as the already-out Jeff Kent kneels to the right. On top of his nifty fielding, Lo Duca hit a blistering .455 in the three-game sweep. *James Keivom/NY Daily News Archive/Getty Images*

Author's collection

pitchers making the majority of the starts were 34 or older: Tom Glavine and Steve Trachsel won 15 apiece; Orlando "El Duque" Hernandez, acquired from Arizona for Jorge Julio, went 9–7; and Pedro Martinez, who won his first five starts, including his 200th career win.

The Mets jumped to a five-game lead quicker than any team in major league history (12 games). They spent all but one day in first place, taking full control in mid-June with a 9–1 road trip that included sweeps in Arizona and Philadelphia. Even when the Mets were swept in Boston at the end of June and then dropped two of three at Yankee Stadium, their double-digit lead decreased by just one game. The Mets led by 13½ at the end of July when they traveled to Atlanta, winners of every NL East title since 1995 and three straight NL West crowns before that. New York left with a sweep. That's when the bullpen was taken for a cab ride.

Duaner Sanchez, whose 18-inning scoreless streak to start his Mets career had New Yorkers working on the proper pronunciation of Dwa-Ner, hopped in a taxi for a late-night meal on an off day in Miami. An accident on I-95 left the pitcher with a separated shoulder and the Mets with just a few hours to try to find a replacement. The deadline-day deal with Pittsburgh cost them Xavier Nady, both

productive and popular in right field, and brought back their 2005 setup man, Roberto Hernandez, along with Oliver Perez, a lefty who'd been demoted after going 2–10 with a 6.63 ERA. Still trying to fill the same holes, the Mets later acquired Guillermo Mota, who was despised at Shea for a beanball war with Mike Piazza, and right fielder Shawn Green, a 300-home-run hitter near the end of a long career. Minaya's biggest in-season move had come in June, when the team bit the bullet on Kaz Matsui and paid his way to Colorado. Jose Valentin played second base for the first time in a dozen years and hit 18 homers while committing just six errors.

Despite their deficiencies, the Mets were never threatened in 2006, mainly because of a powerful offense that set a club record with 200 home runs. The Mets had a franchise high six all-stars, including pitchers Martinez (who skipped the game to rest) and Glavine. Piazza's successor, Paul Lo Duca, garnered his fourth all-star appearance and ended the year with a .318 average. David Wright, the first Met in 20 years to take part in the home run derby and the first since 1979 to homer in an All-Star Game, finished the season with 26 homers and a .311 average. Jose Reyes, who missed the midseason exhibition after injuring his hand, wound up with 122 runs, a .300 average, and a league-best 17 triples and 64 steals; he also hit three homers in a game and hit for the cycle. Carlos Beltran, who was booed on Opening Day and had to be pushed out of the dugout to take a curtain call after his first homer in the season's third game, was cheered thereafter for his franchise-record-tying 41 home runs and team-leading 116 RBI (tied with Wright).

The 97-win Mets went into October cruising but ailing. Pedro, suffering injuries to his hip, calf, and toe, tried a late-season comeback and tore his rotator cuff. El Duque was tabbed to open the postseason, but he hurt his calf jogging the day before the Division Series. So Maine took his place. He

Carlos Delgado heads for home after belting a first-inning, three-run homer to give New York an early lead in Game 2 of the NLCS. The Mets went on to lose the game and the series, but Delgado did his part; his three homers and nine RBI in the seven games led all players. *Nick Laham/ Getty Images*

pitched well in front of a raucous Shea crowd that witnessed two Dodgers tagged out at the plate on the same play in the second inning. Carlos Delgado—who had spurned the Mets as a free agent in 2005, was traded to them in 2006, and crushed 38 home runs as their first baseman—had four hits in his first career postseason game. He drove in the go-ahead run in the seventh for the Mets' first postseason win at home since the 2000 World Series.

Glavine was superb and Billy Wagner picked up his second save the next night. Suddenly, the Mets—left for dead when two pitchers went down just before the series—now had a chance to sweep Los Angeles. They did just that, despite blowing an early four-run lead and going through seven pitchers in Game 3. With the Yankees knocked out by the Tigers in the Division Series that same day, wishful thinking seeped in with the champagne. October baseball, however, is noted for its wakeup calls.

The Cardinals were the foe in the NLCS, as they had been in the Mets' 2000 victory to reach the World Series. Glavine made it look easy in the opener, combining on a four-hit shutout, with Beltran accounting for the only two runs with a homer. The Mets hit Chris Carpenter hard the next night and Maine kept them in the game. New York held a two-run lead with Mota on the mound in the seventh, two on, two out, and two strikes on Scott Spiezio, who launched a ball to deep right that Green got a glove on but could not haul in. The underdog Cardinals tagged Wagner in the ninth and the NLCS was even.

Steve Trachsel, the longest tenured Met, couldn't get out of the second inning in Game 2. Despite the shortage of starters, he never pitched again as a Met. Oliver Perez took the mound the next night and held a 5–3 lead when the Mets scored six times and cruised to a 12–5 win. Delgado drove in five and Beltran slammed two home runs. The second rainout in the series meant that the last three games would

Endy Chavez's leaping, snow-cone catch robbed Scott Rolen of a home run in the sixth inning of Game 7 of the NLCS. St. Louis rallied in the top of the ninth, however, and clinched the pennant. *Nick Laham/Getty Images*

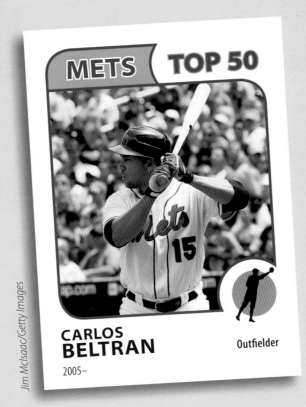

METS | **TOP 50**

CARLOS BELTRAN

Outfielder

2005–

Carlos Beltran can make the game look so effortless that sometimes people question his effort. No one, however, can question his numbers. Since joining the Mets in 2005, Beltran holds or shares the single-season marks for homers (41), extra-base hits (80), and runs (127), and he is second only to Mike Piazza in slugging (.594). Those figures were reached in 2006, when he joined David Wright and Carlos Delgado as the first Mets trio with 20 homers at the All-Star break. He also earned his first Gold Glove and Silver Slugger Awards, all while helping the Mets win their first division title in 18 years.

In the team's stressful finishes in 2007 and 2008, Beltran was front and center trying to will the team across the finish line, but to no avail. Beltran was the final Met to score at Shea Stadium, crossing home on the last Mets home run at the stadium.

A quiet man from the pineapple-growing region of Puerto Rico, Carlos Ivan Beltran did not arrive in New York softly. Coming off a stellar postseason in Houston following a trade from Kansas City, he signed a seven-year, nine-figure deal in 2005 with the "New Mets" (a moniker he promoted). He played through injuries, including a horrific collision with Mike Cameron. Only once had Beltran played fewer than 140 games since being 1999 American League Rookie of the Year, but knee procedures kept him off the field for the equivalent of a full season in 2009 and 2010.

be played in as many days—not helping the already depleted Mets staff. Glavine, so good in his first two postseason starts, had a 2–0 lead in the fourth but gave the runs right back, and the Cards needed to win just once in New York to claim the pennant.

Maine wouldn't let them get it so easily. The rookie received a rousing ovation as he left in the sixth with a man on and a 2–0 lead in Game 6. Chad Bradford ended the threat with a double-play grounder. Wagner allowed a two-run double to So Taguchi, whose homer had beaten him five nights earlier, but he saved the 4–2 win.

Whereas Mets greats Jon Matlack (1973) and Ron Darling (1986, 1988) had started the other Game 7s in franchise history, the team had no choice but to go with Oliver Perez in the 2006 NLCS. He outdid his predecessors, but series MVP Jeff Suppan was just as good for St. Louis. Endy Chavez's leap high over the fence turned Scott Rolen's home run into a double play, but he could only watch Yadier Molina's drive in the ninth off Aaron Heilman. Adam Wainwright caught Carlos Beltran looking with the bases loaded to clinch the pennant. Shea Stadium went deathly quiet, as if she knew she would never see another October game.

That's Why They Call It the Blues

History lumps the 2007 and 2008 Mets together because of the final day failure against the same team with the same prize on the line, but how the Mets arrived at each season finale against the Marlins are two completely different tales.

The 2007 Mets had the swagger of a team that had ended Atlanta's long run and showed the confidence that they could take the next step with better luck and pitching. In the end, they had neither. The Mets sure could hit, though. Their .275 mark was second to the 1999 club's for best in franchise history, and their 200 steals led the majors and eclipsed the

Moises Alou's two-run homer against the Nationals extended his personal hitting streak to 30 games, but it couldn't stop the Mets' freefall during the final month of the 2007 season, as New York lost to Washington 9–6 on September 26 at Shea. *Al Bello/ Getty Images*

1987 club mark by 41. Despite a midseason spat with his manager and a brutal finish, Jose Reyes set the Mets single-season record with 78 steals, drew almost as many walks, and scored 119 runs. The offense also got 30 homers, 42 doubles, 107 RBI, and a .325 average from Wright; 33 homers and 112 RBI from Beltran; and a 30-game hitting streak and .341 average from 40-year-old Moises Alou, who missed two and a half months due to injury. Luis Castillo chipped in 10 steals and 37 runs in 50 games after coming over from Minnesota to man second base when Jose Valentin's knee gave out for good, and the Mets saw contributions off the bench from infielder Ruben Gotay (.295), midseason waiver acquisition Marlon Anderson (.319), rapping prospect Lastings Milledge (.272), and Damion Easley, whose 10 homers, .280 average, and determined approach were sorely missed when he went down for the year in August.

Oh, but the pitching. The team ERA went up every month, from 2.96 in April to 5.27 in September. With two starters over 40 and three inexperienced starters under 26—Maine and Perez did win 15 apiece—the Mets did not toss a nine-inning complete game all year for the first time in team history. The bullpen just wore out. Three relievers pitched at least 70 times and Billy Wagner (66), would have reached that number if an aggravated back hadn't kept him out of several key games.

All the Mets needed to avoid disaster was one more win against the Phillies, the team christened by MVP Jimmy Rollins in spring training as the "Team to Beat" amid scoffing and derision from New York. Even after a four-game sweep by Philly in August cut the division lead to one, the Mets built the lead back up to seven 7 with 17 remaining. The percentages all tilted the other way as the Phillies won their last eight games against the Mets, five games decided by one or two runs. Southpaw reliever Pedro Feliciano, who had his finest season, allowed three home runs all year, all to Philly:

In his final start as a Met, Tom Glavine hands the ball over to manager Willie Randolph after yielding seven runs in the first inning against the Florida Marlins. It was a grim end to a tough season for all Mets and their fans. *Chris Trotman/Getty Images*

one in June in the 11th inning to Chase Utley to complete a sweep at Shea, one in the 8th inning to Jimmy Rollins in August to break up a shutout as Philadelphia went on to tie the game and win in 10, and one to Aaron Rowand at Shea on September 14 to tie the game in the 8th after Pedro Martinez, who missed the first five months, had pitched superbly. The biggest home run, however, had come on September 13,

when Tom Glavine, cruising with a shutout in the 6th inning, surrendered a two-run shot to Utley to tie the game. An inch higher on the bat or an inch more inside, and it's a pop-up and the Mets might have won the division without a sweat. Instead, it started a 5–12 finish—while Philadelphia went 13–4—and commenced a horrific ending for Glavine, who had been hailed in August for career win number 300.

On the final day of the season, after John Maine took a no-hitter into the eighth the previous day to end a five-game losing streak, and Glavine was charged with seven runs in the first inning of a must-win game. The two men who became scapegoats for all that went wrong in 2007 stood together on the mound: Glavine and Randolph. Glavine never pitched again in New York, leaving for Atlanta as a free agent and retiring. Randolph was sent home the following June.

The Last Roundup at Shea

The Mets filled the void at the top of the rotation with Johan Santana, acquired from Minnesota in January when the experts said GM Omar Minaya had no chance at landing the highly sought after free agent. That put the pressure on manager Willie Randolph, who had been left to twist in the wind the day after the 2007 disaster until Minaya pronounced his job safe. The crushing blow of the previous year's collapse, piled on top of the NLCS disappointment of 2006, made for an anxious start to the final season at Shea Stadium.

The Phillies rubbed salt in the wound by upstaging the home team on Shea's final Opening Day with a 5–2 win that dropped the Mets to 2–4. New York took four of their next five against Philly and stood just a game out of first on May 19 after walloping the Yankees, 11–2. The next day, however, Randolph's comments that he thought were off the record turned out to be big news in the *Bergen County Record*. Already under pressure to produce a winner, the manager got himself in hot water by bringing up race as a factor in how he was perceived by the media and the way the cameras filmed him on SNY. The situation quickly worsened when the Mets embarked on a 1–6 road trip in which they lost Ryan Church, their best hitter of the first quarter of the season, when he sustained a concussion in Atlanta; the injury got far worse after he ill advisedly flew to Denver with the club.

In mid-June, Randolph, pitching coach Rick Peterson, and first-base coach Tom Nieto were fired in the middle of the night during the club's fourth western swing in seven weeks. Bench coach Jerry Manuel, the 2000 American

League Manager of the Year with the White Sox, took charge. After a couple of up-and-down weeks, the Mets reeled off 10 straight wins in early July. Barely a month after standing seven and a half games out, they were now tied for first.

A half game separated the Mets and Phillies when the teams met for a two-game series in Philadelphia in late August. With Pedro Martinez on the mound, the Mets went up 7–0 but lost the lead in the 9th and eventually fell in 13 innings. The Mets rallied late to win the next night, and New York went 5–1 the rest of the trip to build a three and a half game lead with 17 games remaining—the same number of games that marked the start of the team's undoing in 2007. Like the previous year, there were no days off. And with a decimated bullpen—Billy Wagner was done for the year with elbow surgery—they needed every break possible. Instead they suffered more injuries and more heartbreak.

The Mets tried to make do with fill-ins Daniel Murphy and Nick Evans from Double-A Binghamton (dubbed the "Bingo Twins" by Howie Rose) and retreads like Fernando Tatis, who was staging an impressive comeback after missing all of 2007 until he went down again in mid-September. Carlos Delgado collected 24 homers and 69 RBI in a 67-game span, earning MVP consideration, but that talk stopped along with his bat in the final three weeks. The bullpen, consisting of a rag-tag assortment of nondescript and overused arms, proved incapable of getting hitters out.

The Mets ended 2008 by losing 10 of their last 17, with relievers taking half of those losses. But the offense shared in the blame as well. New York scored just five runs in the last three games of the season against Florida in front of packed houses as the Mets pushed past four million attendance for the only time in club history. On the penultimate day of the season, Santana almost single-handedly put the Mets in a flat-footed tie with the Brewers in the Wild Card race with

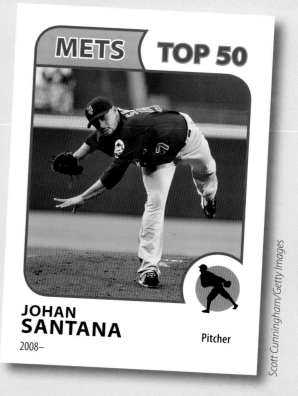

METS TOP 50

JOHAN SANTANA
2008–

Pitcher

Johan Santana arrived in New York amid fanfare and oodles of money. He did not disappoint. In an earlier era before pitch counts, Santana would have easily won 20 and probably the Cy Young Award as well in 2008. Instead he won 16, and the bullpen's seven blown saves not only cost him the hardware, it cost his team a postseason berth.

A native of Venezuela, Johan Alexander Santana did not win a game in his first professional season in the United States in 1997. The Astros left him unprotected in 1999 and the Marlins took him in the Rule V draft. He was immediately traded to the Twins, but he did not crack their rotation full-time until 2004. That year he won 20 games and the first of two Cy Youngs. A standoff by the Yankees and Red Sox enabled Omar Minaya to acquire the talented southpaw from Minnesota for a list of lesser prospects: Carlos Gomez, Deolis Guerra, Philip Humber, and Kevin Mulvey.

Armed with a six-year, $137.5 million contract extension, Santana had one of the best seasons in club history. He captured his third ERA crown with a career-best 2.53 and also led the league in starts (34) and innings (234⅓). He did not lose a game in the second half and ended the year with a complete-game shutout on short rest to keep Mets hopes alive. He began the 2009 season with a 0.71 ERA over his first seven starts, but he wound up having elbow surgery. A solid 2010—2.98 ERA in 199 innings—ended abruptly with shoulder surgery.

Former Mets from throughout the team's history gathered at Shea Stadium for a final farewell on September 28, 2008. Among those on hand were Jesse Orosco, John Franco, Keith Hernandez, Lenny Dykstra, Tom Seaver, Jerry Koosman, Dwight Gooden, Darryl Strawberry, Yogi Berra, Gary Carter, Rusty Staub, Edgardo Alfonzo, Bud Harrelson, and Ed Kranepool. *Jim McIsaac/Getty Images*

one game left to play. Having volunteered to pitch on short rest despite a left knee that required surgery a few days later, Santana pitched a three-hit, complete-game shutout against the Marlins.

Everyone that filed in for the last scheduled game at Shea Stadium hoped that there would be more baseball to be played at the old park. Perhaps a one-game playoff with Milwaukee; there was even the possibility that the Mets could clinch a postseason berth on that final Sunday, in front of former Mets greats and dignitaries on hand to honor the 44-year-old park.

Like Santana the day before, Oliver Perez offered to pitch on short rest. He tied Santana for the league lead with 34 starts. The Marlins took a 2–0 lead in the top of the sixth, but the Mets tied it in the bottom of the inning on Carlos Beltran's home run that shook the Shea foundation for the final time. Endy Chavez made a near carbon copy catch of his 2006 NLCS leap to preserve the tie in the seventh, but successive home runs off successive Mets relievers put Florida up by two the following inning. Representing the tying run in the ninth, Church's fly ball to right-center ended the Mets' postseason hopes, as well as Shea's run as a sporting facility.

Shea's final hour belonged to the people who came before, players who had been champions and those who'd suffered through the difficult losing years. Forty-three former Mets lined the infield and then touched home plate a final time, one by one. Shea was far from the greatest stadium ever built, but the fans and the players made the place memorable. Keith Hernandez, beloved as both a player and broadcaster, summed up how the great 1980s teams felt about the people that filled Shea: "Their passion fed our passion."

New Home, Same Neighborhood

One of the hallmarks of Omar Minaya's tenure as general manager is fixing a problem the year after it crops up. The Mets bullpen blew 29 saves in 2008. With Billy Wagner undergoing surgery late in the year to repair the torn medial collateral ligament in his left arm, the Mets had no assurance they would have their closer at all in 2009, the final year of his contract. So the Mets went pen shopping at the winter meetings and came back with Francisco "K-Rod" Rodriguez, coming off a record 62-save season for the Angels, for a three-year, $37 million deal. Then the Mets got another closer. A 12-player, three-team trade sent out Aaron Heilman, Joe Smith, Endy Chavez, and four others for Seattle closer turned setup man J. J. Putz (plus Sean Green and Jeremy Reed). But as fate would have it, the bullpen wasn't the biggest worry in 2009. Everything else was.

When healthy, the 2009 Mets were a flawed team, but once the injuries started mounting, the inaugural season at Citi Field went right down the state-of-the-art no-flush toilet. Mets players made 22 trips to the disabled list, falling (for lack of a better word) one DL stint short of the 2008 club as the most injured team in Mets history. Still, New York was in the thick of the NL East race for the first half.

A 19–9 May, featuring two game-winning hits in one week by catcher Omir Santos, put the Mets in a virtual tie with the Phillies for first place. Despite going 9–18 in June, they still stood just one game out on July 2. The Mets then sunk through the standings like an anvil, going 31–52 from that point on. The Phillies, who started the Mets on the road to oblivion by sweeping them over July Fourth weekend, had the best record in the league from that point on and rolled to their third straight division crown. For good measure, the Phils knocked off the Mets the night they celebrated the 40th anniversary of the 1969 club. Recently signed Phillie Pedro Martinez beat the Mets the next afternoon, with Eric Bruntlett turning the first game-ending unassisted triple play since 1927 to top it off.

The Mets were abysmal on the road in 2009 (29–52), but Citi Field wasn't that favorable either. The new stadium played extremely big, which didn't help the popgun army of replacements the Mets trotted out after most of their regulars got hurt. Though the Mets tied the Dodgers for the highest average in the majors at .270, the team's 95 home runs were the fewest by far in the majors. The 12 home runs by Daniel Murphy was the lowest total for a club home run leader since the trio of Steve Henderson, John Milner, and John Stearns each hit a dozen in 1977. Speaking of blasts from the past, the Mets brought in Gary Sheffield in 2009. Rumored to be coming to the Mets in his twenties and thirties, he finally arrived at age 40 and was one of the team's more durable players until he too got hurt in July. Sheffield's first homer as a Met was a game-tying blast the week Citi Field opened; it was also his 500th career home run. The first Met to homer at Citi, however, had plenty of problems in the park's inaugural season. David Wright, coming off a gargantuan 33-homer, 124-RBI season in 2008, homered just four times at Citi Field after Opening Day. Even more alarmingly, he homered just five times on the road. Though

he batted over .300 for the fifth straight year, all his numbers were lower at Citi Field than on the road. He also endured the most frightening injury of his career when he was beaned by San Francisco's Matt Cain and landed on the disabled list with a concussion.

Those first-year jitters faded early in year two at Citi Field. Any trepidation about the deep dimensions was transferred to the opposition. The Phillies were shut out three straight games in May at Citi Field, New York's first shutout sweep since the 1969 Mets did the same thing in Philadelphia. While the original was pulled off by Tom Seaver, Jerry Koosman, and Gary Gentry, the 2010 trio (all of whom combined with relievers) was R. A. Dickey, Ken Takahashi, and Mike Pelfrey. The first two of those pitchers were mid-thirties journeymen who started the year in the minors, while Pelfrey won as many games in the first half of 2010 as he did in all of 2009, when the easily rattled Big Pelf led the league in balks and allowed a home run to the first batter in Citi Field history (Jody Gerut). The 2010 Pelfrey even added a save in his first career relief outing, finishing New York's 20-inning win in St. Louis in April. He was responsible for the only three wins in an early 11-game stretch before the Mets turned things around. At home.

CITI FIELD

Citi Field was a long time coming. Mets ownership spruced up Shea Stadium, did the dance with politicians, and tried not to deride its team's home, but the Wilpons are builders, and they were eager to build. It didn't take a real estate background to see that building a new stadium was a team's best revenue source.

It was inevitable that the new Mets stadium would be built in the same part of Long Island and that it would resemble Ebbets Field, the Brooklyn ballpark where a young Fred Wilpon first fell for the game. In 1998 the Mets unveiled plans for a Ebbets-esque, retractable-roof, natural-grass facility with the field sliding out (like the Arizona Cardinals eventually built for football) to accommodate conventions, NCAA basketball's Final Four, and other events. Mayor Rudy Giuliani struck tentative agreements with both the Mets and Yankees for new stadiums in his final year in office in 2001. After September 11, those plans came off the board.

It was the Olympics that brought a new Mets stadium back in the public debate. New York's bid for the 2012 Summer Olympic was a reach for several reasons, but any bid required plans for a stadium that could house the opening and closing ceremonies, plus track and field events. If the bid had been successful, the stadium would have been expanded to more than 80,000 seats, with the Mets playing at Yankee Stadium during the Olympic games. After London won the bid in July 2005, the Mets forged ahead with their own ballpark plans. On March 18, 2006, the Mets unveiled a ballpark model, and later that summer preliminary work was underway in the parking lot of Shea Stadium.

Even as Shea closed and the finishing touches were put on Citi Field, the as-yet unopened facility saw its share of controversy. With troubled Citicorp receiving $350 billion in taxpayer funds during the financial crisis, politicians called to strike down the $400 million, 20-year naming-rights deal agreed to in 2006. Citi assured that no TARP (Troubled Asset Relief Program) funds were used to sponsor Citi Field. The name remained, but that was not the end of the taxpayer gripes. The $800-million price tag included $138 million in public monies, a figure due to grow with all the tax breaks received over time.

The 42,000-seat park (15,000 smaller than Shea) opened with a college baseball game, St. John's vs. Georgetown, on March 29, 2009, followed by two exhibition games between the Mets and the Red Sox the first weekend in April. It opened for real against San Diego on April 13 (three days before the new Yankee Stadium).

From the start, the food was one of the most popular and celebrated amenities at the new ballpark. The gourmet items available at all levels of Citi can't even be compared with Shea Stadium's nondescript fare. Still, complaints on other matters did quickly materialize. Many seats did not afford views of the foul lines, and ticket prices were high. Tickets in 2009 averaged $37, though that is skewed somewhat by the large number of seats at the premium level, which averaged $149; ticket prices did drop marginally in 2010. Others lamented the expansive playing dimensions, and perhaps most galling to Mets fans was that the new park celebrated Brooklyn Dodgers history more than anything associated with the Mets. It did not help that the 2009 Mets posted the club's worst record in five years.

Heading into the ballpark's second season, the Mets did much to introduce more team history into the décor of Citi Field. In addition to banners around the exterior celebrating former players, a Mets Hall of Fame and Museum offers numerous displays on the great moments and individuals from throughout the franchise's 50 seasons. *Matthew Silverman*

After drawing 3,154,262 in 2009, attendance dropped in 2010. A 16-foot rise in the center field wall was lowered to 10 feet, but the dimensions were unchanged: 335 to left, 379 to left-center, 408 to center, 415 to deepest right-center, 383 in the power alley, and 330 in right. The lone "easy" target is still down the right-field line, where David Wright homered in his first at bat in 2010 and Johan Santana hit the foul pole. The 12½- to 15-foot wall in left and left-center remains—in the words of radio announcer Howie Rose, "The Great Wall of Flushing." The home team's acceptance of the spaciousness showed in the Mets' superb play early in 2010, even as the club fared poorly on the road.

As for celebrating the current tenant, the team installed images of great Mets throughout the stadium in 2010, unveiled a Mets Hall of Fame and Museum in the Jackie Robinson Rotunda, and christened the expanse beyond the stands in distant right-center "Shea Bridge"—a favorite target for lefty-swinging Ike Davis.

Food has always been one of the fine amenities at Citi Field, and no concessions stand is more popular than the Shake Shack, offering sumptuous burgers and its famous milk shakes. *Matthew Silverman*

1 Mets fans were fired up to open the new decade with their first trip to the World Series in 14 years, but the 2000s would prove to have as many lows as highs as the team went through four different managers and only one postseason appearance following the 2000 season. *Keith Torrie/ NY Daily News Archive/Getty Images*

2 Cliff Floyd (30) and Mike Cameron (44) were brought to New York in the hopes of reviving the lineup, and although each had a season with 30 or more homers with the Mets—Cameron in 2004 and Floyd in 2005—neither proved to be part of the long-term plan. *Jim McIsaac/Getty Images*

3 The transition from Shea Stadium to Citi Field toward the end of the decade was a historic moment for the franchise. *Nick Laham/Getty Images*

4 In the last game at Shea Stadium, one Mets legend threw out the ceremonial "last pitch" to another Mets legend. Here Mike Piazza and Tom Seaver walk off the mound following the closing ceremonies. *Corey Sipkin/ NY Daily News Archive/Getty Images*

Looking ahead to the second half century of Mets baseball, fans are counting on the speed and glovework of Jose Reyes, the power and leadership of David Wright, and the dominating arm of Johan Santana, among others, to bring the team back to the top.

5 *Mike Ehrmann/WireImage/ Getty Images*

6 *Brad Mangin/MLB Photos/ Getty Images*

7 *Jim McIsaac/Getty Images*

Journeyman pitcher R. A. Dickey found a home with the Mets in 2010. After going 22–28 with a 5.43 ERA in parts of seven seasons, the 35-year-old knuckleballer went 11–6 with a 2.80 ERA in 23 starts in New York. *Mike Zarrilli/Getty Images*

Ike Davis receives a congratulatory pie in the face after going two for four with an RBI in his major league debut on April 19, 2010. Wearing number 42 in honor of Jackie Robinson Day at Citi Field, the rookie first baseman finished the year with 19 homers. *Jim McIsaac/Getty Images*

The Mets equaled the best homestand in franchise history by going 9–1 in April 2010 while winning three of four from the Cubs and sweeping the Braves and Dodgers. That homestand also marked the debut of first base prospect Ike Davis, son of former Yankees pitcher Ron Davis. The rookie not only showed an ability to launch balls to distant locales at Citi Field, but he also perfected the flip-over-the-rail-into-the dugout-catch, doing so three times in his first couple of months on the job. Jose Reyes, who did not play after May in 2009 because of hamstring problems, got a late start on the year because of a thyroid issue, but he quickly looked the Jose of old and was even named to the all-star team, though he didn't play due to an oblique problem.

For the second straight year, Johan Santana had a superb first month in 2010, but then tailed off and ended the year with surgery (elbow in 2009, shoulder in 2010). After a tough June, pitching coach Dan Warthen got Santana to hold his hands differently, because he thought Santana was tipping his pitches. He threw 16 innings of shutout ball over his next two starts.

Also for the second straight year, the Mets tailed off in July. A 2–9 West Coast trip doomed their second half. The Mets went from July 25 to August 31 without going one game above or below .500. Consistent mediocrity, and a second-straight fourth-place finish, wound up costing both manager Jerry Manuel and GM Omar Minaya their jobs following the 2010 season. As the franchise celebrates its 50th year, Mets baseball starts all over again with a few fresh faces and a clean slate.

The personnel, the uniform, even the ballpark changes, but after a half century the feeling is still the same. "Let's Go Mets!"

2000s METS YEAR-BY-YEAR

YEAR	W–L	PCT.	GB	FINISH	
2000	94–68	.580	1	2nd*	In the decade known for the Mets finishing one game short, the 2000 team was the first Mets club to do so. After winning the Wild Card, they ended the year with five straight wins. The Braves lost their last five after clinching the division and then dropped three straight to St. Louis in the NLDS.
2001	82–80	.506	6	3rd	In the final weekend, Lenny Harris singled off Montreal's Carl Pavano for his 151st career pinch hit to surpass Manny Mota as the all-time leader. Harris finished the season with 21, three short of Rusty Staub's single-season team mark from 1983. Harris would play four more years in the majors and amass 212 pinch hits.
2002	75–86	.466	26 ½	5th	The 40th anniversary Mets team as voted by fans: 1B K. Hernandez; 2B E. Alfonzo; SS B. Harrelson; 3B H. Johnson; OF M. Wilson, L. Dykstra, and D. Strawberry; C M. Piazza; RHP T. Seaver; LHP J. Koosman; RHRP R. McDowell; LHRP J. Franco; PH E. Kranepool and R. Staub; Manager G. Hodges.
2003	66–95	.410	34 1 ½	5th	With Mike Piazza out for three months, backup catchers Vance Wilson and Jason Phillips played every day for the last-place club. Wilson set a career high with 89 games caught while novice first baseman Phillips batted a career-best .298 and hit the 5,000th homer in Mets history.
2004	71–91	.438	25	4th	Todd Zeile hadn't strapped on catching gear since converting to third base in 1990, but he wanted to catch in his final season, and he did so in mid-September. Then a rash of injuries forced him to catch again in the season finale. His last play was a foul pop, and he homered in his final career at bat.
2005	83–79	.512	7	3rd	Known as one of the great hitting catchers of all time, Mike Piazza did not have too many miscues in the field (stolen bases against him aside). After putting first base behind him, Piazza made just two errors in his last 101 games caught as a Met, a .997 fielding percentage, tying his 2000 mark for best by any Mets catcher in a season.
2006	97–65	.599	–	1st	The Mets set a club record with 10 grand slams, including two in one inning. Trailing the Cubs 5–2 in the sixth at Wrigley, Cliff Floyd's slam gave the Mets the lead. One out and an Endy Chavez RBI-single later, Carlos Beltran hit another grand slam. David Wright's two-run homer made it a club record 11-run inning.
2007	88–74	.543	1	2nd	John Maine went 7⅔ hitless innings on September 29 in a crucial game against Florida. Maine's earlier one-hitter vs. Washington went five innings, and Tom Glavine's complete-game one-hitter against St. Louis went six. Both were shortened by rain, the only season the Mets had no nine-inning complete game.
2008	89–73	.549	3	2nd	Fernando Tatis had scarcely played in the majors since 2003, including two years that he didn't pick up a bat. Hoping to earn enough to build a church near his Dominican home, Tatis joined the Mets and was NL Comeback Player of the Year, batting .297 with 11 homers and 47 RBI.
2009	70–92	.432	23	4th	With Johan Santana heading the staff, you'd think he'd have had some famous firsts at Citi Field, but the first win by a Met was by Oliver Perez, the first Mets complete game belonged to Livan Hernandez, and the first complete-game shutout was Nelson Figueroa's. Santana did pitch the first day game at Citi, and won, 1–0.
2010	79–83	.488	18	4th	On June 10 the Mets had the best home record in the majors (24–10) and the fewest road wins in the NL (8–18). They traveled to Baltimore, Cleveland, and the Bronx and reeled off seven straight road wins (and eight wins overall), including their first road sweeps since 2008.

*Won Wild Card.

Debby Wong/Shutterstock

New York Mets

All-Time Record Book

Honors and Awards

Mets in the Baseball Hall of Fame, Cooperstown, NY

Richie Ashburn	outfielder 1962	1995
Yogi Berra	catcher 1965; coach 1965–1971; manager 1972–1975	1972
Gary Carter	catcher 1985–1989	2003
Rickey Henderson	outfielder 1999–2000; coach 2007	2009
Willie Mays	outfielder 1972–1973; coach 1974–1979	1979
Eddie Murray	first baseman 1992–1993	2003
Nolan Ryan	pitcher 1966, 1968–1971	1999
Tom Seaver	pitcher 1967–1977, 1983	1992
Duke Snider	outfielder 1963	1980
Warren Spahn	pitcher/coach 1965	1973
Casey Stengel	manager 1962–1965	1966
George Weiss	president and general manager 1961–1966	1971

Mets Broadcasters Honored with the Ford Frick Award

Bob Murphy, 1994

Lindsey Nelson, 1988

Note: Broadcaster Ralph Kiner was inducted into the Hall of Fame as a player in 1975.

The New York Mets Hall of Fame, Flushing, NY

Joan Payson	owner 1960–1975	1981
Casey Stengel	manager 1962–1965	1981
Gil Hodges	first baseman 1962–1963; manager 1968–1971	1982
George Weiss	president and general manager 1961–1966	1982
William A. Shea	pioneer	1983
Johnny Murphy	executive 1961–1967; general manager 1968–1970	1983
Ralph Kiner	broadcaster 1962–2010	1984
Bob Murphy	broadcaster 1962–2003	1984
Lindsey Nelson	broadcaster 1962–1978	1984
Bud Harrelson	shortstop 1965–1977; coach 1982, 1985–1990; manager 1990–1991	1986
Rusty Staub	outfielder 1972–1976, 1981–1985	1986
Tom Seaver	pitcher 1967–1977, 1983	1988
Jerry Koosman	pitcher 1967–1978	1989
Ed Kranepool	first baseman/outfielder 1962–1979	1990
Cleon Jones	outfielder 1963–1975	1991
Jerry Grote	catcher 1966–1977	1992
Tug McGraw	pitcher 1965–1967, 1969–1974	1993
Mookie Wilson	outfielder 1980–1989; coach 1997–2002	1996
Keith Hernandez	first baseman 1983–1989	1997
Gary Carter	catcher 1985–1989	2001
Tommie Agee	outfielder 1968–1972	2002
Frank Cashen	general manager 1980–1991	2010
Dwight Gooden	pitcher 1984–1994	2010
Davey Johnson	manager 1984–1990	2010
Darryl Strawberry	outfielder 1983–1990	2010

Rookie of the Year

Tom Seaver, 1967

Jon Matlack, 1972

Darryl Strawberry, 1983

Dwight Gooden, 1984

Cy Young Award

Tom Seaver, 1969

Tom Seaver, 1973

Tom Seaver, 1975

Dwight Gooden, 1984

Gold Glove Award

Tommie Agee, OF, 1970

Bud Harrelson, SS, 1971

Doug Flynn, 2B, 1980

Keith Hernandez, 1B, 1983–1988

Ron Darling, P, 1989

Rey Ordonez, SS, 1997–1999

Robin Ventura, 3B, 1999

Carlos Beltran, OF, 2006–2008

David Wright, 3B, 2007–2008

Silver Slugger

(awarded to best offensive player at each position since 1980)

Keith Hernandez, 1B, 1984

Gary Carter, C, 1985–1986

Darryl Strawberry, OF, 1988, 1990

Howard Johnson, 3B, 1989, 1991

Dwight Gooden, P, 1992

Mike Piazza, C, 1998–2002

Edgardo Alfonzo, 2B, 1999

Mike Hampton, P, 2000

Jose Reyes, SS, 2006
Carlos Beltran, 2006–2007
David Wright, 2007–2008

Rolaids Relief Man of the Year

John Franco, 1990
Armando Benitez, 2001

Career Batting Records

(through 2010)

Bold denotes player was active for team in 2010

Games

Ed Kranepool (1962–1979)	1,853
Bud Harrelson (1966–1977)	1,322
Jerry Grote (1966–1977)	1,235
Cleon Jones (1963, 1965–1975)	1,201
Howard Johnson (1985–1993)	1,154
Mookie Wilson (1980–1989)	1,116
Darryl Strawberry (1983–1990)	1,109
Edgardo Alfonzo (1995–2002)	1,086
David Wright (2004–2010)	**1,004**
Lee Mazzilli (1976–1981, 1986–1989)	979

At Bats

Ed Kranepool	5,436
Bud Harrelson	4,390
Cleon Jones	4,223
Mookie Wilson	4,027
Howard Johnson	3,968
Jose Reyes	**3,916**
Darryl Strawberry	3,903
Edgardo Alfonzo	3,897
Jerry Grote	3,881
David Wright	**3,772**

Hits

Ed Kranepool	1,418
Cleon Jones	1,188
David Wright	**1,149**
Edgardo Alfonzo	1,136
Jose Reyes	**1,119**
Mookie Wilson	1,112
Bud Harrelson	1,029
Mike Piazza	1,028
Darryl Strawberry	1,025
Howard Johnson	997

Runs

Darryl Strawberry	662
David Wright	**639**
Jose Reyes	**634**
Howard Johnson	627
Edgardo Alfonzo	614
Mookie Wilson	592
Cleon Jones	563
Ed Kranepool	536
Mike Piazza	532
Bud Harrelson	490

Doubles

David Wright	**258**
Ed Kranepool	225
Howard Johnson	214
Edgardo Alfonzo	212
Mike Piazza	193
Jose Reyes	**191**
Darryl Strawberry	187
Cleon Jones	182
Carlos Beltran	**178**
Mookie Wilson	170

Triples

Jose Reyes	**83**
Mookie Wilson	62
Bud Harrelson	45
Cleon Jones	33
Steve Henderson	31
Darryl Strawberry	30
Lance Johnson	27
Doug Flynn	26
Ed Kranepool	25
Lee Mazzilli	22

Home Runs

Darryl Strawberry	252
Mike Piazza	220
Howard Johnson	192
David Wright	**169**
Dave Kingman	154
Carlos Beltran	**134**
Todd Hundley	124
Kevin McReynolds	122
Edgardo Alfonzo	120
Ed Kranepool	118

At Bats Per Home Run

Dave Kingman	15.1
Darryl Strawberry	15.5
Mike Piazza	15.8
Carlos Delgado	16.9
Bobby Bonilla	18.7
Robin Ventura	19.6
Cliff Floyd	20.3
Todd Hundley	20.6
Howard Johnson	20.7
Carlos Beltran	**20.7**

Runs Batted In

Darryl Strawberry	733
David Wright	**664**
Mike Piazza	655
Howard Johnson	629
Ed Kranepool	614
Edgardo Alfonzo	538
Cleon Jones	521
Carlos Beltran	**493**
Keith Hernandez	468
Kevin McReynolds	456

Total Bases

Ed Kranepool	2,047
Darryl Strawberry	2,028
David Wright	**1,946**
Mike Piazza	1,885
Howard Johnson	1,823
Edgardo Alfonzo	1,736
Cleon Jones	1,715
Jose Reyes	**1,698**
Mookie Wilson	1,586
Carlos Beltran	**1,386**

Batting Average

John Olerud	.315
David Wright	**.305**
Keith Hernandez	.297
Mike Piazza	.296
Edgardo Alfonzo	.292
Dave Magadan	.292
Steve Henderson	.287
Jose Reyes	**.286**
Wally Backman	.283
Ron Hunt	.282

On-Base Percentage

John Olerud	.425
Dave Magadan	.391
Keith Hernandez	.387
David Wright	**.383**
Mike Piazza	.373
Edgardo Alfonzo	.367
Luis Castillo	**.366**
Carlos Beltran	**.366**
Steve Henderson	.360
Robin Ventura	.360

Slugging Percentage

Mike Piazza	.542
Darryl Strawberry	.520
David Wright	**.516**
Carlos Delgado	.506
John Olerud	.501
Carlos Beltran	**.499**
Bobby Bonilla	.495
Cliff Floyd	.478
Robin Ventura	.468
Bernard Gilkey	.461

On-Base Plus Slugging

John Olerud	.926
Mike Piazza	.915
David Wright	**.899**
Darryl Strawberry	.878
Carlos Beltran	**.864**
Carlos Delgado	.857
Bobby Bonilla	.851
Cliff Floyd	.832
Robin Ventura	.828
Bernard Gilkey	.818

Bases on Balls

Darryl Strawberry	580
Bud Harrelson	573
Howard Johnson	556
David Wright	**483**
Wayne Garrett	482
Keith Hernandez	471
Edgardo Alfonzo	458
Ed Kranepool	454
Lee Mazzilli	438
Mike Piazza	424

Hit by Pitch

Ron Hunt	41
Cleon Jones	39
Cliff Floyd	37
Felix Millan	36
Carlos Delgado	33
David Wright	**30**
Edgardo Alfonzo	29
Jeff Kent	28
John Olerud	26
Darryl Strawberry	26

Strikeouts

Darryl Strawberry	960
Howard Johnson	827
David Wright	**800**
Cleon Jones	697
Mookie Wilson	692
Dave Kingman	672
Todd Hundley	624
Bud Harrelson	595
Ed Kranepool	581
Tommie Agee	572

At Bats per Strikeout

Felix Millan	29.1
Doug Flynn	13.5
Gregg Jefferies	12.8
Ron Hunt	12.7
Rusty Staub	12.6
Ken Boswell	10.2
Rey Ordonez	9.4
Ed Kranepool	9.4
John Stearns	9.1
Rafael Santana	8.9

Stolen Bases

Jose Reyes	**331**
Mookie Wilson	281
Howard Johnson	202
Darryl Strawberry	191
Lee Mazzilli	152
David Wright	**138**
Lenny Dykstra	116
Bud Harrelson	115
Wally Backman	106
Roger Cedeno	105

Pinch Hits

Ed Kranepool	90
Rusty Staub	77
Matt Franco	58
Ron Hodges	48
Marlon Anderson	38
Bruce Boisclair	38
Lee Mazzilli	38
Mookie Wilson	37
Lenny Harris	35
Mackey Sasser	32

Sacrifice Flies

Ed Kranepool	58
David Wright	**50**
Howard Johnson	50
Cleon Jones	41
Edgardo Alfonzo	40
Darryl Strawberry	39
Rusty Staub	37
Carlos Beltran	**34**
Kevin McReynolds	33
Gary Carter	31
Keith Hernandez	31

Single-Season Batting Records

Rate stats based on 502 plate appearances in a season as a Met

Games

Felix Millan	162 (1975)
John Olerud	162 (1999)
Carlos Beltran	161 (2008)
Jose Reyes	161 (2005)
Robin Ventura	161 (1999)

At Bats

Jose Reyes	696 (2005)
Jose Reyes	688 (2008)
Lance Johnson	682 (1996)
Jose Reyes	681 (2007)
Felix Millan	676 (1975)

Hits

Lance Johnson	227 (1996)
Jose Reyes	204 (2008)
John Olerud	197 (1998)
David Wright	196 (2007)
Jose Reyes	194 (2006)

Runs

Carlos Beltran	127 (2006)
Edgardo Alfonzo	123 (1999)
Jose Reyes	122 (2006)
Jose Reyes	119 (2007)
Lance Johnson	117 (1996)

Doubles

Bernard Gilkey	44 (1996)
David Wright	42 (2008)
David Wright	42 (2007)
David Wright	42 (2005)
Edgardo Alfonzo	41 (1999)
Howard Johnson	41 (1989)

Triples

Lance Johnson	21 (1996)
Jose Reyes	19 (2008)
Jose Reyes	17 (2006)
Jose Reyes	17 (2005)
Jose Reyes	12 (2007)

Home Runs

Carlos Beltran	41 (2006)
Todd Hundley	41 (1996)
Mike Piazza	40 (1999)
Darryl Strawberry	39 (1988)
Darryl Strawberry	39 (1987)

At Bats per Home Run

Carlos Beltran	12.4 (2006)
Mike Piazza	12.7 (2000)
Dave Kingman	12.8 (1976)
Todd Hundley	13.2 (1996)
Mike Piazza	13.3 (1999)

Runs Batted In

David Wright	124 (2008)
Mike Piazza	124 (1999)
Robin Ventura	120 (1999)
Bernard Gilkey	117 (1996)
Howard Johnson	117 (1991)

Total Bases

David Wright	334 (2008)
David Wright	330 (2007)
Jose Reyes	327 (2008)
Lance Johnson	327 (1996)
Bernard Gilkey	321 (1996)

Batting Average

John Olerud	.354 (1998)
Cleon Jones	.340 (1969)
Lance Johnson	.333 (1996)
Magadan	.328 (1990)
David Wright	.325 (2007)

On-Base Percentage

John Olerud	.447 (1998)
John Olerud	.427 (1999)
Edgardo Alfonzo	.425 (2000)
Rickey Henderson	.423 (1999)
Cleon Jones	.422 (1969)

Slugging Percentage

Mike Piazza	.614 (2000)
Carlos Beltran	.594 (2006)
Darryl Strawberry	.583 (1987)
Mike Piazza	.575 (1999)
Mike Piazza	.573 (2001)

On-Base Plus Slugging

Mike Piazza	1.012 (2000)
John Olerud	.998 (1998)
Carlos Beltran	.982 (2006)
Darryl Strawberry	.981 (1987)
Edgardo Alfonzo	.967 (2000)

Bases on Balls

John Olerud	125 (1999)
Darryl Strawberry	97 (1987)
Keith Hernandez	97 (1984)
John Olerud	96 (1998)
Carlos Beltran	95 (2006)
Edgardo Alfonzo	95 (2000)
Bud Harrelson	95 (1970)

Hit by Pitch

John Olerud	13 (1997)
Ron Hunt	13 (1963)
Cliff Floyd	12 (2006)
Fernando Vina	12 (1994)
Felix Millan	12 (1975)

Strikeouts

David Wright	161 (2010)
Dave Kingman	156 (1982)
Tommie Agee	156 (1970)
Dave Kingman	153 (1975)
Todd Hundley	146 (1996)

At Bats per Strikeout

Felix Millan	37.0 (1974)
Felix Millan	29.0 (1973)
Felix Millan	27.9 (1976)
Felix Millan	24.1 (1975)
Lance Johnson	17.1 (1996)
Doug Flynn	17.1 (1981)

Stolen Bases

Jose Reyes	78 (2007)
Roger Cedeno	66 (1999)
Jose Reyes	64 (2006)
Jose Reyes	60 (2005)
Mookie Wilson	58 (1982)

Pinch Hits

Rusty Staub	24 (1983)
Lenny Harris	21 (2001)
Matt Franco	19 (1997)
Jeff McKnight	19 (1993)
Marlon Anderson	18 (2005)
Rusty Staub	18 (1984)

Sacrifice Flies

Howard Johnson	15 (1991)
Gary Carter	15 (1986)
David Wright	12 (2010)
Bernard Gilkey	12 (1997)
David Wright	11 (2008)

Single-Game Hitting Records

Hits	6	Edgardo Alfonzo (8/30/1999 at Astros)
Runs	6	Edgardo Alfonzo (8/30/1999 at Astros)
Singles	5	Jim Hickman (9/30/1964 at Milwaukee Braves); Gary Carter (7/4/1985 at Braves, 19 innings); Dave Magadan (7/24/1987 vs. Astros)
Doubles	3	Shared by many players. Most recent: Jose Reyes (5/13/2009 vs. Braves)
Triples	3	Doug Flynn (8/5/1980 at Expos)
Home Runs	3	Jim Hickman (9/3/1965 at Cardinals); Dave Kingman (6/4/1976 at Dodgers); Claudell Washington (6/22/1980 at Dodgers); Darryl Strawberry (8/5/1985); Gary Carter (9/3/1985); Edgardo Alfonzo (8/20/1999 at Astros); Jose Reyes (8/15/2006 at Phillies)
Runs Batted In	9	Carlos Delgado (6/27/2008 at Yankees)
Extra-Base Hits	4	Shared by many players. Most recent: Edgardo Alfonzo (8/30/1999 at Astros)
Total Bases	16	Edgardo Alfonzo (6/27/1999 at Astros)
Bases on Balls	4	Shared by many players. Most recent: David Wright (8/22/2007 vs. Padres)
Most Strikeouts	5	Ron Swoboda (6/22/1969 vs. Cardinals, Game 1); Frank Taveras (5/1/1979 vs. Padres); Dave Kingman (5/28/1982 vs. Astros); Ryan Thompson (9/29/1993 vs. Cardinals)
Sacrifice Hits	3	Sid Fernandez ((7/24/1987 vs. Astros); Livan Hernandez (4/11/2009 at Marlins)
Sacrifice Flies	2	Shared by many players. Most recent: Omir Santos (5/15/2009 at Giants)
Hit by Pitch	2	Shared by many players. Most recent: Fernando Tatis (7/2/2009 at Pirates)
Grounded into Double Play	4	Joe Torre (7/21/1975 vs. Astros)
Stolen Bases	4	Vince Coleman (6/26/1992 at Cardinals; 6/23/1993 vs. Expos); Roger Cedeno (5/14/1999 at Phillies); David Wright (5/14/2009 at Giants)
Hitting for the Cycle		Jim Hickman (8/7/1963 vs. Cardinals) Tommie Agee (7/6/1970 vs. Cardinals) Mike Phillips (6/25/1976 at Cubs) Keith Hernandez (7/4/1985 at Braves, 19 innings) Kevin McReynolds (8/1/1989 at Cardinals) Alex Ochoa (7/3/1996 at Phillies) John Olerud (9/11/1997 vs. Expos) Eric Valent (7/29/2004 at Expos) Jose Reyes (7/21/2006 vs. Reds)
Hitting Streak		Moises Alou, 30 games (8/23–9/26/2007)

Inside the Park Home Runs

Gil Hodges (5/16/1962 vs. Cubs)
Richie Ashburn (6/28/1962 vs. Colt .45s)
Charlie Neal (5/7/1963 vs. Phillies)
Ron Hunt (6/5/1966 vs. Dodgers)
Bud Harrelson (8/17/1967 at Pirates)
Don Hahn (9/5/1971 at Phillies)
Doug Flynn (6/12/1979 vs. Reds)
Gil Flores (8/19/1979 at Reds)
Lee Mazzilli (6/27/1980 at Phillies)
Steve Henderson (8/12/1980 at Pirates)
Wally Backman (7/31/1982 vs. Pirates)
Dave Kingman (9/10/1982 at Cardinals)
Mark Bradley (8/31/1983 vs. Dodgers)
Darryl Strawberry (6/17/1984 at Cardinals)
Howard Johnson (9/20/1987 at Pirates)
Darryl Strawberry (5/3/1989 vs. Reds)
Kevin Elster (6/26/1990 at Cardinals)
Tim Bogar (8/14/1993 at Phillies)
Edgardo Alfonzo (5/6/1995 at Reds)
Timo Perez (9/24/2000 at Phillies)
Marlon Anderson (6/11/2005 vs. Angels)
Kazuo Matsui (4/20/2006 at Padres)
Jose Reyes (9/7/2006 vs. Dodgers)
Damion Easley (8/2/2007 vs. Brewers)
Angel Pagan (8/23/2009 vs. Phillies)
Angel Pagan (6/19/2010 at Nationals)

Career Pitching Leaders

Based on at least 500 career innings as a Met.

Wins

Tom Seaver	198
Dwight Gooden	157
Jerry Koosman	140
Ron Darling	99
Sid Fernandez	98
Al Leiter	95
Jon Matlack	82
David Cone	81
Bobby Jones	74
Steve Trachsel	66

Losses

Jerry Koosman	137
Tom Seaver	124
Dwight Gooden	85
Jon Matlack	81
Al Jackson	80
Sid Fernandez	78
Jack Fisher	73
Craig Swan	71
Ron Darling	70
Al Leiter	67

Win-Loss Percentage

Dwight Gooden	.649
Rick Reed	.621
Johan Santana	**.615**
Tom Seaver	.615
David Cone	.614
Ron Darling	.586
Al Leiter	.586
Bret Saberhagen	.580
Bobby Jones	.569
Bobby Ojeda	.560

Earned Run Average

Tom Seaver	2.57
Jesse Orosco	2.73
Johan Santana	**2.85**
Jon Matlack	3.03
Jerry Koosman	3.09
John Franco	3.10
Dwight Gooden	3.10
Bobby Ojeda	3.12
David Cone	3.13
Sid Fernandez	3.14

Games

John Franco	695
Pedro Feliciano	**459**
Tom Seaver	401
Jerry Koosman	376
Jesse Orosco	372
Tug McGraw	361
Armando Benitez	333
Dwight Gooden	305
Aaron Heilman	305
Jeff Innis	288

Innings Pitched

Tom Seaver	3,045
Jerry Koosman	2,545
Dwight Gooden	2,169⅔
Ron Darling	1,620
Sid Fernandez	1,584⅔
Jon Matlack	1,448
Al Leiter	1,360
Craig Swan	1,230⅓
Bobby Jones	1,215⅔
David Cone	1,209⅓

Strikeouts

Tom Seaver	2,541
Dwight Gooden	1,875
Jerry Koosman	1,799
Sid Fernandez	1,449
David Cone	1,172
Ron Darling	1,148
Al Leiter	1,106
Jon Matlack	1,023
Bobby Jones	714
Craig Swan	671

Strikeouts per 9 Innings

David Cone	8.722
Nolan Ryan	8.700
Oliver Perez	**8.536**
Sid Fernandez	8.229
Dwight Gooden	7.778
John Maine	**7.755**
Jesse Orosco	7.645
John Franco	7.582
Tom Seaver	7.509
Al Leiter	7.319

Strikeouts per Bases on Balls

Bret Saberhagen	5.039
Rick Reed	3.734
Johan Santana	**3.024**
Tom Seaver	3.000
Dwight Gooden	2.880
Frank Viola	2.745
David Cone	2.719
Jon Matlack	2.442
Sid Fernandez	2.431
Jerry Koosman	2.194

Walks Plus Hits per Inning

Bret Saberhagen	1.076
Tom Seaver	1.079
Sid Fernandez	1.113
Rick Reed	1.155
Dwight Gooden	1.175
Johan Santana	**1.175**
Bobby Ojeda	1.182
Jim McAndrew	1.184
David Cone	1.192
Jon Matlack	1.195

Hits per 9 Innings

Nolan Ryan	6.512
Sid Fernandez	6.628
Tom Seaver	7.184
Jesse Orosco	7.254
David Cone	7.524
Gary Gentry	7.605
Tug McGraw	7.777
John Maine	**7.854**
Dwight Gooden	7.873
Jerry Koosman	8.068

Bases on Balls per 9 Innings

Bret Saberhagen	1.322
Rick Reed	1.600
Ed Lynch	1.947
Frank Viola	2.241
Jack Fisher	2.338
Johan Santana	**2.460**
Jim McAndrew	2.467
Tom Seaver	2.503
Bobby Ojeda	2.509
Jon Matlack	2.604

Games Started

Tom Seaver	395
Jerry Koosman	346
Dwight Gooden	303
Sid Fernandez	250
Ron Darling	241
Al Leiter	213

Jon Matlack 199
Bobby Jones 190
Craig Swan 184
David Cone 169

Complete Games
Tom Seaver 171
Jerry Koosman 108
Dwight Gooden 67
Jon Matlack 65
Al Jackson 41
Jack Fisher 35
David Cone 34
Roger Craig 27
Ron Darling 25
Craig Swan 25

Shutouts
Tom Seaver 44
Jerry Koosman 26
Jon Matlack 26
Dwight Gooden 23
David Cone 15
Ron Darling 10
Al Jackson 10
Sid Fernandez 9
Bobby Ojeda 9
Gary Gentry 8

Home Runs Allowed
Tom Seaver 212
Jerry Koosman 187
Ron Darling 155
Sid Fernandez 138
Bobby Jones 137
Steve Trachsel 124
Dwight Gooden 123
Al Leiter 118
Rick Reed 116
Craig Swan 112

Hits Allowed
Tom Seaver 2,431
Jerry Koosman 2,281
Dwight Gooden 1,898
Ron Darling 1,473
Jon Matlack 1,312
Bobby Jones 1,255
Al Leiter 1,222
Craig Swan 1,191
Sid Fernandez 1,167
Tom Glavine 1,057

Bases on Balls Allowed
Tom Seaver 847
Jerry Koosman 820
Dwight Gooden 651
Ron Darling 614
Sid Fernandez 596
Al Leiter 546
David Cone 431

Jon Matlack 419
Craig Swan 368
Steve Trachsel 354

Earned Runs
Jerry Koosman 875
Tom Seaver 870
Dwight Gooden 747
Ron Darling 630
Bobby Jones 558
Sid Fernandez 553
Al Leiter 517
Craig Swan 508
Jon Matlack 488
Al Jackson 464

Batters Faced
Tom Seaver 12,191
Jerry Koosman 10,517
Dwight Gooden 8,898
Ron Darling 6,807
Sid Fernandez 6,456
Jon Matlack 5,953
Al Leiter 5,774
Bobby Jones 5,154
Craig Swan 5,140
David Cone 5,008

Saves
John Franco 276
Armando Benitez 160
Jesse Orosco 107
Billy Wagner 101
Tug McGraw 86
Roger McDowell 84
Neil Allen 69
Skip Lockwood 65
Francisco Rodriguez 60
Braden Looper 57

Games Finished
John Franco 484
Armando Benitez 266
Jesse Orosco 246
Tug McGraw 228
Roger McDowell 189
Ron Taylor 184
Skip Lockwood 164
Neil Allen 160
Billy Wagner 150
Doug Sisk 128

Wild Pitches
Tom Seaver 81
Jerry Koosman 66
Ron Darling 63
David Cone 62
Dwight Gooden 47
Tug McGraw 44
Jon Matlack 42
John Franco 39

Jim McAndrew 34
Pete Falcone 31

Hit Batsmen
Al Leiter 63
Tom Seaver 52
Jerry Koosman 49
Dwight Gooden 41
Mike Pelfrey **38**
Ron Darling 36
Sid Fernandez 36
Bobby Jones 33
Al Jackson 32
Oliver Perez **29**
David Cone 28

Single-Season Pitching Records
For rate stats, pitchers must have thrown one inning for every game played by team

Wins
Tom Seaver 25 (1969)
Dwight Gooden 24 (1985)
Tom Seaver 22 (1975)
Jerry Koosman 21 (1976)
Tom Seaver 21 (1972)

Losses
Jack Fisher 24 (1965)
Roger Craig 24 (1962)
Roger Craig 22 (1963)
Jerry Koosman 20 (1977)
Al Jackson 20 (1965)
Al Jackson 20 (1962)
Tracy Stallard 20 (1964)

Win-Loss Percentage
David Cone .870 (1988)
Dwight Gooden .857 (1985)
Bobby Ojeda .783 (1987)
Tom Seaver .781 (1969)
Bret Saberhagen .778 (1994)

Earned Run Average
Dwight Gooden 1.53 (1985)
Tom Seaver 1.76 (1971)
Tom Seaver 2.08 (1973)
Jerry Koosman 2.08 (1968)
Tom Seaver 2.20 (1968)

Games
Pedro Feliciano 92 (2010)
Pedro Feliciano 88 (2009)
Pedro Feliciano 86 (2008)
Mike Stanton 83 (2004)
Joe Smith 82 (2008)

Innings Pitched
Tom Seaver 290⅔ (1970)
Tom Seaver 290 (1973)
Tom Seaver 286⅓ (1971)
Tom Seaver 280⅓ (1975)
Tom Seaver 278⅔ (1968)

Strikeouts

Tom Seaver	289 (1971)
Tom Seaver	283 (1970)
Dwight Gooden	276 (1984)
Dwight Gooden	268 (1985)
Tom Seaver	251 (1973)

Strikeouts per 9 Innings

Dwight Gooden	11.395 (1984)
David Cone	9.907 (1990)
David Cone	9.793 (1992)
Sid Fernandez	9.511 (1985)
David Cone	9.322 (1991)

Strikeouts per Bases on Balls

Bret Saberhagen	11.000 (1994)
Rick Reed	5.276 (1998)
Tom Seaver	4.738 (1971)
Pedro Martinez	4.425 (2005)
Tom Seaver	4.271 (1968)

Walks Plus Hits per Inning

Tom Seaver	0.946 (1971)
Pedro Martinez	0.949 (2005)
Dwight Gooden	0.965 (1985)
Tom Seaver	0.976 (1973)
Tom Seaver	0.978 (1968)

Hits per 9 Innings

Sid Fernandez	5.707 (1985)
Sid Fernandez	6.112 (1988)
Dwight Gooden	6.441 (1985)
Sid Fernandez	6.442 (1989)
Sid Fernandez	6.526 (1990)

Bases on Balls per 9 Innings

Bret Saberhagen	0.660 (1994)
Rick Reed	1.229 (1998)
Ed Lynch	1.272 (1985)
Rick Reed	1.339 (1997)
Tom Seaver	1.554 (1968)

Games Started

Tom Seaver	36 (1975)
Tom Seaver	36 (1973)
Tom Seaver	36 (1970)
Jack Fisher	36 (1965)
35 starts achieved 13 times	

Complete Games

Tom Seaver	21 (1971)
Tom Seaver	19 (1970)
Tom Seaver	18 (1973)
Tom Seaver	18 (1969)
Tom Seaver	18 (1967)

Shutouts

Dwight Gooden	8 (1985)
Jon Matlack	7 (1974)
Jerry Koosman	7 (1968)
Jon Matlack	6 (1976)
Jerry Koosman	6 (1969)

Home Runs Allowed

Roger Craig	35 (1962)
Pedro Astacio	32 (2002)
Jay Hook	31 (1962)
Rick Reed	30 (1998)
Pete Harnisch	30 (1996)

Hits Allowed

Roger Craig	261 (1962)
Fran Viola	259 (1991)
Jerry Koosman	258 (1974)
Jack Fisher	256 (1964)
Jack Fisher	252 (1965)

Bases on Balls Allowed

Nolan Ryan	116 (1971)
Ron Darling	114 (1985)
Mike Torrez	113 (1983)
Oliver Perez	105 (2008)
Ron Darling	104 (1984)

Earned Runs

Roger Craig	117 (1982)
Jack Fisher	115 91967)
Jay Hook	115 (1962)
Al Jackson	113 (1962)
Jack Fisher	111 (1965)

Batters Faced

Tom Seaver	1,173 (1970)
Tom Seaver	1,147 (1973)
Jerry Koosman	1,118 (1974)
Tom Seaver	1,115 (1975)
Tom Seaver	1,103 (1971)

Saves

Armando Benitez	43 (2001)
Armando Benitez	41 (2000)
Billy Wagner	40 (2006)
John Franco	38 (1998)
John Franco	36 (1997)

Games Finished

Armando Benitez	68 (2000)
Francisco Rodriguez	66 (2009)
Armando Benitez	64 (2001)
Braden Looper	60 (2004)
Billy Wagner	59 (2006)

Wild Pitches

Jack Hamilton	18 (1966)
David Cone	17 (1991)
Jason Isringhausen	14 (1996)
David Cone	14 (1989)
Jon Matlack	13 (1976)

Hit Batsmen

Pedro Astacio	16 (2002)
Kevin Appier	15 (2001)
Nolan Ryan	15 (1971)
Victor Zambrano	15 (2005)
Mike Pelfrey	13 (2008)

Single-Game Pitching Records

Innings Pitched	15	Al Jackson (8/14/1962 vs. Phillies); Rob Gardner (10/2/1965 vs. Phillies)
Consecutive Innings Without Allowing a Run	31⅔	Jerry Koosman (August 19– September 7, 1973)
Hits Allowed	15	Tom Seaver (5/25/1976 at Phillies)
Runs Allowed	11	Craig Anderson (8/26/1962 at Phillies); Jack Fisher (6/3/1967 at Giants, 1st Game); Orlando Hernandez (8/15/2006 at Phillies)
Earned Runs Allowed	11	Orlando Hernandez (8/15/2006 at Phillies)
Home Runs Allowed	5	Roger Craig (5/4/1963 vs. Giants)
Strikeouts	19	Tom Seaver (4/22/1970 vs. Padres); David Cone (10/6/1991 at Phillies)
Consecutive Strikeouts	10	Tom Seaver (4/22/1970 vs. Padres)
Bases on Balls	10	Mike Torrez (7/21/1983 at Reds)
Hit Batsmen	3	Shared by many players; most recently Oliver Perez (9/27/2007 vs. Marlins)
Balks	3	Mike Pelfrey (5/17/2009 at Giants)

New York Mets Managers

	Years	Wins	Losses	Pct.	Postseason App
Casey Stengel	1962–1965	175	404	.302	
Wes Westrum	1965–1967	142	237	.375	
Salty Parker	1967	4	7	.364	
Gil Hodges	1968–1971	339	309	.523	1
Yogi Berra	1972–1975	292	296	.497	1
Roy McMillan	1975	26	27	.491	
Joe Frazier	1976–1977	101	106	.488	
Joe Torre	1977–1981	286	420	.405	
George Bamberger	1982–1983	81	127	.389	
Frank Howard	1983	52	64	.448	
Davey Johnson	1984–1990	595	417	.588	2
Bud Harrelson	1990–1991	145	129	.529	
Mike Cubbage	1991	3	4	.429	
Jeff Torborg	1992–1993	85	115	.425	
Dallas Green	1993–1996	229	283	.447	
Bobby Valentine	1996–2002	536	467	.534	2
Art Howe	2003–2004	137	186	.424	
Willie Randolph	2005–2008	302	253	.544	
Jerry Manuel	2008–2010	204	213	.489	

Team Single-Season Records

General

Most Games	164 (1965)
Most Wins	108 (1986)
Most Losses	120 (1962)
Highest Winning Percentage	.667 (1986)
Lowest Winning Percentage	.250 (1962)
Longest Winning Streak	11 (5/28–6/10/1969; 5/12–5/21/1972; 4/18–4/30/1986; 6/17–6/29/1990)
Longest Losing Streak	17 (5/21–6/6/1962)
Highest Attendance	4,042,043 (2008)
Lowest Attendance (full season)	788,905 (1979)
Lowest Attendance (shortened season)	701,910 (1981— 51 home games)

Batting Records

Runs	953 (1999)
Runs per Game	5.88 (1999)
Hits	1,553 (1999)
Batting Average	.279 (1999)
On-Base Percentage	.363 (1999)
Slugging Percentage	.445 (2006)
OPS	.797 (1999)
Doubles	323 (2006)
Triples	49 (2009)

Home Runs	200 (2006)
Bases on Balls	717 (1999)
Most Strikeouts	1,203 (1968)
Fewest Strikeouts	735 (1974)
Most Stolen Bases	200 (2007)
Fewest Stolen Bases	27 (1973)

Pitching Records

Lowest Earned Run Average	2.72 (1968)
Highest Earned Run Average	5.04 (1962)
Most Hits Allowed	1,577 (1962)
Fewest Hits Allowed (full season)	1,217 (1969)
Most Bases on Balls Allowed	617 (1999)
Fewest Bases on Balls (full season)	404 (1988)
Most Home Runs Allowed	192 (1962)
Fewest Home Runs Allowed (full season)	78 (1968)
Complete Games	53 (1976)
Shutouts	28 (1969)
Scoreless Streak	42 innings (9/23–9/28/1969)
Saves	51 (1987)
Strikeouts	1,217 (1990)
Pitchers with 10+ Wins	6 (1986)

Fielding Records

Most Errors	210 (1962, 1963)
Fewest Errors	68 (1999)
Double Plays	171 (1966, 1983)
Fielding Percentage	.989 (1999)

Team Single-Game Records

General

Longest Game (innings)	25 innings (9/11/1974 vs. Cardinals)
Longest Game (time)	7:23 (5/31/1964 vs. Giants, 23 innings)
Shortest Game (time)	1:36 (4/27/1973 at Braves)
Biggest Winning Margin	18 runs (5/26/1964 at Cubs, 19–1)
Biggest Losing Margin	19 runs (6/11/1985 at Phillies, 26–7)
Biggest Shutout Victory	14 (7/29/1965 at Cubs, 1G; 4/19/1998 at Reds)
Biggest Shutout Defeat	16 (7/2/1999 vs. Braves)

Batting Records

Runs	23 (8/16/1987 at Cubs)
Runs in an Inning	11 (7/16/2006 at Cubs, sixth inning)
Runs, Doubleheader	24 (6/13/1990 at Cubs, 15 in 1G, 9 in 2G)
Runs Batted In	22 (8/16/1987 at Cubs)
At Bats	48 (4/17/1976 at Pirates)
At Bats, Extra Innings	89 (9/1//1974 vs. Cardinals, 25 innings)
Hits	23 (5/26/1964 at Cubs; 4/29/2000 at Rockies)
Hits, Extra Innings	28 (7/4/1985 at Braves, 19 innings)
Singles	18 (8/7/1971 at Braves)
Singles, Extra Innings	23 (7/4/1985 at Braves, 19 innings)
Doubles	10 (9/27/2001 at Expos)
Triples	4 (5/23/1970 at Cubs)
Home Runs	7 (4/19/2005 at Phillies)
Walks	16 (6/29/1962 at Dodgers)
Stolen Bases	7 (5/14/2009 at Giants)
Left on Base	16 (7/25/2001 at Marlins)
Left on Base, Extra Innings	25 (9/11/1974 vs. Cardinals)

Pitching Records

Runs Allowed	26 (6/11/1985 at Phillies)
Hits Allowed	27 (6/11/1985 at Phillies)
Home Runs	7 (6/11/1967 at Cubs; 9/8/1998 at Phillies)
Strikeouts	19 (4/22/1970 vs. Padres; 10/6/1991 at Phillies)
Bases on Balls	12 (8/21/1998 vs. Cardinals— 1st Game; 3/31/2003 at Cubs)
Bases on Balls, Extra Innings	14 (4/12/1986 at Phillies, 13 innings)
Hit Batsmen	4 (4/6/2006 vs. Nationals)
Pitchers Used	8 (Many times, most recently 9/26/2008 vs. Marlins)
Pitchers Used, Extra Innings	9 (Many times, most recently 9/23/2007 at Marlins, 11 innings)

$\mathcal{I}ndex$